Merry Christmas 1998
from the Gessel family

BRIGHAM YOUNG

*An Inspiring
Personal Biography*

Published by Covenant Communications, Inc.
American Fork, Utah

Printed in the United States of America
First Printing: August 1996
Second Printing: February 1998

03 02 01 00 99 98 97 96 10 9 8 7 6 5 4 3 2

ISBN 1-55503-986-3

Library of Congress Cataloging-in-Publication Data

McCloud, Susan Evans.
     Brigham Young: a personal portrait / Susan Evans McCloud.
        p. cm.
     ISBN 1-55503-986-3
     1. Young, Brigham, 1801-1877. 2. Church of Jesus Christ of Latter-Day Saints—Presidents—Biography.
     3. Mormon Church—Presidents—Biography.   I. Title
BX8695.YM25   1996
289.3'092—dc20   96-41390
                                                           CIP

BRIGHAM YOUNG

An Inspiring
Personal Biography

Susan Evans McCloud

Covenant Communications, Inc.

To
Margaret Adams

whose estimable womanhood
has graced the Beehive House
and my life

I respectfully and lovingly
dedicate this book

Table of Contents

Foreword

Brigham Young is best known to the world as the great colonizer, the builder of a huge material commonwealth in the American desert. But he had a very different idea of what he was doing. He called Utah "a good place to make Saints" and often said that the immigrants streaming in from Europe and the East were "like potter's clay," people who "have got to be ground over and worked on the table, until they are made perfectly pliable, and in readiness to be put on the wheel, to be turned into vessels of honor."

As Susan Evans McCloud, one of Mormonism's most versatile and beloved authors, documents fully in this "personal portrait," Brother Brigham was himself common American clay, ground over and worked on the table of life by experience, hardship, and the Lord's callings, until he was a vessel of honor—one of the world's great leaders and orators and a prophet of God. As one who, like Susan, loves this man and his remarkable sermons, I am grateful for the inspiration of the First Presidency in choosing his teachings for the first two-year period of joint study of the latter-day prophets by the men and women of the Church. Susan's book provides a well-crafted, helpful companion for that study.

Brigham Young grew up, without formal education, on a series of hardscrabble homesteads in western New York; he apprenticed himself out and became one of the finest craftsmen of elegant windows, fireplaces, furniture in the area, skills he used with pride all his life, including designing parts of the Kirtland, Salt Lake, and St. George temples. He confessed he was, as a young man, "about as destitute of language as a man could well be" and that he always "had the headache, when [he] had ideas to lay before the people"; but he was also "so gritty that [he] always tried [his] best," and he became the most voluminous, wide-ranging, and, in my judgment, the most conceptually powerful orator the restored Church has produced—in fact, one of the most original, entertaining, and personally expressive of all those who have used the English language. His daughter Susa Young Gates reported one way he did it: "He had acquired the habit of copying the definition of any new word (or one new to him) on a slip of paper; and a conversation well guided, or a later public discourse would furnish a form in which to wrestle with the word and make it his own through use."

Brigham Young was a careful, somewhat skeptical "seeker," one of many in the early nineteenth century who were looking for more truth than they could find in traditional Christianity, and he took two years after reading the Book of Mormon to convert, waiting to see "if good sense was manifest." He is still known, even to Mormons, as a practical man and a good administrator. This book will help you see that he was, in fact, very much like his mentor, Joseph Smith—emotionally responsive to friends and family, witty, and a deeply spiritual man: the first to speak in tongues in the presence of Joseph, capable of rich flights of imaginative language, the receiver of many revelations and visions, including the remarkably moving and comprehensive section 136 of the Doctrine and Covenants—which gave practical details for the trek West (including helping the poor and ceasing drunkenness), the Lord's assurance that "my arm is stretched out in the last days, to save my people Israel," and a rousing, poetic call to "praise the Lord with singing, with music, with dancing."

Susan has documented all this in plentiful detail, focusing on the positive story of Brigham's development and achievements but willing to look at his struggles and occasional errors—such as his self-confessed loss of temper and hurting people "with this unruly member, the tongue" (p. 153), his failure to be as kind and forebearing with Emma as Joseph would have been (p. 129), and his tragically divided loyalties, to the Church and John D. Lee, after the Mountain Meadows Massacre (p. 211). She brings particular strengths—wide-ranging research for anecdotes from people who knew Brother Brigham, and her own inclination, as a mother of six and as a docent at the Beehive House, to focus on Brigham's complex and remarkably successful relations with his wives and many children and the details and quality of his home life, both his amazing feats of organization and gentle personal attention (p. 250) and his mistakes and self-corrections (pp. 258).

There are now many biographies of Brigham Young, of a great range of purpose and spirit and quality. Susan's *Brigham Young: An Inspiring Personal Biography* is a particularly good one to read during this time of joint study of the latter-day prophets because of her empathetic sensitivity to Brother Brigham's experiences with women, from his heartbreak over his mother's early death and his tender care of his dying first wife to his generous, inventive setting a broken bone and contriving a hammock for a young girl injured on the trek west to his championing in Utah of the vote for women and their own independent paper, *The Women's Exponent*. This is a good book for men and women to read together as we come to know and appreciate the teachings of a great prophet, a man whose life is a model for us and whose teachings still challenge us with insights into our attempts to live as God would have us.

Eugene England

Author's Note

I have served as a docent (tour guide) at Brigham Young's home, the Beehive House, since 1965 when I was twenty years old and expecting my first child; all my adult life I have spent under the very real influence of his spirit. One of my desires in preparing this book was to attempt a more personal, more intimate portrait of the man. Many great people are presented in light of their public accomplishments, their role in society or business—against the backdrop of the world, as it were. Yet our curiosity, our longing to see into the personality behind the achievements is very strong. The testimony of personal relationships is the most vital and real, and grants us insight which our spirits crave as we seek for examples, for role models, for faith and courage to strive a little harder, reach a little higher, drawn on by the beauty and power of another's triumphs over all the odds of mortality. As Longfellow expressed it: "Lives of great men all remind us, We can make our lives sublime. . . ."[1]

I discovered very soon in the writing process that, in the space allowed me, taking all practical considerations into account, I could only touch upon those things into which I had wanted to delve so deeply and satisfyingly. Even a narrowly focused volume entitled "Brigham Young's Family and Home Life" could easily stretch to be two or three times the length of this book. It was frustrating and disappointing to reconcile myself to this eventuality.

Yet, I believe that what I have begun here can achieve a good of its own. If my work stirs the mind of the reader to seek further into the heart of this great leader; further into his or her own heart; further into the heart of the gospel which Brigham Young lived to magnify, then it shall have achieved a desired end.

Having been a "part of his household" these many years, I love and honor Brigham Young; I delight in this opportunity to present him, albeit in sketchy and imperfect form, to his people, whose right it is to be blessed by the magnificent legacy of his testimony, faith and love.

Susan Evans McCloud

Notes

1. Lines quoted from the poem "A Psalm of Life" by Henry Wadsworth Longfellow, as printed in *One Hundred and One Famous Poems* (Chicago: Reilly & Lee Co., 1958).

Chapter One

Having Been Born of Goodly Parents

Brigham Young's parentage – early childhood – family relationships – some personal characteristics – death of Brigham's mother

. . . If the Lord has placed me to be the head of a family, let me be so in all humility and patience, not as a tyrannical ruler, but as a faithful companion, an indulgent and affectionate father, a thoughtful and unassuming superior; let me be honored in my station through faithful diligence, and be fully capable, by the aid of God's Spirit, of filling my office in a way to effect the salvation of all who are committed to my charge.

Journal of Discourses, 9:307

Brigham Young once stated—emphatically, as was his custom—that he would "rather be annihilated than be deprived of [his] family in eternity."[1] He was a strong, aggressive patriarch who was vitally interested in every aspect of his family's lives and welfare, keeping a private store for the use of his own households, maintaining an "open door" policy with his fifty-six children so that he was available to them at any hour if they were to

come seeking his aid. "He was so affectionate and understanding," wrote his fifty-first child, Clarissa, "that we always looked
forward to his coming among us and partaking of our pleasures
and fun."[2]

Brigham sent warm, affectionate letters to his sons when they
were absent, extending his care and fatherly influence. To his
eldest, Joseph, serving a mission in England, he wrote:

> We feel proud before the Lord when we think what you are doing in
> the great cause and Kingdom of our God. Be faithful my son. You
> went out as a child. We trust you will return a flaming Elder of salva-
> tion. Keep yourself pure before the Lord. Your Father before you has
> done it, and my constant prayer is that you may. With all my heart I
> believe you will. May God bless you forever and ever. O how glad we
> will be to see you. Brigham Young.[3]

With corresponding affection and candor, Joseph confessed in
a letter to his father:

> When I first came to England, I thought I could have taken charge of
> the British mission with the greatest ease. I have now, however, not
> quite such an exalted opinion of myself, for castles in the air will not
> stand the cold and chilling influences of the sneers of the world; and
> in fact, the more I learn the less I know. I can now in some degree
> realize the benefit to be derived from those counsels and teaching[s]
> you bestowed so liberally upon me, both in private and in public.
> When I left home I was an ignorant unthinking boy, but I shall try to
> return a man of God, one whom he will delight to own and bless.[4]

Brigham's daughter, Clarissa, was effusive in her expressions of
affection for him:

> No child ever loved, revered, and cherished a father more than I did
> mine, but how could I do otherwise, knowing him as I did? My
> mother looked upon him as the embodiment of all that was good and
> noble. He could be stern when occasion demanded but he was the
> wisest, kindest, and most loving of fathers. His constant thoughtful-
> ness for our happiness and well-being endeared him to all of us. The
> bond between my father and me was as close as if I had been his only

child, and I am sure that each of the other children felt the same way. I shall always be grateful that I was born his daughter.[5]

Susa Young, daughter of Brigham and Lucy Bigelow, suffered an unhappy marriage in her early womanhood. While still tender from the effects of her suffering, she wrote to her mother from the Academy at Provo in April of 1879: "The only desire I know of at present or at any time, is to live so that father will meet and welcome me."[6] And again, in June of that same year:

God help me to be worthy of the good opinion of all of the true Saints. For verily I want to be as near what father would wish me to be, as it is possible for my weak queer disposition to be. Oh mother, don't you long to see father to[o], clasp his arms around your neck, and hear his blessed voice pronounce those sweet words "Welcome, my beloved, to your home." Oh I know I am young and have a destiny in this Church to fulfill, but how I would love to go to father![7]

What were the forces which worked upon the humble carpenter from New England? What were the inner characteristics fostered and developed in early life which could bring the mature Brigham Young to feel in his later years, as his daughter, Susa, recorded, "that her father was great in his handling of large affairs, in his infinite power to mould men and measures, but that 'if he had failed, as he himself once said, in his duties as husband and father, he would have waked up in the morning of the first resurrection to find that he had failed in everything'"?[8]

Brigham, who succeeded in more things than most men attempt in a lifetime, had depths of commitment and dedication which are illuminated only in the personal, not the public, struggles of the man. In going back to his family background and upbringing, we gain the first insights into early influences which initially shaped his character and his ideals.

Brigham was the ninth of eleven children born to John and Abigail Howe between 1787 and 1807, a span of twenty-one years. His father was a "small, nimble, wiry man"[9] who had been but six years old in 1769 when his father, Dr. Joseph Young, was killed by the falling of a fence rail and his mother, Elizabeth Hayden Young, was forced to send her children out to help earn their living. John and his eight-year-old brother, Joseph, were "bound out" to Colonel John Jones, and worked in harsh conditions alongside his servants, both black and white. Colonel Jones was a wealthy landowner in Hopkinton, Massachusetts, and it must have been difficult for the young brothers to suffer whippings and other indignities at his hand, knowing their own father had been one of the early and prominent settlers of the little community, and well respected among his friends. Indeed, Dr. Young had a reputation for the successful treatment of cancer, and it was while treating one of his patients, Mr. John Hayden, that he met the man's widowed daughter, Betsy, and fell in love. They were married, and their union was blessed with six children: Suzannah, William, John, Joseph J., Anna, and Ichabod, born only a year before his father's untimely death.

John stuck out his apprenticeship under Colonel Jones for ten years. Then, in 1780, at the age of seventeen, he ran away and joined the Continental Army under General Washington's command. He served in three campaigns, and though he never actually fought in a battle, he lay ill with yellow fever in a hospital in Peekskill and learned well the hardships of a soldier's life. When he returned at the war's end he was able to demand wages from Colonel Jones, and under these improved conditions completed his apprenticeship, from which he was finally released in the spring of 1874 when he turned twenty-one.

Before long, his eye was caught by Abigail, the prettiest of the five popular Howe sisters, who lived in Shrewsbury, just outside Hopkinton. The sisters were described as "pretty girls, vivacious, musical. . . . All were very devout and concerned with Puritan religious life." Nabby, as she was affectionately called, was "a little above medium height. She had blue eyes, with yellowish brown hair, folded in natural waves and ringlets across her shapely brow,"[10] her beauty having been described as almost "doll-like."[11] The nineteen-year-old girl was known as well for her kindly disposition and genial personality, and these qualities were enhanced by an orderly and disciplined nature.

The couple were married at Hopkinton on October 31, 1785; it was All-Hallows Eve, when the vivid splendors of a New England autumn played upon their young senses. This seemed a propitious time in which to be starting a family. The colonies had just won their independence, the Constitution had been drawn up and signed by the delegates in Philadelphia, and Hopkinton was close enough to Boston to be in the mainstream of the anticipated growth and progress. However, the farming soil of Massachusetts was rocky and hard to coax a crop from—and, within a short twenty-four months following their marriage, John and Nabby had two additional mouths to feed: Nancy, born August 6, 1786, and Fanny, who arrived on November 8, 1787.

Nabby's parents had not approved of her marrying an orphan with an inconsequential past and a future which appeared uncertain. Now John took their daughter and new grandchildren to Durham, New York, in his efforts to support them. Here he cleared land for farming, and here their third daughter, Rhoda, named after Abigail's sister, was born. They did not stay in their new location for long. By 1790 they had returned "home" to Hopkinton, where they remained for the next ten years. The following year their first son, John Jr., was born on May 27, with Nabby following two years later on April 23, 1793. Then came Suzannah, June 17, 1795; Joseph, April 7, 1797; and Phinehas Howe, February 16, 1799.

The challenge of feeding eight hungry mouths was not easy for John Young. But the frequent, punishing intervals of childbirth were even more trying for the delicate Nabby, who had begun to suffer severe coughing spells and the weakness of tuberculosis, which was then called consumption—a deadly and wasting disease, common to that day and much dreaded.

In the middle of the winter of 1800-1801, John moved his family to Whitingham, Vermont. This meant a journey of roughly one hundred miles through the New England countryside, now held tightly in the grip of winter. For ten days they endured snow, bitter temperatures, and perhaps blizzards or freezing rains, subsisting on a diet which likely contained salt pork, jerky, corn cakes, and an occasional freshly killed rabbit or fox. They traveled in two bobsleds, which were simple wagon boxes affixed to runners. Apparently there was one horse-drawn sled to carry Nabby and the youngest children, and another pulled by oxen and loaded with all of the family's worldly goods. The frozen earth, however, supported the heavy loads easily, and the travelers escaped the nightmares of spring mud, when the quagmires were so slippery and deep that logs had to be laid in order to make any passage possible. During spring travel, there arose the danger of a horse or ox getting his foot lodged between two loosely set logs, and the long delay of lifting the wood and freeing the beast. The mud dried into deeply carved ruts, which made movement a torture. And in summer the pressed earth rose in clouds of dry dust, raised by the laboring draft animals; dust which choked the throat and nostrils, coated skin and clothing, and worked its grit into the very food the travelers ate. Perhaps this is why John Young opted for the winter in which to make his journey, though Nabby, four months pregnant, must have suffered intensely from the cold, the diet, and lack of the comforts of home and hearth.[12]

Nor was it as though they had a cozy home prepared to receive them. "The Youngs arranged to stay in the cabin of an earlier migrant until they could build their own dwelling."[13] Spring no doubt found them constructing a cabin of their own—cutting logs and clearing land for planting, filling mattresses with corn shucks, supplementing their diet with quail and partridge, deer and bear. In March and April they would have participated in the "sugaring off," when the maple trees were tapped with hollow tubes made from sumac. The sap was emptied into homemade wooden troughs which were emptied into buckets, then poured into large iron kettles, kept boiling night and day so the liquid would thicken into solid maple sugar. This precious commodity could be traded for other goods, and was poured with relish over hot oatmeal and cornbread "dodgers," staples of the family's diet throughout the year.[14]

It was New England summer—soft and fragrant, but not too hot yet, or sore with insects—when Brigham was born on the first day of June, 1801. His father had bought a fine cow from his neighbor, Caleb Murdock, and the animal proved a good producer, which meant cream, butter, and cheese for the family. Fanny, not quite fourteen, had the care of the cow, as well as the infant Brigham, who could not be nursed by his invalid mother. Between milking the cow and helping her sister, Nancy, with the housework, Fanny carried the baby around in her arms or propped on her hip, for he soon made clear his stubborn preference for her, "crying lustily if the others sought to relieve the burdened little sister of her constant charge."[15]

Conditions were harsh and the work demanding, but there was love and unity in the Young home, cooperation and an underlying sense of loyalty which would prove staunch and unchanging in the years to come. Religion was taken seriously and respect for God taught as part of their daily fare; in both speech and behavior care was taken to preserve dignity, respect, and strict morals. Some, hearing Brigham's own description, might call his childhood repressed: "My parents were devoted to the Methodist religion and their precepts of morality were sustained by their good example . . . I was taught by my parents to live a strictly moral life."[16]

As far as matters of discipline were concerned, his father was stern, almost harsh. "Brigham once remarked: 'It was a word and a blow with my father, but the blow came first.'"[17] Interestingly, his brother, Lorenzo, maintained that Brigham was "a favorite of father's, who I never knew to find fault with him but once."[18] And surely, the respect Brigham had for his father was evident. "My Father was a poor, honest, hard-working man," Brigham stated later in his life. "And his mind seemingly stretched from east to west, from north to south; and to the day of his death he wanted to command worlds; but the Lord would never permit him to get rich."[19] Life was a continual struggle for John Young against poverty and illness, but he taught his children, both by example and precept, the value of perseverance and hard work.

Said Lorenzo of his father:

> He had light hair and blue eyes. He had a small mouth and thin lips denoting considerable firmness of character. He was strong and active;

very few men of his size being able to perform the same amount of labor. He lived in the days when they cut hay with a hand scythe. I can remember him as the best mower in the section where he lived. After he was fifty years old I remember a young man saying: "Uncle John Young is the best mower in this town."[20]

Nabby, with a woman's understanding and sympathy, softened her husband's strict ways, though she was deeply religious in her own nature. Lorenzo remembered his mother as

a praying, fervent woman. "She frequently called me to her bedside," he later wrote, "and counseled me to be a good man that the Lord might bless my life. On one occasion she told me that if I would not neglect to pray to my Heavenly Father, he would send a guardian angel to protect me in the dangers to which I might be exposed."[21]

These were strangely prophetic words, considering the future experiences of the Young brothers. They must have made a great impact on Lorenzo's boyish mind, and been recalled with sweet remembrance many a time throughout his eventful life.

Although laughing or playing on the Sabbath day were frowned upon, and the strains of the violin considered evil, Nabby brightened her children's lives by singing about the home and also in the Methodist choir. Brigham's large frame and dignity of appearance was said to have come from his mother's side, but his strong, true musical voice and the love of music were also inherited from his gentle mother. As an adult he often performed informally for friends and small gatherings, and in later years he and his brothers enjoyed singing in unison together, quartet fashion.

After only three years in Whitingham, John moved the family to Sherburne, Chenango County, New York, where he again cleared land, hoping to make a success of farming. Here Nabby's last two children were born—Louisa in 1804, Lorenzo Dow in 1807. Here, too, fourteen-year-old Nabby, named after her mother, died of consumption, most probably contracted from her mother. This was a blow to the entire family, but perhaps most of all to the mother who, suffering patiently herself, must have been horrified to watch disease blight and eventually destroy her cherished daughter's fair promise.

In more natural ways, Nabby's other children were also beginning to leave her. In 1803, when Brigham was only two, the eldest daughter, Nancy, who had been such a mainstay to her mother, married Daniel Kent, and later the same year Fanny, the second child, only sixteen years old, married Robert Carr. Now Rhoda, fifteen, would try to fill their place.

The Young family lived in the area of Sherburne for nine years. Here Brigham grew into young manhood, joining his father and brothers clearing land and performing the countless demanding tasks of farm life. Years later in Salt Lake City, recalling those days, Brigham said:

> Brother Heber and I never went to school until we got into "Mormonism"; that was the first of our schooling. We never had the opportunity of letters in our youth, but we had the privilege of picking up brush, chopping down trees, rolling logs, and working amongst the roots and getting our shins, feet and toes bruised. The uncle of Brother Merrill, who now sits in the congregation, made the first hat that my father ever bought me, and I was then about eleven years of age. I did not go bareheaded previous to that time, neither did I call on my father to buy me a five-dollar hat every few months, as some of my boys do. My sisters would make me what was called a Jo Johnson cap for winter, and in the summer I wore a straw hat which I frequently braided for myself. I learned how to make bread, to wash the dishes, milk the cows and make butter; and can make butter and beat most of the women in this community at housekeeping. Those are about all the advantages I gained in my youth. I know how to economize, for my father had to do it.[22]

In 1813 Rhoda left the family to marry a Methodist minister, John P. Greene, and the same year John, Jr., married Theodocia Kimball. Father Young decided to follow newly married Rhoda and her husband to the community of Aurelius, perhaps hoping to rely upon her care for his ailing wife and her loving support of her brothers and sisters. In 1814 Suzannah, aged nineteen, married James Little.

In June of the following year, 1815, Nabby at last gave up the struggle. She was forty-nine years old at the time of her death. She had borne eleven children, buried a daughter, and left five partially raised young ones behind—Joseph, Phinehas, Brigham, Louisa, and Lorenzo, who was not quite eight years old.

Nabby's death was a terrible blow to Brigham. Throughout his life he held her in the highest esteem, using her as a standard to measure by—so much so that he could declare at a later date, "The man who treats a woman disrespectfully does not know that his mother and sisters were women."[23] Fourteen is an impressionable age at which to lose one's mother, and Brigham would have been well aware of the terrible suffering she endured as she died slowly before their eyes. In his reactions to this experience, the shape of his character was beginning to be formed. He did not become withdrawn and embittered, and he did not reject the faith that she had taught him. Instead, he allowed his soul to be drawn out in compassion—a quality he would need in abundance throughout his life.

Brigham paid his beloved mother a reverent and touching tribute in a sermon delivered August 15, 1852:

> Of my mother—she that bore me—I can say, no better woman ever lived in the world than she was. . . . My mother, while she lived, taught her children all the time to honor the name of the Father and the Son, and to reverence the Holy Book. She said, "Read it, observe its precepts and apply them to your lives as far as you can. Do everything that is good; do nothing that is evil; and if you see any persons in distress, administer to their wants; never suffer anger to arise in your bosoms, for if you do, you may be overcome by evil."[24]

It is not difficult to see how much a part of Brigham's personal creed this counsel became. Time after time in his life he would magnify it, perhaps unconscious of the fact that the light of Nabby Young's spirit was shining through his, that in this one son she had borne and given the world, the best of herself lived on, and all her patience, suffering, and toil were amply requited.

Notes

1. Dean C. Jessee, "Brigham Young's Family, Part 1, 1824-45," *BYU Studies* 18:3, pp. 312-13.
2. Clarissa Young Spencer in collaboration with Mabel Harmer, *Brigham Young at Home* (Salt Lake City: Deseret Book, 1963), p. 61.
3. Dean C. Jessee, ed., *Letters of Brigham Young to His Sons* (Salt Lake City: Deseret Book, 1974), p. 16.
4. Ibid., p. 10.
5. Spencer and Harmer, *Brigham Young at Home,* pp. 16, 35-36.
6. Kenneth W. Godfrey, Audrey M. Godfrey, and Jill Mulvay Derr, *Women's Voices: An Untold History of the Latter-day Saints, 1830-1900* (Salt Lake City: Deseret Book, 1982), p. 333.
7. Ibid., p. 336.
8. Jessee, "Brigham Young's Family," p. 312.
9. Journal of Franklin Wheeler Young, holograph, p. 5, Church Archives.
10. Susa Young Gates, "Mothers of the Latter-day Prophets," *Juvenile Instructor,* January 1924, pp. 4-5.
11. S. Dilworth Young, *Here Is Brigham: Brigham Young, the Years to 1844* (Salt Lake City: Bookcraft,1964), p. 17; hereafter referred to as *Here Is Brigham.*
12. Ibid., pp. 18-21.
13. Leonard J. Arrington, *Brigham Young: American Moses* (Urbana and Chicago: University of Illinois Press, 1986) p. 9; cited hereafter as *American Moses.*
14. Ibid., p. 9.
15. Susa Young Gates in collaboration with Leah D. Widtsoe, *The Life Story of Brigham Young* (New York: The MacMillan Company, 1931) p. 2; cited hereafter as *Life Story.*
16. S. DilworthYoung, *Here Is Brigham,* p. 27.
17. Gates and Widtsoe, *Life Story,* p. 2.
18. Richard F. Palmer and Karl D. Butler, *The New York Years: Brigham Young* (Charles Redd Center for Western Studies; with distribution by Signature Books, Midvale, Utah, 1982), p. 2; cited hereafter as *New York Years.*
19. *Journal of Discourses,* 26 vols. (London: Latter-day Saints' Book Depot, 1854-86) 10:360; cited hereafter as *JD.*
20. Palmer and Butler, *New York Years,* p. 102.
21. Ibid., p. 4.
22. *JD,* 5:97.
23. *JD,* 3:137.
24. Preston Nibley, *Brigham Young: The Man and His Work* (Salt Lake City: Deseret Book, 1970), p. 2; hereafter referred to as *Brigham Young.*

Chapter Two

Coming into His Own

Family moves – early work experiences,
carpentry and craftsmanship –
courtship and marriage – struggles and trials –
caring for his family

He gives a little to his humble followers today, and if they improve
upon it, tomorrow he will give them a little more, and the next day a
little more. He does not add to that which they do not improve upon.
Journal of Discourses, 2:2

During Nabby's last illness, her daughter, Fanny, was there to
nurse her. Fanny's husband had been unfaithful to her and she had
left him, returning home to the family who needed her. It was Fanny
who had been a second mother to Brigham; her presence at such a
crucial time would have helped to soften the trials he endured.

In the wake of Nabby's death, John, succumbing to his old
restlessness, or perhaps to the new fears that haunted him, left the
farm he had worked so hard to settle and improve and moved
thirty-five miles west to what was then considered the Far West—
the unsettled frontier of the "Sugar Hill" district near Tyrone and

only eighteen miles from the Indian trading center called Painted Post. The one hundred acres he purchased cheaply were in a dense forest and contained a grove of maple trees. Life here was primitive, and more demanding than ever. Brigham's daughter, Susa, described typical conditions of that time:

> The diet of these migrating pioneers was that of their condition and inheritance. They invariably had baked potatoes, plenty of eggs, milk and cheese, "Johnny cake" and buttermilk, varied by "garden-sass" in summer, and ginger bread and squash pie and dried beans put into the brick oven on Saturday night for the Sabbath dinner so that no cooking and work should mar the sacred peace of that day.[1]

Perhaps Fanny succeeded in providing some of this fare for the diminished family, but Brigham remembers laboring all winter under the exacting eye of his father, and one time in particular toward spring, when he and young Lorenzo were left alone for several days while their father tramped fifteen miles to the nearest settlement for food. Lorenzo related the experience in his journal:

> We had eaten the last flour the day father left, and had not had a bite all day except what sugar we had eaten and were very faint, but as night drew nigh we started for the house and to our joy a little robin came flying along and lit on a tall tree near the house. Brigham ran to the house and got the gun, and if I ever prayed in my life, I did then that he might kill the poor little robin. The gun cracked and down came the robin. We soon had it dressed and boiling in the pot, and when we thought it cooked we then wished for flour enough to thicken the broth. Finally brother Brigham got the flour barrel and told me to set a pan on the floor and he held up the barrel and I thumped it with a stick and the flour came out of the cracks and we got two or three spoonfuls and thickened the broth, and then with thanks to God for his mercy, we ate and seemed to have all we wanted, a full meal for two hungry boys.—We had a good night's rest, and the next morning went to work and worked all day until almost night on the strength of our little robin."[2]

"The grimness of such an experience was intensified," Eugene England explains, "by the father's continuing insistence that the children not indulge in any pastimes or amusements. Brigham remembers that his brother Joseph, older by four years, seemed never to smile 'during some four or five years.'"[3]

The privation Lorenzo described was not an isolated experience. Brigham himself referred to hauling as much as fifty or sixty pounds of sugar on his back and walking into the settlement in order to exchange it for flour. Breakfasts were commonly bread and porridge, with only water to drink. "I used to work in the woods logging and driving a team," Brigham said, "summer and winter, not half clad, with insufficient food until my stomach would ache."[4] Brigham was also familiar with the despondency and gloom common to the isolated frontiersman; he knew what it was to be lonely and downcast, and learned to handle such debilitating influences by the strength of his own will and determination of spirit.

One of the challenges he faced was yet another move to Tyrone, New York, and his father's remarriage in 1817 to a widow named Hannah Brown, who had several children of her own. The following year, at the age of nineteen, Phineas married Clarissa Hamilton. Joseph and Lorenzo were taken in by their sister, Suzannah, and Brigham says of himself:

> When I was sixteen years of age, my father said to me, "You can now have your time; go and provide for yourself;" and a year had not passed away before I stopped running, jumping, wrestling and the laying out of my strength for naught; but when I was seventeen years of age, I laid out my strength in planning a board, or in cultivating the ground to raise something from it to benefit myself.[5]

These words speak of a commendable maturity for a boy of that age, despite the frank admission which follows, and proves little more than that Brigham was normal and human, as most young boys are:

> I applied myself to those studies and pursuits of life that would commend me to every good person who should become acquainted with me, although like other young men, I was full of weakness, sin, darkness and ignorance, and labored under disadvantages which the

young men of this community have not to meet. I sought to use language on all occasions, that would be commendable, and to carry myself in society, in a way to gain for myself the respect of the moral and good among my neighbors.[6]

The teachings of his parents were bearing fruit, and Brigham's fine rational mind taking precedence over emotional needs and the inclinations of the flesh.

Brigham located himself in the frontier village of Auburn along the Seneca Turnpike, where some of his family already lived. It was a plain town of about a thousand residents, with muddy streets and a stream of hopeful immigrants swelling its ranks. Here he became apprenticed to a carpenter, glazier, and painter by the name of John Jeffries. Under his watchful tutelage, Brigham developed rapidly and succeeded in turning out quality work.

The first job my boss gave me was to make a bedstead out of an old log that had been on the beach of the Lake for years, water-logged and watersoaked. Said he—"There are tools, you cut that log into right lengths for a bedstead. Hew out the side rails, the end rails and the posts; get a board for the head board, and go to work and make a bedstead." And I went to work and cut up the log, split it up to the best of my ability, and made a bedstead that, I suppose, they used for many years. I would go to work and learn to make a washboard, and make a bench to put the wash tub on, and to make a chair.[7]

Brigham's skill and dependability quickly gained him a reputation and opportunities to work on many prominent building projects in the area, including "the first marketplace in Auburn, the prison, the theological seminary, and the home of 'Squire' William Brown (later occupied by William H. Seward, who served as Governor of New York and Lincoln's secretary of state)."[8]

The mantelpieces, doorways, and staircases constructed during this era are still considered showpieces by their owners today. Many old houses in the community boast chairs and desks reputedly fashioned by the youthful Brigham Young, although their chaste lines and beautiful workmanship cannot be adequately documented.

Brigham was well-liked in the community and known, even in these early times, for his congenial nature, dependability, and versatility:

> Auburn folklore has it that he helped landscape homes and plant gardens and orchards about the town. As a laborer, townspeople would remember him as "an energetic, active and capable young man," and his services were in demand for as long as he remained in Auburn.[9]

Throughout his life, Brigham retained a certain pride in these accomplishments of his youth. His daughter, Susa, said of him: "He became an expert carpenter and cabinet-maker, as some of his early work exists to testify, and he was wont to mention the fact that his best accomplishment was painting and glazing."[10]

> Brigham continued to expand and mature. After leaving Auburn, he moved several times, trying to find a profitable location. Sometime in 1823 he went to work for Charles Parks, whose shop was just over a mile outside Bucksville. Parks paid him $2.50 a week and, recognizing his outstanding craftsmanship, gave him increasing responsibility and diversity of jobs. With the ingenuity which would become characteristic of him, Brigham invented a water-powered pigment crusher to aid in the tedious task of mixing paint, using one of the cannon balls his father had brought home from the revolution as the pestle in his homemade device. Impressed, Parks promoted him to carpenter, and Brigham began trying his hand at furniture pieces, cupboards, frames, and doors.

His qualities of character and spirit were developing during this time as well. When his brother-in-law, James Little, was killed when his wagon overturned, Brigham was named one of the executors of his estate—a serious matter for a young man of twenty-one. At one time he saved the mill where he worked when lightning struck the chimney and sparks from the stovepipe scattered all about. Another time he attempted to save a drowning baby, stopping the mill wheel and diving to the bottom of the flume where he located the child and pulled it out. He began at once to apply mouth-to-mouth resuscitation to the infant, but the mother was too distraught to see the value of what he was doing. She snatched the baby from him and returned to her house, where the little one died.[11]

At this time in his life, Brigham saw himself as awkward of speech and presentation when he was attempting to deal with others. Yet some inner urge prompted him to help organize the Bucksville Forensic and Oratorical Society, where he also participated, upsetting one irate listener by the wit and clarity of his arguments to such a degree that he removed his coat and "vowed to whip Brigham then and there. Brigham reportedly took it calmly, saying that, although he was not a fighting man, he would defend himself and leave it to observers to determine who received the whipping. He was not attacked."[12]

We see emerging a young man who would assert himself for whatever he thought worth doing, a man who could think calmly in a crisis and control both himself and circumstances before they were allowed to control him. He began at an early age to study people as seriously as he did all else. His daughter, Susa, relates:

> He cultivated contact with intelligent men older than himself, yet retained lively relationships with youth. Always fond of children, he drew them naturally into the radius of his magnetic friendship. As a youth, he gathered little boys around him, telling them patriotic stories, inciting them to deeds of valour, and raising their ideals of life.[13]

This glowing appraisal may not be exaggerated when one considers the attitude of Brigham's children toward their father— one of consistent trust and respect mingled with delight in his company and a desire to please him, as revealed in their written memories and the letters which passed between them. Even nineteen-year-old Ellis Reynolds, one of a number of young people taken into Brigham's household and offered assistance of one kind or another, left an in-depth appraisal which is consistent with the high praise his children bestowed upon him:

> How kind and fatherly Brigham Young was to me. My heart warms and my eyes moisten to the big heart, the generous consideration of

that great man who lived to bless all the world as far as mortal power could reach. Directed by what seemed a divine instinct he could read and understand the human heart. His vision could encompass all of mortal need in the great and vital things, and even unto the smallest detail of everyday life.[14]

During this period, Brigham began to court a young woman named Miriam. There were opportunities to court her at the dances held in upper stories of the local inns, where a spirit of easy companionship prevailed. Miriam, according to Susa Young, was "a beautiful blonde, with blue eyes, a finely chiselled face and wavy hair. She possessed a gentle, uncomplaining spirit and was in every way most lovable."[15] Susa described Brigham as "tall, five feet ten in youth, vigorous, handsome and magnetic, his physical comeliness was severely adorned with a cleanliness which was at times radiant."[16] At the time they began courting, Miriam was nearly eighteen, Brigham nearly twenty-three, both June babies born within days of each other.

Their backgrounds were also similar. Miriam's father had fought in the Revolutionary War, as had Brigham's. They both enjoyed music and would often sing together, as well as discuss the things they considered important in life. Susa claimed that the courtship, though short, was "most romantic."[17] Surely Brigham considered the selecting of a wife a very weighty matter, and he must have appreciated the prospect of a woman's presence in his life again—her voice and her laughter, things he had missed since his mother's death and the breaking up of his family.

He married Miriam Angeline Works on October 8, 1824, when the autumn world was crowned with as much joy and beauty as were their hearts. Their sense of celebration must have been heightened by the fact that Gilbert Weed, the Justice of the Peace who married them, presided at the wedding of Brigham's sister, Louisa, the following day.

The couple, it seems, spent their first few days in semi-reclusion in a little log house situated at the back of the Hayden farm, then set up housekeeping on their own. William Hayden, who owned a mill in Port Byron, described the Young house, situated across from the pail factory where Brigham worked, as being small and "devoid of paint inside or out." He continued in detail:

> In the east end was an old-fashioned fire place and large chimney, with stairway on one side and a small pantry on the other. Two rooms were partitioned off on the west end for bedrooms, being about seven feet square. The intervening space was parlor, sitting room, dining room and kitchen combined. The lower rooms of the house were roughly plastered; but were without the luxury of a cellar.[18]

Soon after their marriage, Brigham and Miriam joined the Methodist church, and prepared for the birth of their first child, a daughter who arrived on September 26, 1825. They named her Elizabeth.

Surely these two enjoyed peace and a sense of purpose together. Brigham was a great reader, and perhaps he read aloud to her while she cared for their child, rocking back and forth in the soft gray twilight beside a warm fire. They labored and planned together, secure in their mutual goals and desires. They did not know at this time how life would take hold of them, and higher forces alter their plans.

The Youngs moved briefly with their new daughter to Oswego, a beautiful location on the shore of Lake Ontario. Although they stayed here only a short time, good things were remembered and spoken of Brigham:

> One associate there, Hiram McKee, who later became an evangelical preacher, recalled that Brigham had been exemplary in his conduct and conversation, "humble and contrite," had demonstrated "deep piety and faith in God," and had joined in "fervent prayers and enlivening songs."[19]

Brigham now begins to emerge as a young man both gentle and forceful, enterprising and astute, his personality warmed with a genuine curiosity and interest in others.

In less than a year, Brigham moved his family again, this time to Mendon. Did he possess his father's restlessness? He was definitely searching for something, his "life's work" in a sense beyond trade or profession, though he devoted his best efforts to anything which had the mark of his workmanship on it and would reflect the integrity so important to him.

Moving to Mendon was a return to family for Brigham. His widowed sister, Suzannah, was there, as were his father, Louisa and Rhoda with their husbands and families, and his sister, Fanny, living with the Heber C. Kimball family. John and Phineas lived in nearby communities, Joseph lived with his father and stepmother, and even young Lorenzo was there part of the time.

The prospects for farming in the area were excellent and the future must have seemed hopeful, despite their history of struggle and poverty. Heber Kimball's assessment of Brigham's family at this period is enlightening. "They were in low circumstances," he said, "and seemed to be an afflicted people in consequence of having a great deal of sickness and sorrow to pass through; and of course were looked down upon by the flourishing church where we lived."[20]

Brigham built a house for Miriam which his daughter described as "a charming bit of early Colonial cottage workmanship."[21] On June 1, 1830, Miriam gave birth to their second daughter and named her Vilate, after Heber's wife, who must have already befriended the frail woman who was struggling to care for her little ones and face the terrible reality of her chronic tuberculosis.

We can only imagine Brigham's feelings when he learned that his young wife was doomed to suffer much as his own mother had; a cruel fate for him to watch the two women he loved sink into a death which he had no power to prevent, or even to soften very much. But he did not allow himself to fall into despondency or relax his efforts. He labored with the same consistent will, doing a variety of "custom" work, from putting in staircases, fireplace mantels, doorways and windowpanes to making tables, chairs, chests, and other pieces of furniture. His friend Heber later described those days:

> Brother Brigham and myself used to work hard, side by side, for fifty cents a day and board ourselves; we had seventy-five cents a day when we worked in the hayfield; we would work from sunrise to sunset, and until nine o'clock at night if there was sign of rain. We would rake and bind after a cradler for a bushel of wheat a day, and chop wood, with snow to our waist for eighteen cents a cord, and take our pay at seventy-five cents a bushel.[22]

Years later, Heber and Brigham would lament the "carelessness of hired men" and the easily obtained, store-bought goods the Saints of Salt Lake desired. It is consistently obvious that Brigham never forgot his humbler days and the standards they taught him. There were times, while living in Mendon, when he went seeking assistance by borrowing from his neighbors:

> George Hickox, whose descendants still live in the area, declared that Brigham once approached him about borrowing a dollar. "Chop wood with me and earn it," was Hickox's reply. On another occasion Brigham owed Hickox a bill and made a dozen chairs to satisfy the account.[23]

It is interesting to note how Brigham applied this principle in the early days of Salt Lake, providing destitute immigrants who entered the valley with work and a means of earning something, be it only wages in foodstuffs, and getting on their feet, rather than belittling them with an outright dole. He remembered the lessons of self-reliance and accountability he learned through his own struggles, and realized their universal value:

> I build walls, dig ditches, make bridges, and do a great amount and variety of labor that is of but little consequence only to provide ways and means for sustaining and preserving the destitute. . . . Why? I have articles of food, which I wish my brethren to have; and it is better for them to labor . . . so far as they are able to have opportunity, than to have them given to them.[24]

Brigham also shouldered the care of his invalid wife during this period. He would arise early in the morning, get breakfast for

Miriam, the little girls, and himself, then he would dress the children and do what was necessary in tidying and cleaning up the house, then carry his wife to her rocking chair beside the fireplace before leaving the house for his day's labors. When he returned in the evening, he had to cook a meal for the family, finish up the household labors, see to the needs of his daughters, and put both wife and children to bed.[25] No wonder he felt qualified in later years to counsel, perhaps even needle women on the performance of their duties:

> Why do not women learn to be housekeepers? They may reply—
> "Brother Brigham, if you will teach us, we will keep our houses
> according to your instructions." I could go into your houses and tell
> you item by item. . . . Not one woman in ten, that I ever saw, thor-
> oughly understands keeping a house.[26]

He could not at times resist a little boasting of the large range of his own powers and abilities.

Yet the matter of his personal life at this time, and the manner in which he handled it, are key to the man. Wrote Susa Young:

> He loved the peaceful seclusion of a home, yearned for the domestic
> independence which alone fosters character development and the self-
> expression which had been denied him since his mother's long illness
> and her final death in his early life. . . . The love he gave his young
> wife was deep and abiding, and his loyalty to her was unquestioned.[27]

Perhaps all the more so because of the bittersweet nature of those painful and uncertain days.

A letter to the Ontario *Republican Times* recorded the impressions of a Canandaigua citizen who recalled Brigham Young:

> . . . There could scarcely be a more kind and affectionate husband and
> father than he [Brigham] was, and few men in his circumstances
> would have provided better for their families. Mrs. Young was sick,
> most of the time unable to do any kind of work, but she was a wor-
> thy woman, and an exemplary Christian; she was well deserving of his

care and attention, and she had it while she lived in Canandaigua. . . .
We never thought him fanatical, . . . he was looked upon by his neighbors generally to be a consistent Christian.[28]

Brigham possessed no greater powers than any other to look around the corners to what lay ahead. He could never have anticipated the life that awaited him, the variety of weighty responsibilities which would be his to bear. Surely, at this stage of his life he met with the first approval of heaven for the kindly and patient way in which he accepted and functioned within the painful confinements of his daily life. He was already proving how well-tuned were his sensitivities, his commitment to duty, his ability to project beyond self. For all Brigham knew, this would be the pattern of his days for long years to come. He accepted the limitations and disappointments nobly, concentrating on the opportunities placed in his path, loving and serving as his mother, in her own patience and gentleness, had taught him to do, magnifying those qualities which were beginning to emerge as distinctly his.

Notes

1. Gates and Widtsoe, *Life Story,* p. 3.
2. Palmer and Butler, *New York Years,* p. 7.
3. Eugene England, *Brother Brigham* (Salt Lake City: Bookcraft,1980), p. 3; cited hereafter as *Brother Brigham.*
4. Palmer and Butler, *New York Years,* pp. 7-8.
5. *JD,* 10:360.
6. *JD,* 10:360.
7. *JD,* 18:76.
8. Arrington, *American Moses,* p. 13.
9. Ibid., p. 14.
10. Gates and Widtsoe, *Life Story,* p. 3.
11. S. DilworthYoung, *Here Is Brigham,* p. 41.
12. Arrington, *American Moses,* p. 15
13. Gates and Widtsoe, *Life Story,* p. 4.
14. Susan Evans McCloud, *Not in Vain* (Salt Lake City: Bookcraft,1984), p. 52.
15. Gates and Widtsoe, *Life Story,* p. 5.
16. Ibid., p. 4.

17. Ibid., p. 5.
18. Palmer and Butler, *New York Years,* p. 21.
19. Arrington, *American Moses,* p. 16.
20. Heber C. Kimball, "History," manuscript, book 94-B, Heber C. Kimball Papers, Church Archives.
21. Gates and Widtsoe, *Life Story,* p. 5.
22. *JD,* 9:329.
23. Arrington, *American Moses,* p. 17.
24. Journal History of Brigham Young, 8 June 1856, Church Archives.
25. Gates and Widtsoe, *Life Story,* p. 5.
26. *JD,* 8:296.
27. Gates and Widtsoe, *Life Story,* p. 5.
28. Letter of Unnamed Correspondent, *Ontario Republican Times,* 7 September 1857, Church Archives.

Chapter Three

Embracing Mormonism

Book of Mormon and missionaries come to the Youngs –
Brigham's personal conversion – early missionary labors –
death of wife, Miriam

I will tell you in a few words what I understand "Mormonism" to
be. . . . It embraces every fact there is in the heavens and in the heaven
of heavens—every fact there is upon the surface of the earth, in the bow-
els of the earth, and in the starry heavens; in fine, it embraces all truth
there is in all the eternities of the Gods. How, then, can we deny it?
Journal of Discourses, 9:148

The publication of *the Book of Mormon* in March of 1830 created a great wave of excited reaction in the Palmyra area. Brigham,
as well as others, was aware of the stir. "I was somewhat acquainted
with the coming forth of the Book of Mormon," he told the Saints
in Salt Lake years later, "not only through what I read in the newspapers, but I also heard a great many stories and reports which
were circulated as quick as the Book of Mormon was printed, and
began to be scattered abroad."[1] The experience of the Book of
Mormon became a family happening for the Youngs, in that pecu-

liar way in which they all interacted with one another, supporting each other and learning from one another's experiences.

All the Young brothers considered religion a solemn and serious matter. John, Joseph, and Phinehas became earnest followers of Methodism, each one at length receiving the license necessary to talk and teach in public. The Young family had all gathered in the Mendon area by the spring of 1828. Phinehas reported that they opened a house for preaching and began to teach with what light they felt they had. Although their efforts were blessed and they continued in the work, as early as the spring of 1830, when The Church of Jesus Christ of Latter-day Saints was being officially organized, there seemed no progress in the reformation they were attempting to effect. "I, as an individual," Phinehas wrote, "felt that we had arrived at the zenith of our enjoyment in the course we were pursuing."[2] His brother, Joseph, who also labored as a Methodist preacher, had felt strongly the lack in what organized religion had to offer. "There is not a Bible Christian in the world," he once said to Brigham. "What will become of the people?"[3]

The youngest son, Lorenzo, reluctant to align himself with any organized religion, was given, at the age of nineteen, a dream which presaged the work of his family:

> I thought I stood in an open space of ground and saw a good, well defined road leading, at an angle of forty-five degrees, into the air as far as I could see. I heard a noise similar to that of a carriage in rapid motion, at what seemed the upper end of the road. In a moment it came into sight, drawn by a pair of beautiful white horses. The carriage and harness appeared brilliant with gold, and the horses traveled with the speed of the wind. It was manifested to me that the Savior was in the carriage, and that it was driven by His servant. It stopped near me and the Savior inquired, "Where is your Brother Brigham?" After answering His question he inquired about my other brothers, and concerning my father. His queries being answered satisfactorily, He stated that He wanted us all, but especially my brother Brigham. The team then turned about and returned the way it came. . . . Subsequent events proved that it foreshadowed our future. It was evidently fulfilled, when my father and all of his family entered into the new and everlasting Covenant [Mormonism].[4]

In August, scant months following the organization of the Church, Joseph Smith's young brother, Samuel, was on the road as a missionary. On the second day of his journey he came to the home of Rhoda Young Greene and her husband, John, who was also a Methodist preacher, and attempted to sell them a Book of Mormon. John was not interested, but kindly agreed to take a few and attempt to sell them himself. Curious, both he and his wife read the book, and found themselves deeply moved by it.

At Tomlinson's Inn, near the same time, Phinehas purchased a copy of the same book from Samuel and intended to read it in order to expose its errors, feeling that the testimony the young man bore of his brother's mission was "very strange" and "rather ridiculous." But his experience was quite different from what he had expected:

> "I commenced and read every word in the book in the same week," Phinehas confessed. "The week following I did the same, but to my surprise, I could not find the errors that I anticipated, but felt a conviction that the book was true. . . . My father then took the book home with him, and read it through. He said it was the greatest work and the clearest of error he had ever seen, the Bible not excepted. . . . I then lent the book to my sister, Fanny Murray. She read it and declared it a revelation. Many others did the same.[5]

What was happening with Brigham as all this was going on? He was taking his own more careful, more thorough route. He was, as he called himself, "a person of observation," priding himself on being able to discern the spirit of a man from his countenance. From a young age he had observed and formed his own opinions about all sorts of things. He did not like to be "crowded" or forced into doing anything. As he once explained it:

> Young men would say to me, "Take a glass." "No, thank you, it is not good for me!" "Why, yes, it is good for you." "Thank you, I think I know myself better than you know me.". . . I recollect my father urged me [to sign the temperance pledge]. "No sir," said I, "if I sign the temperance pledge I feel that I am bound, and I wish to do just right, without being bound to do it; I want my liberty"; and I have con-

ceived from my youth up that I could have my liberty and independence just as much in doing right as I could in doing wrong.[6]

Such independence, fortunately, rested on Brigham's mature,
tenacious code of honor and morality. "From the days of my
youth," he maintained, "there never was a boy, a man, either old
or middle aged, that ever tried to live a life more pure and refined
than your humble servant."[7] His brother, Lorenzo, agreed:

> Brigham was a boy of strictly moral habits as far as I ever knew. I do
> not think he was ever known to drink or use profane language. He
> was very industrious and hard working. As to his faults, I never knew
> of anything particular. I never knew of his having difficulty with his
> associates or his brothers and sisters. . . . I never knew of his getting
> angry but once in his youthful days when I thought he was violent.[8]

In typical fashion Brigham recalled: "I was not disposed to
attach myself to any church, nor to make a profession of religion,
though brought up from my youth amid those flaming, fiery
revivals so customary with the Methodists."[9]

It was not from immature arrogance that Brigham made these
assertions. As he later explained,

> I have often prayed—if there is a God in heaven save me, that I may
> know all and not be fooled. I saw them get religion all around me—
> men were rolling and hollering and bawling and thumping but had
> no effect on me—I wanted to know the truth that I might not be
> fooled.[10]

His discernment is evident in this recollection of listening to a
popular preacher of the day, Lorenzo Dow:

> . . . I asked myself, "What have you learned from Lorenzo Dow?" and
> my answer was, "Nothing, nothing but morals." He could tell the
> people they should not work on the Sabbath day; they should not lie,
> swear, steal, commit adultery, etc., but when he came to teaching the
> things of God he was as dark as midnight.[11]

Brigham had great confidence in his older brothers, even pride in their fine, spiritual qualities. He called his brother, Joseph, the most serious-minded of men, and said of him, "I knew that he was solemn and praying all the time. I had more confidence in his judgment and discretion, and in the manifestations of God to him, than I had to myself."[12] Despite this, he did not follow their examples and affiliate himself with Methodism until he was twenty-three. But he needed to have the experience, the inner change himself. His quest for truth was a real one, generated from deep inside his own being. He was trying sincerely to forsake his sins and live on a higher level, desiring to be "as good as I know how while here."[13]

But what Brigham found in the Methodist church did not satisfy him:

> As I became acquainted with smart, intelligent, literary priests . . . I thought, Now I can obtain some intelligence from this or from that man; and I would begin to ask questions on certain texts of Scripture; but they would always leave me as they found me, in the dark.[14]

He decried the hypocrisy he saw in the Christian clergy, until at length he became disgusted with their lack of sincerity and power. "I would as lief go into a swamp at midnight to learn how to paint a picture," he explained, "as to go to the religious world to learn about God, heaven, hell or the faith of a Christian."[15]

During this period, Brigham was restless and vaguely discontented, at times feeling "cast-down, gloomy, and despondent . . . lonesome and bad." His inner life seemed veiled with "a dark shade, like the shade of the valley of death."[16] He was disappointed, even disgusted with what he saw in the world. Concern for Miriam was mingled with this restless concern for his own soul. The powers within him were beginning to stir, to awaken, yet they had no place to go, no threshold for growth or action.

Although several members of Brigham's family had read the Book of Mormon and were deeply impressed by its "plain, biblical style; its answers to questions of life and afterlife that had vexed them; its clarification of obscure passages in Isaiah, Revelation, and other books in the Old and New Testaments,"[17] Brigham exhibited his usual caution in approaching it: "Says I, 'Wait a little while; what is the doctrine of the book, and of the revelations the Lord has given? Let me apply my heart to them;' and after I had done this, I considered it to be my right to know for myself as much as any man on earth."[18]

This statement gives vital insight into the power of the man. Even at this early stage of development, he believed in his literal right and ability to gain spiritual direction—to communicate, as it were, with Deity. This is strongly borne out by the discovery he made and recorded in his own powerful manner:

> When I undertook to sound the doctrine of 'Mormonism,' I sup-posed I could handle it as I could the Methodist, Presbyterian, and other creeds of Christendom. . . . I found it impossible to take hold of either end of it; I found it was from eternity, passed through time, and into eternity again. When I discovered this, I said, "It is worthy of the notice of man."[19]

Brigham "took note of it" when the missionaries came through the area in the fall of 1831, roughly a year after Samuel Smith left copies of the Book of Mormon with his brother and brother-in-law. He took notice enough to state that they "came to Mendon to preach the Everlasting Gospel, as revealed to Joseph Smith, the Prophet, which I heard and believed"[20]; enough to con-cur with his brother Phinehas, who returned from an uneasy, inef-fective preaching mission during which he could think of nothing but the Book of Mormon and what he had heard of Mormonism, only to have Brigham tell him "that he was convinced that there was something to Mormonism. I told him I had long been satis-fied of that."[21]

Brigham's study of human nature naturally made him inter-ested in the people who espoused Mormonism and were drawn to it. When the missionaries returned to Mendon several months later, he watched them as closely as he listened to them. He was considering what commitment would cost him in personal terms: forsaking his friends, perhaps even his family or wife—forsaking all, if need be, for the sake of the gospel. He felt he needed to make this decision within his own heart, even if such a sacrifice was never required of him. His answer to himself was a resounding "yes." Then, true to form, he requested concurring action on the part of heaven. He hurried home to pray in private.

> "If this religion is true, send the missionaries to my home, that they might pray for my sick wife and also explain the gospel to her." Next evening, according to a statement of one of the elders, they happened to pass by Brigham's property. The thought came to them that the tidiness of the yard bespoke a person worth visiting. From the window Brigham saw them approach his door; he hurriedly welcomed them in and invited them to give Miriam a blessing. They were, he assured them, the answer to his prayer.[22]

Brigham's unerring discernment allowed him to recognize that he, who had never really preached, could easily out-talk these missionaries; but that was of little consequence in view of the fact that "their testimony was like fire in my bones; I understood the spirit of their preaching; I received that spirit; it was light, intelligence, power, and truth."[23]

Conversion meant action as far as Brigham was concerned. Three weeks after his encounter with the elders, he and his brother Phinehas and their wives, along with his dear friend, Heber Kimball, traveled to Bradford County, Pennsylvania, where they might observe a Mormon meeting. It was January of 1832, and the small group traveled by horse and sleigh across snow and ice, fording rivers when they had to, sustained by the excitement of their mission and a sweet camaraderie. Miriam undoubtedly suffered more than the others, but how sweet to her must have been the love and unity of the experience. Vilate Kimball remained at home, presumably to care for the children; but Miriam would not be restrained from accompanying her husband. Though it probably cost her dearly, she was granted this brief time away from the demands of daily life to spend with Brigham—a rare treat, indeed. They visited Brigham's sister, Nancy, and stayed six days with the Saints, attending their meetings, hearing them speak in tongues, rejoicing with them in the beauty of truth.

Only days after their return home, Brigham set off alone on an arduous journey of 250 miles to Kingston, Ontario, to share what he had learned with his brother, Joseph, who was living and preaching there. Joseph was ready. The message Brigham brought was to him a "spiritual jubilee—a deliverance from a long night of darkness and bondage."[24] He and Brigham returned to Mendon together in March.

In April, Joseph, Phinehas, and their father, John, were baptized in the Bradford branch. Ten days later—Sunday, April 15, 1832—the missionaries baptized Brigham in the waters of his own millpond. By the end of 1833, the entire Young family and most of their spouses, constituting some seventeen persons, had come into the Church. This family was instrumental, to an impressive degree, in building up the early kingdom, in sustaining and supporting one another and the gospel in its formative years. Lorenzo, the last living child of Father Young, wrote at the age of eighty-three:

> My father, my step-mother, Hannah Brown, my four brothers and five sisters, with their wives and husbands, were all members of the Church, carried out their professions and lived like true Saints, with the exception of two brothers-in-law. Of a family of twenty three, twenty one of them, if I pass away in the faith, will have lived and died Latter Day Saints.[25]

Of the experience of baptism, Brigham recorded:

> I was baptized by Eleazer Miller, who confirmed me at the water's edge. We returned home, about two miles, the weather being very cold and snowy; and before my clothes were dry on my back he laid his hands on me and ordained me an Elder, at which I marvelled. According to the words of the Savior, I felt a humble, child-like spirit, witnessing unto me that my sins were forgiven.[26]

Brigham was more prepared, more ready than he realized. The following day his friend Heber was baptized, but felt unworthy of immediate ordination. Heber's wife, Vilate, was baptized within two weeks, and Miriam Young within another, being forced to wait until the weather softened enough that her weakened system could endure the experience.

Brigham must have felt whole. Surely he continued to rejoice, overcome by the exuberance of his own soul. As he later reflected,

> I wanted to thunder and roar out the Gospel to the nations. It burned in my bones like fire pent up, so I [commenced] to preach the Gospel of life to the people. . . . Nothing would satisfy me but to cry abroad in the world, what the Lord was doing in the latter days . . . I had to go out and preach, lest my bones should consume within me.[27]

Although he suffered with fears, headaches, and feelings of terrible inadequacy when he first attempted to speak publicly, from the very beginning Brigham experienced what was to sustain him every time he gave a sermon during his lifetime. "I opened my mouth," he said, "and the Lord filled it."[28] We have over eight hundred of Brigham's sermons on record; according to him, they were all delivered without prepared notes or text. He learned from the outset the value of teaching by the Spirit, overcoming his fears, and depending on the inspiration which he never doubted would attend him.

Brigham delivered his first sermon only one week after his baptism in the small Mendon branch which consisted of fifteen families—eight of them Youngs. Some dedicated women members would walk barefoot from Victor, a town three miles away, in order to attend the meetings. Their devotion did not go unnoticed. While gathering wood one day, Brigham, his father and brother, and Heber were pondering and discussing the faithfulness of the Saints and the possibilities of the work they were engaged in,

> when the glory of God shone upon us, and we saw the gathering of the saints to Zion, and the glory that would rest upon them; and many more things connected with that great event, such as the sufferings and persecutions that would come upon the people of God, and

the calamities and judgments that would come upon the world. These things caused such great joy to spring up in our bosoms that we were hardly able to contain ourselves, and we did shout aloud "Hosannah to God and the Lamb."[29]

Experiences such as these helped to sustain the men through the persecutions of their neighbors, spurred largely by the leaders of the town's powerful Baptist church. Disdaining their bigotry, Brigham did not let it deter or even alarm him. With a faith sweetly idealistic, Brigham gave his whole heart—which in his case meant all the efforts of his hands—to the work of the gospel:

I commenced to contract my business operations and dealings, and laid away my ledger, and notebooks, saying, "I shall never want you anymore" . . . I expected we should be one family, each seeking to do his neighbor good, and all be engaged to do all the good possible.[30]

Leaving Miriam and his children in the care of Vilate Kimball, Brigham spent the summer of 1832 doing missionary work with Heber. They canvassed the small townships of western New York: Reading, Hornby, Patten, Avon, Hector, and others. During this time, Brigham discovered that his powers were growing. "For me to travel and preach without purse or scrip, was never hard," he explained:

I never saw the day, I never was in the place, nor went into a house, when I was alone, or when I would take the lead and do the talking, but what I could get all I wanted. Though I have been with those who would take the lead and be mouth, and been turned out of doors a great many times, and could not get a night's lodging. But when I was mouth I never was turned out of doors; I could make the acquaintance of the family, and sit and sing to them and chat with them, and they would feel friendly towards me; and when they learned that I was a "Mormon" Elder it was after I had gained their good feelings.[31]

Brigham's knowledge of human nature is clearly revealed here. Yet he did not take personal credit for this growing power. He knew his limitations, and he knew the source of his strength:

. . . had it not been that I clearly saw and understood that the Lord Almighty would take the weak things of this world to confound the mighty, the wise, and the talented, there was nothing that could have induced me or persuaded me to have ever become a public speaker.[32]

Trusting as surely that their wants would be supplied, though they traveled without purse or scrip, he and Heber baptized at least seven people before returning home, where Brigham found his frail, patient wife to be dying. He nursed Miriam through her final weeks there in the Kimball home; the added strength and assistance of Heber and Vilate must have made a difference which he felt and appreciated for the rest of his life.

Miriam's death brought a confrontation Brigham could not avoid. The unresolved grief over his mother's death, the scars and frustrations of his youth and boyhood—all culminated in this intensely personal trial. Brigham makes it clear in his own history that Miriam died "in the faith." "In her expiring moment," he wrote, "she clapped her hands and praised the Lord and called upon Brother Kimball and all around to praise the Lord."[33] The doctrines taught by this new faith were deep and compelling. His daughter, Susa, explained:

The new Church taught that life before this earth was individually lived, and life, after death, would continue personality, progress, and intellectual growth; that such life was and would be as eternal as God was eternal; that women were to share in all the blessings and gifts of life here and hereafter . . . while the sealing ordinance which bound together husbands and wives, parents and children, continued in force and efficacy throughout eternity; that through this key his own beloved mother and wife . . . would be his companions and associates throughout an active eternity. These principles hung suspended on the thread of his reasoning faculties which had been trained in the school of Protestant rejection of revelation.[34]

Brigham's testimony in these matters was now assured. "I weighed the matter studiously for nearly two years," he once declared, "before I made up my mind to receive that Book." Continuing, he explained,

> I looked at it on all sides. All other religions I could fathom . . . but this new one I reasoned on month after month, until I came to a certain knowledge of its truth. Had this not been the case I never would have embraced it to this day. I wished time sufficient to prove all things for myself.[35]

This knowledge was part of the catharsis which took place for him now, part of the healing, uplifting power of this gospel in his life. His active involvement in the Church gave him a healthy outlet for his energies and passions, as well as the sensitive assurances and comforts his spirit needed at this time. He did not look back now; he was never to look back—not once after he had set his foot on this road. His allegiance, his faith were unswerving, unassailable. No man or woman, more easily won, possessed the tenacity and surety which Brigham displayed, as expressed in this powerful avowal:

> Were you to ask me how it was that I embraced "Mormonism," I should answer, for the simple reason that it embraces all truth in heaven and on earth, in the earth, under the earth, and in hell, if there be any truth there. There is no truth outside of it; there is nothing holy and honorable outside of it; for, wherever these principles are found among all the creations of God, the Gospel of Jesus Christ, and his order and Priesthood, embrace them. [36]

Brigham's intellect, as well as his spirit, was expanding to comprehend and embrace the solemnities of eternity, the truths which were as sweet as the taste of honey on his tongue.

Notes

1. *JD*, 2:249.
2. *Manuscript History of Brigham Young*, 1801-1844, comp. by Elden J. Watson (Salt Lake City, 1967), p. xviii; cited hereafter as *Ms. History*.
3. Arrington, *American Moses*, p. 22.
4. James A. Little, "Biography of Lorenzo Dow Young," *Utah Historical Quarterly*, vol. 14, 1946.

5. Leonard J. Arrington and JoAnn Jolley, "The Faithful Young Family: The Parents, Brothers, and Sisters of Brigham," *Ensign* (10 August 1980), p. 55.
6. *JD*, 14:225.
7. Palmer and Butler, *New York Years,* pp. 33-34.
8. Ibid., p. 34.
9. Ibid., p. 35.
10. Minutes of Young Family Meeting, 18 January 1845, Church Archives.
11. *JD*, 14:197-98.
12. *JD*, 8:37.
13. *JD*, 14:197.
14. *JD*, 5:73.
15. *JD*, 14:198.
16. *JD*, 3:310-21.
17. Arrington, *American Moses,* p. 27.
18. *JD*, 3:91.
19. *JD*, 2:123-24.
20. Palmer and Butler, *New York Years,* p. 63.
21. Miriam Maxfield, "A Compiled History of Phinehas Howe Young," typescript, pp. 3-6, Church Archives.
22. Eunice E. Curtis, "The Ancestors of Enos Curtis and Ruth Franklin: Utah Pioneers, 1783-84, and Related Families," p. 13, Church Archives.
23. *JD*, 9:141.
24. *Millennial Star,* vol. 25 (4 July 1863), p. 424.
25. James A. Little, "Biography of Lorenzo Dow Young," *Utah Historical Quarterly,* vol. 14 (1946), p. 209.
26. *JD*, 9:219.
27. *JD*, 1:313-14.
28. *JD*, 13:211.
29. Palmer and Butler, *New York Years,* p. 70.
30. *Millennial Star,* vol. 25 (11 July 1863), p. 438.
31. Palmer and Butler, *New York Years,* p. 74.
32. *JD*, 4:21.
33. Preston Nibley, *Brigham Young,* p. 10.
34. Gates and Widtsoe, *Life Story,* p. 8.
35. Ibid., p. 9.
36. *JD*, 11:213.

Chapter Four

Joining with the Saints

Brigham meets Brother Joseph, speaks in tongues –
missions to Canada – moves family to Kirtland – tireless support
of the Prophet – marriage to Mary Ann Angell –
Zion's Camp, lessons learned

I have Zion in my view constantly. . . . Our work is to bring forth
Zion, and produce the Kingdom of God in its perfection and beauty
upon the earth. . . . When the wicked have power to blow out the sun,
that it shines no more; when they have power to bring to a conclusion the operations of the elements, suspend the whole system of
nature. . . then they may think to check "Mormonism" . . . and thwart
the unalterable purposes of heaven. . . . Jehovah is the "Mormonism"
of this people, their Priesthood and their power.
Journal of Discourses, 9:293

With his passion to examine and prove all things to his own
satisfaction, it was impossible for Brigham to "put the gospel to
rest" until he had personally met Joseph Smith, the Prophet.

Confident of the love and tenderness his little daughters
would receive from Vilate Kimball, he left them in her care and
prepared to journey to Kirtland. Miriam died on September 8th.

About three weeks later, Brigham, his brother Joseph, and Heber Kimball set out on the 325-mile journey to Ohio, driving Heber's wagon and visiting friends and branches of the Church along the way. They exhorted the Saints and prayed with them, and Brigham spoke in tongues—a phenomenon some pronounced to be of the Lord, others of the devil. It must have been strange for Brigham to experience this outpouring of speech, this sudden ability to express himself after years of hesitation and halting efforts. He had first spoken in tongues only weeks after his baptism, while gathered at Heber's house for family prayer. "The Spirit came on me," he said simply, "and I spoke in tongues, and we thought only of the day of Pentecost."[1] The excesses of the Pentecostal religions were repulsive to Brigham, but he seemed to show no concern for the way in which this gift was bestowed upon him and other early Saints. Indeed, he took heed and magnified this directive of the Spirit by developing and respecting the power of "the word," both written and spoken.

On his own initiative, Brigham committed himself to a series of proselyting missions. He also began to keep his first personal journal, which extended through 1835—a factual, straightforward account of his doings recorded in a small notebook. During the years until 1844, when the Prophet Joseph Smith died, he filled three additional notebooks. Although not introspective, they give us some of his perceptions of the things he was experiencing. Here, as in his letters and in accounts others have given of him, we see the continuing development of his tender and feeling spirit, blending and merging with the power of conviction and strength of action which characterized his life.

Brigham's sister Rhoda and her husband, John Greene, had moved to Kirtland during the summer, so the young visitors had a place to stay. "We went to his [Joseph Smith's] father's house, and learned that he [Joseph] was in the woods, chopping," Brigham recorded. What were his feelings as he walked into the cool quiet of the woods in search of the Mormon prophet, a man but twenty-six years old, yet responsible for the mighty changes which were being wrought in Brigham's life?

> We immediately repaired to the woods, where we found the Prophet, and two or three of his brothers, chopping and hauling wood. Here my joy was full at the privilege of shaking the hand of the Prophet of God, and received the sure testimony, by the Spirit of prophecy, that he was all that any man could believe him to be, as a true Prophet. He was happy to see us, and bid us welcome. We soon returned to his house, he accompanying us.[2]

If the recording of so momentous a meeting seems a little commonplace, lacking anticipated sensation, it is well to remember that the most weighty sense of awareness was present—the testifying power of the Spirit, which bespeaks dignity and reverence; and this is the feeling one gets from Brigham's simple, unembellished account. This is the formula Brigham used with pure, almost childlike faith throughout his life; once he had proven it, he not only never doubted its validity, but he was wise enough to call upon that power whenever he had need of its aid. As he told his daughter, Susa, when she longed to

> know that the Gospel was true, that Jesus was the Christ and that Joseph Smith was divinely ordained to re-establish His church in latter days; not merely to hope and try to believe it, but to know as her father *knew* its truth. He said, "Daughter, there is only one way to find it out. And that is the way I found it out and the way your mother found it. Get down on your knees and ask God to give you that testimony and knowledge which Peter had when Christ asked the Apostles: 'Whom do ye say that I am?'"[3]

That evening, the visitors were still in the company of the Prophet. As Brigham describes it:

> In the evening a few of the brethren came in and we conversed together upon the things of the Kingdom. He [Joseph] called upon me to pray; in my prayer I spoke in tongues. As soon as we arose from our knees the brethren flocked around him, and asked his opinion concerning the gift of tongues that was upon me. He told them that it was the pure Adamic language. Some said to him they expected he would condemn the gift brother Brigham had, but he said, "No, it is of God, and the time will come when Brother Brigham Young will

preside over this Church." The latter part of this conversation was in my absence.[4]

From the very beginning, Joseph discerned the stature of this man who was to become his most stalwart disciple and defender, and he was given definite confirmation by the Spirit. What did Brigham, himself, think to hear such words spoken concerning him? Surely he treasured them up in his heart; then, in his practical manner, he went forward to do the work—no matter how tedious or humble or demanding it might prove.

In December, Brigham and his brother Joseph traveled to Kingston in upper Canada on foot, through snow and mud, at one time traveling six miles over ice. They baptized about forty-five converts and organized branches. "When we left there," Brigham recalled, "the Saints gave us five York shillings with which to bear our expenses two hundred and fifty miles on foot, and one sister gave me a pair of woolen mittens two-thirds worn out. I worked with my own hands and supported myself."[5] This was how Brigham liked it. He was as gritty, as self-dependent as any New Englander could be, and he carried an assurance of the importance of the work which he did:

> Men who understand language, who were taught it in their youth, who have had the privilege of schools and good education, [amaze me when they] get up and tell how they shrink from addressing this people.
>
> When I think of myself, I think just this—I have the grit in me, and I will do my duty any how. When I began to speak in public, I was about as destitute of language as a man could well be. But tell about being bashful, when a man has all the learning and words he can ask for! With scores and hundreds of thousands of words with which to convey one's ideas, and then tell about being bashful before a people! How I have had the headache, when I had ideas to lay before the people, and not words to express them; but I was so gritty that I always tried my best.[6]

Brigham apparently possessed the sense of vision great men must own, which enabled him to see all things in perspective and hone every skill and ability for its use in the whole. Part of doing his best was to continuously improve and expand, wherever he saw the need for it, or wherever a weakness was recognized. His daughter, Susa, related that "he had acquired the habit of copying the definition of any new word (or one new to him) on a slip of paper; and a conversation well-guided, or a later public discourse would furnish a form in which to wrestle with the word and make it his own through use."[7]

Brigham's desire to be his best was powerfully welded with his own formula of doing all within his own power, then trusting very literally to his Heavenly Father to make up the rest: "My faith is, when we have done all we can, then the Lord is under obligation, and will not disappoint the faithful; he will perform the rest."[8] Later in his life, he taught the Saints by the power of personal experience:

> There are a great many men who know but little what they can do, and there are a great many women that never consider what they can perform; people do not fully reflect upon their own acts, upon their own ability, and therefore do not understand what they are capable of doing.[9]

From the beginning, Brigham made it a conscious point to come to know himself and to learn and expand the capabilities and gifts which were his.

Upon returning from Canada, Brigham rested a few weeks at Heber's home, playing with his motherless children and building up the Church in that area. Then he set off alone for Canada, once more on foot, and preaching along the way. Arriving in Loughbrough, he discovered that seventeen people had been baptized during the four months since he and Joseph had been there. He remained in the area, baptizing, teaching, and sustaining the members until the first of July, when he decided to accompany some of his converts to Kirtland to help them relocate there.

At this time in his life, Brigham was his own man, with a freedom of action he would not have enjoyed if he had been married. In struggling to define himself, he confessed his determination "that I would be governed by certain principles and among them I decreed that women should not govern me neither should my passions of lust or anger, but I would be boss over myself my passions and appetites."[10] His single life was uncluttered by emotional commitments and gave him a clarity which was rare and of great value.

In Kirtland, Brigham had the opportunity to spend time with the Prophet Joseph and get to know him on a more personal level. Solidifying some of Brigham's own determinations, Joseph challenged a group of elders at that time with a level of dedication to the work which was a bit overwhelming, but one which Brigham was prepared to embrace.

> It was simply this: Never do another day's work to build up a Gentile [non-Mormon] city; never lay out another dollar while you live, to advance the world in its present state. . . . It is the word and command-ment of the Lord to his servants that they shall never do another day's work, nor spend another dollar to build up a Gentile city or nation.[11]

The word of the Lord was something Brigham took seriously and literally. He returned to Mendon only to make plans to move his little family to Kirtland, as the Prophet had directed, following the revelation he had received early in 1833 that a stake of Zion be established there.

At this time, Brigham's family and that of his friend, Heber, were virtually one and the same. Vilate was essentially a second mother to Brigham's growing daughters, and within the confines of that household he could find a little of the rest and sustenance which he would otherwise have gone entirely without. In September of 1833 they all moved together to Kirtland, where Brigham's father had already taken up residence, though his sec-ond wife refused to accompany him, choosing to live in Tyrone with one of her sons.

Northeastern Ohio, originally part of the Western Reserve, was first settled in 1796; the Kirtland area as early as 1811. Newel

K. Whitney, who would later play a prominent part in the Mormon community, was one of the earliest pioneer businessmen who, in 1823, established the first general store in the settlement. He was still running the store in early February 1831, when a sleigh stopped in front of his establishment. A young man jumped out and approached him, extending his hand in a friendly manner and calling him by name.

Newel was bewildered. "I could not call you by name as you have me," he responded.

"I am Joseph the Prophet," the stranger said. "You have prayed me here, now what do you want of me?"[12]

Newel's wife, Elizabeth, testified that Joseph's arrival was "the fulfillment of the vision we had seen of a cloud as of glory resting upon our house."[13]

The Whitneys were ready, and received the Prophet with great kindness, as did others, Parley Pratt notable among them. A converted Campbellite, through the preaching of Sidney Rigdon, Parley had heard of the Book of Mormon while on a canal boat en route to New York. He recorded what occurred once he started to read it:

> I read all day; eating was a burden, I had no desire for food; sleep was a burden when the night came, for I preferred reading to sleep. As I read, the Spirit of the Lord was upon me, and I knew and comprehended that the book was true, as plainly and manifestly as a man comprehends and knows that he exists.[14]

Such were some of the brethren Brigham was to encounter in Kirtland. As to the place itself, one early pioneer paints an impressive description:

> The country for many miles around had been for centuries the hunting-ground of the Indians. . . . The forest-trees were of endless variety and of the tallest kinds. A thick growth of underbrush grew beneath, flowers of rare beauty blushed unseen, birds of varied plumage filled the air with their music, the air itself was fragrant and invigorating.[15]

At the time of Brigham's arrival, Kirtland was a village of about thirteen hundred people, with converts constantly arriving from the New England states; by 1838, the number of Mormons would increase to over two thousand. Housing was nearly impossible to find, and the majority of the Saints, though many had possessed means at the outset, were poor. Brigham describes his own pathetic state at the time:

> . . . if any man that ever did gather with the Saints was any poorer than I was—it was because he had nothing. . . . I had two children to take care of—that was all. I was a widower. "Brother Brigham, had you any shoes?" "No; not a shoe to my foot, except a pair of borrowed boots." I had no winter clothing, except a homemade coat that I had had three or four years. . . . I had travelled and preached and given away every cent of my property . . . until I had nothing left to gather with; but Joseph said, "come up," and I went up the best I could.[16]

Heber rented a small house, where the two families crowded in together. Brigham was certain of one thing: he was not afraid to work, and he possessed skills which were in great demand. He began at once to build Heber a house, which he completed in April of 1834, working at the same time on houses for Andrew Cahoon and John Smith, the Prophet's uncle, for much-needed pay.

We read the facts, and they sound a bit grim and demanding. Brigham seemed to progress quickly and surely; however, the reality, if we consider it, was much different than that. He progressed by dint of faith, perseverance, and humility, as this account of Jonathan Crosby's shows:

> Shortly after we got to Kirtland, Brother B. Young, H. C. Kimball, [and] P. P. Pratt came to me to borrow money. I had nearly 100 dol[lars]. . . . They were very poor. Pres. Young said he had nothing in the house to eat, and he knew not where to get it. . . . He stood in the door of the printing office thinking of his condition and he felt so bad the sweat [rolled off] him.[17]

It seems reasonable to assume that experiences such as these remained vivid in Brigham's memory and had some impact on many future decisions, such as his determination, supported by solemn vow, to assist all of the poor to remove from Missouri, and his efforts in the early days of the Salt Lake Valley to provide means for all men to work and support themselves.

Brigham's support of the Prophet, his tireless activity, and his energetic and colorful preaching attracted the attention of many, among them a young convert from Rhode Island by the name of Mary Ann Angell. She came from a deeply religious family where both her parents loved the scriptures and would read them to their children and discuss with them the principles they contained.

> She once asked her mother when very young, why the books of the New Testament were so much alike, and her mother replied, "To make the testimony of the Savior stronger, for in the mouth of three or four witnesses the truth is substantiated."[18]

Mary Ann worked in the local Baptist Church until one day in 1830, when she listened to Thomas B. Marsh preach the gospel and obtained from him a Book of Mormon. When she first took the book in her hands, a strong feeling came over her that it was true. Indeed, the witness of the Spirit was so strong that not once, throughout the rest of her life, did she experience a moment of doubt. Her parents were, at the time, in New York visiting friends. The letters she wrote led them to investigate the Church. Mary Ann traveled to New York, where she heard both Phinehas and Lorenzo Young preach. She and her parents were baptized by Brigham's brother-in-law, John P. Greene. Ironically, her life was intertwined with Brigham's family from the very start.

Anxious to join with the Saints in Kirtland, Mary Ann went alone, since her parents were not yet ready. She earned her keep by helping in the homes of established and well-to-do members. When she heard Brigham speak and the Spirit whispered to her that here was the man she had been waiting for, her heart must have thrilled, for she had determined early in life that she would marry only a Christian man of sterling virtue and character. Now, at the somewhat advanced age of twenty-nine, she had found him. Emmeline B. Wells, in her sketch of Mary Ann, observed that

> There is no doubt in the mind of the writer, but that a watchful Providence guided and directed President Young in choosing for his companion for life, one who possessed those sympathetic and generous traits of character which make women motherly in nature before becoming mothers themselves; and also those sublime and heroic attributes that help women to stand firm in times of trial and temptation.[19]

On February 18, 1834, Brigham Young, age thirty-two, and Mary Ann Angell, age thirty, were married; family tradition has it that Sidney Rigdon performed the ceremony. Brigham records none of the relief and gratitude he must have felt—only that he and Mary Ann moved into a house of their own (whether rented or built by him is not known), that she "took charge of my children, kept my house, and labored faithfully for the interest of my family and the kingdom."[20]

The statement is terse, but comprehensive, and it is clear that Mary Ann was capable and willing. Both she and Brigham believed that their marriage was ordained in the heavens, and that it was part of a larger purpose—a larger commitment to a grand design, and an eternal future for which they were willing to labor and sacrifice. Thus she was able to wish Brigham "God speed" when he left on May 1, a little over two months after their wedding, to go up with the camp to redeem Zion. She was pregnant, living in poverty and concern for her husband's welfare, and she had to win the affection of two little girls who had been snatched a second time from the arms of a loving mother, for so Vilate Kimball had been to them. This could not be helped, and Mary Ann had the support and affection of the Kimballs to assist her in the challenge. She succeeded so beautifully that the girls, in their later lives, observed that in every sense of the word, she had been a true mother to them. She gave birth to her first child, a son, shortly after Brigham's return in the autumn. Joseph A. Young was born on October 14, 1834.

Zion's Camp was organized to assist the families in Missouri, many of whom had been driven from their homes the previous November. Governor Dunklin had promised redress if the Church would provide a posse to assist him. Brigham and Heber were among the first to volunteer; Brigham's brother, Joseph, was more reluctant, but a chance encounter with the Prophet more than convinced him. "Brother Brigham and brother Joseph," the Prophet said, "if you will go with me in the camp to Missouri and keep my counsel, I promise you, in the name of the Almighty, that I will lead you there and back again, and not a hair of your heads shall be harmed."[21] The two brothers shook hands with the Prophet to confirm the covenant. Mary Ann's brother, Solomon, wished to go with the camp, as did his friend, Lorenzo Booth. She kindly took in both of their families so the men could do as they desired.

Joseph divided the group (which eventually numbered 205 men, eleven women, and seven children) into companies of twelve. Both Brigham and Heber were appointed captains of twelve. Twenty-five baggage wagons accompanied the camp, but these were loaded with provisions, tools (axes, saws, spades, hoes, etc.) and relief bedding, clothing, and food for the Missouri Saints. Therefore, nearly all of the men walked.

Near the beginning, the men were able to buy bread along the way, or flour with which to bake it, living often on the simple fare of corndodger and johnnycake. George A. Smith, at sixteen the youngest of the group, recorded in his journal for May 26: "The day was exceedingly hot and we suffered much from thirst, and were compelled to drink water which was filled with living creatures. I learned to strain wigglers with my teeth."[22] And Joseph Young recalled vividly:

> I never went through a more severe trial of my faith; it was as much as we all could bear. We performed 100 miles in three days, in the hottest weather, some of us at times carrying our muskets and knapsacks weighing some 20 to 30 pounds on our backs, traveling until the blood could be heard in our boots and shoes.[23]

It was necessary that the purpose of the journey be kept secret, so the men learned how to hedge in answering the questions of curious observers. Despite the rigid routine and organization of the camp, with a trumpet calling the men to rise at four a.m., there was yet opportunity for singing and merrymaking at the end of the day. Brigham and his brother, Joseph, often sang duets together; their voices were very pleasing and uplifting. Their songs, Levi Hancock asserted, "were the sweetest I ever heard in the Camps of Zion."[24] Each Sabbath religious services were held, and Brigham often preached. But despite the camaraderie and spiritual encouragement, there was much complaining and petty backbiting among the men. George A. Smith gave priceless insight into conditions when he wrote:

> The Prophet . . . never uttered a murmur or complaint, while most of the men in the camp complained to him of sore toes, blistered feet, long drives, scanty supply of provisions, poor quality of bread . . . magotty bacon and cheese, etc. Even a dog could not bark at some men without their murmuring at Joseph. If they had to camp with bad water, it would nearly cause rebellion. *Yet we were the Camp of Zion,* and many of us were careless, thoughtless, heedless, foolish or devilish, and yet we did not know it. *Joseph had to bear with us and tutor us like children.*[25]

This was a training and proving ground for the brethren; an obviously necessary one. As the unusual little army neared Jackson County, Joseph appointed Parley and Orson Pratt to sound out the governor, who, true to their fears, pretended concern but refused any real assistance.

The first encounter or "battle" the group faced came on June 19, when five armed men rode into camp, threatening that the Mormons would "see hell before morning." To the amazement of all, a ferocious storm blew up suddenly, though there had not been a cloud in the sky. Their plans spoiled, many of the mobbers found themselves at the mercy of wind, torrential rain, and huge hailstones which beat holes in their hats, broke and dented their guns, and tore down limbs and large trees all around them. Some of the men, overcome by terror, huddled in a cold, empty school-house for protection, marveling at the power of the storm and the hand that had wrought it. Earlier, a group of twelve, in an ugly mood, had started for Independence in hopes of raising an army; but their boat sank in the Missouri, and seven were drowned. A spirit of panic and confusion seemed to seize the mobbers; when they met in committee, one man accidentally stabbed another to death. They were dumfounded by their inability to do anything against the Mormons. The men in the camp spent the night in gratitude, praising God for their deliverance.

But a few days later, a worse enemy attacked the camp: the dreaded cholera, which settles in the stomach and intestines and can kill a person in less than a day. Despite their blessings (at times angels, seen by many, had been with them); despite Joseph's warning that a scourge would come upon them, the men had to see for themselves the chastening hand of God. Seventy men, Heber among them, were stricken; thirteen died. Even the Prophet suffered a violent attack, but both Brigham and his brother Joseph were spared. It was not until the members humbled themselves, covenanting with uplifted hands to obey Joseph's counsel, that the nightmare was lifted.

On July 3, the Prophet formed a high council in Clay County and reorganized and encouraged the Saints. He then told Lyman Wight to discharge every man who had marched in Zion's Camp, giving each a certificate of his faithfulness. The next day, Brigham and several others started for home together, walking all the way to Kirtland, where they arrived, some accounts say, in late August. In Emmeline Wells' sketch of Mary Ann, she writes: "In the fall of the same year Brigham Young returned to his home, and almost immediately after his arrival his eldest son, Joseph A. Young, was born on the 14th of October, 1834."[26]

Neither Brigham nor Mary Ann murmured or complained at the uselessness and waste of the venture for which they had both sacrificed. Brigham recognized its value to him, answering others' assertions of the camp's failure with his own discerning testimony:

When I returned from that mission to Kirtland, a brother said to me, "Brother Brigham, what have you gained by this journey?" I replied, "Just what we went for; but I would not exchange the knowledge I have received this season for the whole of Geauga County; for property and mines of wealth are not to be compared to the worth of knowledge."[27]

Those select men whom Joseph was soon to organize into leaders in the new kingdom learned all they were meant to learn from the Zion's Camp experience. As Wilford Woodruff pointed out:

When the members of Zion's Camp were called, many of us had never beheld each others' faces; we were strangers to each other and many had never seen the Prophet. . . . We gained an experience that we never could have gained in any other way. We had the privilege of beholding the face of the Prophet, and we had the privilege of traveling a thousand miles with him, and seeing the workings of the Spirit of God with him, and the revelations of Jesus Christ unto him and the fulfillment of those revelations. . . . Had I not gone up with Zion's Camp I should not have been here today, and I presume that would have been the case with many others in this Territory.[28]

This process Brother Woodruff described was essential for the survival and growth of the Church. A cohesiveness, a unity of faith, understanding, and purpose was essential; there was so much to learn and digest, and all of it demanding and new.

For Brigham Young, the experience was vital to his ultimate destiny. He bore powerful witness to his experience and the eternal powers behind it, which he willingly acknowledged:

I have travelled with Joseph a thousand miles, as he has led the Camp of Israel. I have watched him and observed every thing he said or did. . . . For the town of Kirtland I would not give the knowledge I got from Joseph from this Journey; and then you may take the State of Ohio and the United States, and I would not give that knowledge for them. It has done me good and you good—and this was the starting point of my knowing how to lead Israel. I watched every word and summed it up, and I knew just as well how to lead this kingdom as I know the way to my own house. It is God within me; and God upon me; God by day and by night, and it is for his kingdom on the earth.[29]

Joseph was his model, yet Brigham understood from the beginning whence came the power, and who was the Head of the work they did.

Notes

1. *Ms. History*, p. 3
2. Ibid., p. 4.
3. Gates and Widtsoe, *Life Story*, p. 9.
4. *Millennial Star*, vol. 25 (11 July 1863), p. 439.
5. *JD*, 6:229.
6. *JD*, 5:96-97.
7. Gates and Widtsoe, *Life Story*, p. 280.
8. *JD*, 4:91.
9. *JD*, 4:101.
10. Diary of Wilford Woodruff, 15 February 1858, Church Archives.
11. *JD*, 11:294-5.
12. "A Leaf from an Autobiography," *Woman's Exponent* 7 (15 August 1878), p. 51.
13. Ibid.
14. Parley P. Pratt, *Autobiography of Parley P. Pratt*, edited by Parley P. Pratt, Jr. (Salt Lake City: Deseret Book, 1950), p. 27; hereafter referred to as *Autobiography*.
15. History of Geauga and Lake Counties, Ohio (Philadelphia, 1878) p. 246, Church Archives.
16. *JD*, 11:295.
17. "Jonathan Crosby Autobiography," 15, in Parkin, *Conflict at Kirtland*, p. 161, Church Archives.
18. Emmeline B. Wells, "Heroines of the Church: Biography of Mary Ann Angell Young," *Juvenile Instructor*, vol. 26 (1 January 1891), p. 16.
19. Ibid., p. 17.
20. *The Journal of Brigham: Brigham Young's Own Story in His Own Words*, comp. by Leland R. Nelson (Provo, Utah: Council Press, 1980), p. 6; cited hereafter as *Journal of Brigham*.
21. Ibid.
22. Arrington, *American Moses*, p. 40.
23. *Deseret News*, 12 October 1865, p. 13, Church Archives.
24. Arrington, *American Moses*, p. 40.
25. George A. Smith, "Memoirs," p. 25, Church Archives; italics author's.
26. Wells, "Biography of Mary Ann Angell Young," *Juvenile Instructor*, p. 14.

27. Heber C. Kimball, "History," *Times and Seasons* 6:839, Church Archives.
28. *JD,* 13:158.
29. Arrington, *American Moses,* pp. 45-46.

Chapter Five

Loyalty to God's Servant and the Work

Council organized – mission to the East –
working on the house of the Lord – dedication of
Kirtland Temple – mission to New England – trials in Kirtland,
life in danger – removal from Kirtland

If we are united, we are independent of the powers of hell and of the world. . . . I wish the people to understand that they have no interest apart from the Lord our God. The moment you have a divided interest, that moment you sever yourselves from eternal principles.
Journal of Discourses, 5:257, 4:31

For Brigham, the return to Kirtland was a return to a multitude of public and private challenges. Making a living and caring for his family had to be worked into the affairs of the kingdom, which included quarrying rock and working on the temple, as well as donating his efforts to complete a school room and a printing office. He also found himself defending the Prophet in legal suits brought against him. He did this with vigor mixed with a sense of humor, as when the court, examining the failed promises made to the members of Zion's Camp, asked him what he perceived "a lot of land" to mean and he replied, "In the cemetery it generally means six feet."[1]

Brigham again enjoyed the association of the Prophet Joseph during this period, meeting with him, working with him, singing for his family at his home of an evening. The temple, three stories high and costing sixty thousand dollars, was a prodigious undertaking for the poor and overburdened Saints who were struggling, among other things, to incorporate the principles of living which Joseph was giving them. During the Kirtland period, virtually all of Joseph's translation of the Bible was completed, as well as the translation of the Egyptian papyrus rolls. He received eighty-four revelations, sixty-four of which were incorporated into the *Doctrine and Covenants*, comprising almost half of the entire volume. These revelations covered a wealth of topics including Christ's mission, the Godhead, Satan's role and mission, the definition of priesthood, priesthood roles and keys, missionary work, the Sabbath day, consecration and stewardship, tithing, accountability, and information concerning the premortal life and creation of the world to the second coming and life after death. The challenges would have been overwhelming if they were looked at as a whole; but wisely, the Saints took them one step at a time, gaining strength with each step mastered, each trial overcome.

On February 14, 1835, nearly five years after the Church was organized, Joseph ordained three witnesses—Oliver Cowdery, David Whitmer, and Martin Harris—who selected and ordained twelve apostles whose sacred work was to carry the gospel to all the nations of the earth. They were to be, as the Prophet told them, "equal in authority and power" to the presiding officers of the Church (Doctrine and Covenants 107:24). Brigham was the second to be called, but he sat third in the council, which was organized according to age. At thirty-four, he was only two years younger than Thomas B. Marsh and David W. Patten, who sat above him. Heber Kimball, only fourteen days younger than Brigham, was next in line. Brigham was promised many things in his ordination, including an influence among "heathen nations," and that he would go forth and "do wonders in the name of Jesus."[2]

The men were immediately appointed to labor in various mission fields. Late on May 2, following a grand council and instruction from the Prophet, Brigham set out on a five-month mission to the East, walking most of the way, suffering hardships and disappointments, staying with those who were willing to take him and his brethren in, meeting with small and large groups (a congregation of over two thousand in Vermont). He met a relative at Dunkirk, on Lake Erie, near the beginning of his mission, but the old man was friendly neither to Brigham nor his message. Near the end of his travels, after preaching in the Boston area in August and September, Brigham took a companion and traveled twenty miles to Hopkinton, where many of his relatives still lived. "I found Grandmother [Howe] alive and comfortable well for her," he wrote. "She expressed great joy for the privilege of seeing one of mother's children once more."[3] They met with a great deal of opposition and rejection, and at times Brigham would resort to the Biblical gesture of shaking the dust of the place from his garments as a testament to the hard-heartedness of the people. He did not record his personal reactions to the difficulties and discoveries, or to the memories which his return to Mendon must have stirred. He was straightforward and matter-of-fact in doing his duty, but his keen, watchful eye stored up the lessons he learned and the insights he gained for future use.

In company with William Smith and Orson Hyde, Brigham returned to Kirtland on September 25. Mary Ann was undoubtedly happy to have him with her once more, providing, albeit inadequately, for the family's needs. He remained home that fall and winter, preaching occasionally in the surrounding areas, seeing to his family, working on the temple, and meeting in council with his brethren. He also attended the Hebrew school which Joseph had started, hiring a Jewish scholar, Joshua Seixas, to teach over forty of the brethren.

Joseph asked Brigham to superintend the painting and finishing work on the temple, which gave him opportunity to add the imprint of his own spirit upon the splendid building, possibly even designing the Federal-style arched windows at each end of the temple, or the intricately sectioned Gothic windows gracing the sides. Artemus Millet, one of Brigham's own converts from Canada, supervised the masonry work, and it was a joy for the two men to work side by side on the house of the Lord. The poverty of his family that winter, on the other hand, bit hard—though not hard enough to force Brigham to accept the church assistance which Joseph had offered to the Twelve. His independence was apparent, but also his direct, straightforward dependence upon the Lord. "Who supported my family? God and I," he stated. "Who found clothing? The Lord and myself."[4] He did occasionally have to resort to accepting the aid of others, with much reluctance borrowing from friends when he had no other recourse. But he had learned well the lesson of his youth, that of working to pay his own way. And with absolute assurance he took all matters to the Lord first, depending on divine assistance before he would think of turning for help to his fellow man.

On January 22, 1836, Joseph called the Twelve and other leaders into the nearly completed temple. There, each received "the ordinance of holy anointing," wherein the Prophet placed his hands on their heads and pronounced individual and marvelous blessings upon each man. Then the Twelve, exercising their authority, anointed the newly selected Seventy, men whose calling was solely to do missionary work. It was pleasing to Brigham when his brother, Joseph, was selected as the first president of the group. Then the gathered brethren feasted on the gifts of the Spirit; some were given visions, some spoke in tongues. Brigham spoke little of these experiences, holding them sacred in his own heart, perhaps following the counsel Joseph had given: "If God gives you a manifestation, keep it to yourselves."[5] The place of the extraordinary, the sensational in matters of the Spirit was clearly understood by Brigham, as exemplified in an instance he related:

> The Twelve "set stakes" to see an angel. They were determined to pray
> until they did so. But they never saw one though [we] prayed ourselves

into darkness. I praid to God with all my heart that I might never again meet with that Quorum with the spirit they possessed and I never did.[6]

The dedication of the Kirtland temple on Sunday, March 27, was a consummation for all of the Saints. Many of them had not only sacrificed of their means that it might be built, but had sacrificed of their pride and worldly desires that they might prepare their hearts for the spiritual blessings the Prophet had promised. And the blessings did come. As Lorenzo Snow enumerated:

> . . . prophecy—the gift of tongues—visions and marvelous dreams . . . the singing of heavenly choirs . . . the sick were healed, the deaf made to hear, the blind to see and the lame to walk . . . a spiritual atmosphere pervaded that holy edifice.[7]

Visions, experienced in eight separate meetings, included one of the Father and Son, and the Savior himself appeared in the temple on five different occasions.

By seven o'clock on the morning of the dedication, over a thousand people were waiting outside the temple doors. The services began at nine a.m. and did not adjourn until four p.m.. Heber C. Kimball recorded in his journal:

> During the ceremonies, an angel appeared and sat near President Joseph Smith, Sen., and Frederick G. Williams, so that they had a fair view of his person. He was a very tall personage, black eyes, white hair, and stoop shouldered; his garment was whole, extending to near his ankles; on his feet he had sandals. He was sent as a messenger to accept of the dedication.[8]

This messenger was identified by Joseph as Peter, the apostle.[9]

In the afternoon, following the Prophet's dedicatory prayer, the choir sang for the first time William W. Phelps' inspired anthem:

> *The Spirit of God like a fire is burning!*
> *The latter-day glory begins to come forth;*
> *The visions and blessings of old are returning;*

And angels are coming to visit the earth. . . .
We'll sing and we'll shout with the armies of heaven,
Hosanna, hosanna to God and the Lamb!
Let glory to them in the highest be given,
Henceforth and forever, Amen and amen![10]

After the singing and the acceptance of the prayer of dedication by the various quorums, Brigham, along with his brethren of the Twelve, administered the sacrament to the large congregation of Saints. Near the very end of the meeting, following the Hosanna Shout, he arose and spoke in tongues, after which David Patten interpreted. What Brigham uttered, what incredible feelings stirred his bosom, we can only imagine. But the solemnity of the occasion was more than surface-deep for him, as his future actions showed.

Of greatest importance to Brigham in his role as apostle were the events which took place in a meeting in the temple on April 3, when Joseph Smith and Oliver Cowdery, separated from the other brethren by drawn curtains, saw the Savior "standing upon the breastwork of the pulpit," saying to them with a voice which was "as the sound of the rushing of great waters":

> I am the first and the last; I am he who liveth, I am he who was slain. . . . Let the hearts of your brethren rejoice, and let the hearts of all my people rejoice . . . For behold, I have accepted this house, and my name shall be here; and I will manifest myself to my people in mercy in this house. (D & C 110:4-7)

In order then, following the manifestation of the Savior, Moses, Elias, and Elijah appeared, committing to Joseph Smith the various keys which they held. Therefore, authority now rested in the hands of the Prophet. Brigham had seen and felt it all; and now its beauty and reality solemnized his commitment to the truth and his loyalty to the young man who had been so honored of heaven—the man who had brought these eternal privileges within Brigham's reach.

In May, Brigham left on a mission to New England, converting relatives in Hopkinton: Uncle John Haven, who proved to be a challenge, and the sons of Rhoda Richards, his mother's sister—Phineas, Levi, and Willard (who would eventually become a powerful missionary in Great Britain, an apostle, and eventually a counselor to Brigham in the First Presidency).

Brigham, it will be remembered, relished missionary work, and was good with people, exerting the magnetic charm he even then possessed, singing and serving and gentling their fears. He was all the more able to do so because he taught from the heart. But he paid a personal price for his successes, leaving a pregnant Mary Ann behind, and his precious children, whose company he missed. "What shall I say to you to comfort your hart?" he wrote to Mary Ann, adding:

> I pray for you and I feel that the Lord will bless you and keep you from danger and bare you upon the arms of faith. Tell the children that I remember them in my prares. I pray the Lord to give you strength and wisdom.[11]

He was certainly aware of their need, and of his responsibility toward them. It was his main objective upon returning home, he wrote, to "pay for my house and I want to repare it this fall so that I can feel contented about my family when I leave them." We can feel Brigham's own loneliness in his concluding lines: "My Dear Mary, I remember you continually in my prayers. My love to all my little children. Be good to your mother and pray for me when I am away. Fairwell. I remane your hosbon and frend."[12]

Shortly after his return home in September, his cousins Levi and Willard Richards arrived and stayed with his family through the fall and winter. Perhaps they lent their strong young backs in helping Brigham patch up his house and provide for the needs of his family. But privacy was a luxury Mary Ann was not to enjoy; not then or for many long years to come. It could not have been easy for her, when her twins were born in December, to have a full and extended household. They named the children after themselves: Mary Ann and Brigham, and the joy of their pure, precious spirits tempered the intense trials they suffered during these months.

Brigham found affairs in a deplorable state when he returned to Kirtland. "We were much grieved," wrote Heber, "to see the spirit of speculation that was prevailing in the Church."[13] Land prices had skyrocketed, a spirit of greed and jealousy had overtaken many of the Saints, and with the failure of the Kirtland Safety Society in the national bank panic of 1837, many were suddenly divested of their supposed wealth and turned all their animosity toward the Prophet, who became an easy scapegoat for their own failures and fears.

Brigham was irate. He made no bones as to where his loyalties lay, taking it upon himself to warn and chastise dissenters. He was practical by nature, yet had cultivated wisdom and discernment. He possessed no weak hero-worship for the Prophet, but a realistic assessment of realities and how the system, under divine direction, should work:

> Though I admitted to my feelings and knew all the time that Joseph was a human being and subject to err, still it was none of my business to look after his faults. . . . It was not for me to question whether Joseph was dictated by the Lord at all times and under all circumstances or not. . . . He was called of God; . . . and if He had a mind to leave him to himself and let him commit an error, that was no business of mine.[14]

One particularly dark day in early January 1837, when Joseph was out of the city, many of the Twelve and other Church leaders—even those men who had been special witnesses to the Book of Mormon—gathered for a council in the upper room of the temple. The purpose of their meeting: how to depose the Prophet Joseph Smith. Brigham states that "Father John Smith, brother Heber C. Kimball and others were present, who were opposed to such measures."[15] He also gives a thrilling and graphic account of what took place:

> I rose up, and in a plain and forcible manner told them that Joseph was a Prophet, and I knew it, and that they might rail and slander

him as much as they pleased, that they could not destroy the
appointment of the Prophet of God, *they could only destroy their own
authority, cut the thread that bound them to the Prophet and to God,*
and sink themselves to hell.

Brigham's spiritual maturity as well as his loyalty are evident
in this defense. As he proceeds, the human Brigham also emerges:

> Many were highly enraged at my decided opposition to their mea-
> sures, and Jacob Bump [an old pugilist] was so exasperated that he
> could not be still. Some of the brethren near him put their hands on
> him, and requested him to be quiet; but he writhed and twisted his
> arms and body saying, "How can I keep my hands off that man?" I
> told him if he thought it would give him any relief he might lay them
> on. That meeting was broken up without the apostates being able to
> unite on any decided measures of opposition. This was a crisis when
> earth and hell seemed leagued to overthrow the Prophet and the
> Church of God. The knees of many of the strongest men in the
> Church faltered.

But Brigham's never did. Though his life was truly in danger,
though he was plagued and despised by those who had before been
his friends, he had set his course and would not deviate from it:

> During this siege of darkness I stood close by Joseph, and, *with all the
> wisdom and power God bestowed upon me, put forth my utmost energies
> to sustain the servant of God and unite the Quorums of the Church.*[16]

Earlier, we quoted Brigham's determination to do good to
others.[17] His loyalty and efforts were not for the Prophet alone,
but for the work. He was committed to the kingdom, and was
not merely aligning himself on one "side" as opposed to another,
but he was aligning himself with what he believed to be God's
work, and, therefore, allowing nothing to discourage him or
stand in his way.

Moreover, he knew how to translate intent into action, which
he had already proven countless times. During this period, he
thought it important to record in his bare-bones biography a time

when he had learned of a plot to waylay and murder Joseph on his return from Michigan. "I procured a horse and buggy," he wrote, "and took brother William Smith along to meet Joseph. We met him returning in the stage coach, Joseph requested William to take his seat in the stage, and he rode with me in the buggy. We arrived in Kirtland in safety."[18]

It is no wonder that when the Prophet asked Heber Kimball to serve a mission in England shortly thereafter and Heber, fearful and needing the strength of his old friend beside him, requested that Brigham might go with him, Joseph replied that he wished Brigham to stay beside him. No man was more qualified or more willing to do just that.

In early September, the Saints met in conference to reorganize the Church. Those authorities who were in good standing were sustained; but it was necessary to disfellowship those, leaders and otherwise, who had sought the overthrow and destruction of the Church. "The apostates and disaffected, not being united, were compelled to endure the chagrin of witnessing the accomplishment of the will of God and his Prophet,"[19] were the words Brigham recorded in his journal concerning the event.

Brigham was too obvious and powerful a supporter to be left alone; he had offended and humiliated too many of the apostates. "On the night of the 22nd of December, 1836, in a cold wintry storm Brigham Young fled for his life from the hands of his enemies, and from his home," wrote Emmeline Wells, "commending to God and to angels his wife and five helpless children." Mary Ann's newly born twins were only four days old at the time. Where her husband was, or what his fate, she knew not from day to day. Her own plight she described as "undoubtedly the severest trial of my life":

She was left alone to struggle as best she could under the complication of adverse circumstances surrounding her, *relying upon God for help, in whom she ever implicitly trusted,* to carry her safely through all the difficulties and trials that beset her way. She suffered intensely from the depredations of those who were filled with bitterness, some of whom had been members of the Church, but had fallen away. The mob came to her house, frequently searching it pretending to believe her husband was hid up there, and frighten her with threats and vile language.[20]

Joseph Smith did not leave Kirtland until January. Kirtland Camp, with the majority of the Saints (515 members), left on the fifth of July. Brigham and Mary Ann, separated from one another, relied upon God for help, proving the powerful words the Prophet Joseph spoke concerning the Kirtland era:

> It was clearly evident that the Lord gave us power in proportion to the work to be done, and strength according to the race set before us, and grace and help as our needs required.[21]

Notes

1. Arrington, *American Moses*, p. 47.
2. Joseph Smith, Jr., *History of the Church of Jesus Christ of Latter-day Saints,* edited by B. H. Roberts, 7 vols. (Salt Lake City: The Church of Jesus Christ of Latter-day Saints, 1948) 2:193-8; cited hereafter as *HC.*
3. *Ms. History*, p. 5.
4. *JD*, 7:229 and 2:18.
5. Diary of Joseph Smith, 12 November 1835, Church Archives.
6. Diary of Wilford Woodruff, 23 February 1859, Church Archives.
7. Karl Ricks Anderson, *Joseph Smith's Kirtland: Eyewitness Accounts* (Salt Lake City: Deseret Book, 1989), p. 170.
8. Orson F. Whitney, *Life of Heber C. Kimball* (Salt Lake City: Bookcraft,1945), p. 91.
9. Truman O. Angell Journal, as cited in Lyndon Cook, *BYU Studies,* vol. 15, no. 4 (Summer 1975), p. 550.
10. *HC,* 2:426.
11. Arrington, *American Moses*, p. 54.
12. Ibid., p. 55.
13. Whitney, *Life of Heber C. Kimball,* p. 99.
14. *JD,* 1:215.
15. *Journal of Brigham*, p. 9.
16. Ibid.; italics author's.

17. Ibid., p. 10.
18. Ibid., p. 10.
19. Ibid., p. 13.
20. Emmeline B. Wells, "Heroines of the Church: Biography of Mary Ann Angell Young," *Juvenile Instructor,* vol. 26 (1 January 1891), pp. 18-19; italics author's.
21. Susan Evans McCloud, *Joseph Smith—A Photobiography* (Salt Lake City: Aspen Books, 1992), p. 55; hereafter referred to as *Joseph Smith.*

Chapter Six

Accomplishing the Objects of the Lord

*Assisting Joseph – treachery and extermination in Missouri –
a sacred oath – removing the Saints from the state –
visiting the prophet and brethren in jail – the banks of the
Mississippi – purchasing land in Illinois – laying the foundation
of the Lord's house – reunion with Joseph Smith*

All intelligent beings who are crowned with crowns of glory, immortality, and eternal lives must pass through every ordeal appointed for
intelligent beings to pass through, to gain their glory and exaltation.
Every calamity that can come upon mortal beings will be suffered to
come upon the few, to prepare them to enjoy the presence of the
Lord. . . . Every trial and experience you have passed through is necessary for your salvation.

Journal of Discourses, 8:150

Brigham, fleeing his detractors, traveled first to Dublin,
Indiana, where he met up with his brother Lorenzo and a number
of families who were wintering there. The Prophet soon joined
him, and wasted no time in looking for work cutting wood or
sawing logs, for he was destitute of means. Brigham records an
enlightening incident which took place:

> The Prophet . . . came up to me and said, "Brother Brigham, I am des-
> titute of means to pursue my journey, and as you are one of the Twelve
> Apostles who hold the keys of the kingdom in all the world, I believe
> I shall throw myself upon you, and look to you for counsel in this
> case." At first I could hardly believe Joseph was in earnest, but on his
> assuring me he was, I said, "If you will take my counsel, it will be that
> you rest yourself and be assured, brother Joseph, you shall have plenty
> of money to pursue your journey."[1]

What prompted Brigham to make such a statement? He was a little uneasy himself. But he had advised a Brother Tomlinson, who had approached him in discouragement about the sale of his tavern stand, to "do right and obey counsel," and he should not only sell soon, but "the first offer he would get would be the best." It worked out even so. He was offered $500, a team, and $250 in store goods. "I told him that was the hand of the Lord," Brigham replied bluntly, "to deliver President Joseph Smith from his present necessity."[2] Brother Tomlinson gave the Prophet $300 that he might proceed on his journey.

Meanwhile, Mary Ann, back in Kirtland, had fallen ill with consumption—a word which must have struck terror to Brigham's heart. Her biographer states that her illness "seemed likely to prove fatal." But she hung on through the dark, bitter winter months, and somehow mustered enough strength to take her five children and travel—by private carriage and then steamboat—to meet Brigham in Richmond, Missouri. When he saw her, "he was so astonished and shocked at the change in her appearance that his first exclamation was, 'You look as if you were almost in your grave.'"[3]

Indeed, Mary Ann's health was to continue fragile, and she was desperately ill throughout that summer and fall—so much so that Joseph released Brigham from the heavy burden of church responsibility he had been carrying, speaking through revelation:

> Verily thus saith the Lord, let my servant Brigham Young go unto the
> place which he has bought, on Mill Creek, and there provide for his

family until an effectual door is opened for the support of his family,
until I command him to go hence, and not to leave his family until
they are amply provided for.[4]

This was a much-needed respite, a time for Brigham to renew
his own greatly depleted resources, for him to spend time with the
children and strengthen the woman who had pledged her life that
he might be able to devote his energies to the work of the Lord.
Despite the extenuating circumstances which often made it necessary for the leaders of the Church to "desert" their families, leaving them to their own resources, Joseph Smith made it clear in his
teachings what a man's duty to wife and family were:

> The Prophet Joseph Smith often referred to the feelings that should
> exist between husbands and wives, that they, his wives, should be his
> bosom companions, the nearest and dearest objects on earth in every
> sense of the word. He said men should beware how they treat their
> wives . . . that many would awake on the morning of the resurrection
> sadly disappointed; for they, by transgression, would have neither
> wives nor children, for they surely would be taken from them and
> given to those who should prove themselves worthy.[5]

In this, as in all things, Joseph demonstrated principle by the
power of his personal example—as in the case related by Jesse W.
Crosby, who took it upon himself to give "corrective advice" to
the Prophet:

> Some of the home habits of the Prophet—such as building kitchen
> fires, carrying out ashes, carrying in wood and water, assisting in the
> care of the children, etc.—were not in accord with my idea of a great
> man's self respect. "Too terrible a humiliation," I [told him], "for you
> who are the head, and you should not do it." The Prophet listened
> quietly to all I had to say, then made his answer in these words: "If
> there be humiliation in a man's house, who but the head of that house
> should or could bear that humiliation? . . . If a man cannot learn in
> this life to appreciate a wife and do his duty by her, in properly tak-
> ing care of her, he need not expect to be given one in the hereafter."[6]

In this, as in countless areas, Brigham reflected the teachings of the Prophet Joseph in the counsel he later gave to the Saints:

It is for the husband to learn how to gather around his family the comforts of life, how to control his passions and temper, and how to command the respect, not only of his family but of all his brethren. . . . The father should be full of kindness, and endeavor to happify and cheer the mother, that her heart may be comforted and her affections unimpaired in her earthly protector.[7]

During this season when Brigham was concentrating on the care of his family—one step back, as it were, from the mainstream of things—he was able to see the inevitability that the Saints would be driven from Missouri, that the tragedy of their experience in that place was drawing to an end.

There were nearly fifteen thousand Mormons in the state. When a group of them attempted to vote at an election in Gallatin, local mobsters attempted to stop them, construing anything as an excuse for further violence—even the brethren's facile attempts to ward off their blows. By September, the violence and the rumors of violence had increased; and on August 30, 1838, Governor Boggs ordered General Atchison to raise within his district four hundred armed and equipped men to stand in readiness to quell the Mormon troubles. (This was the same Lilburn W. Boggs who had been lieutenant governor of the state when the Saints were driven from Jackson County, and who had secretly encouraged the mobs in their violent and frenzied acts.) The attacks on Mormon settlements culminated with the burning and destruction of DeWitt, forcing more and more homeless Saints to gather for safety in Far West.

In October, Brigham thought it prudent to move his family to the protection of the city—but not before viewing with his own eyes the treachery of Missouri settlers who would gather their belongings in preparation to leave the county, then burn their own homes and barns behind them, reporting with glee that the Mormons had burned them out. The madness spread, fed by political and religious leaders who wished to be rid of the threat to their power and control which the Mormons posed.

Dissension and apostasy within the ranks of the Church increased the sense of insecurity and unrest. On or about October 18, leading apostles Orson Hyde and Thomas Marsh left the Church and the area. Brother Marsh had struggled to overcome his own weaknesses, admitting that "I had become jealous of the Prophet, and then I saw double and overlooked everything that was right, and spent my time looking for evil."[8] The advice Brigham gave him, when approached, could stand as the consummate word by which he lived his own life: "Brother Brigham, with a cautious look, said, 'Are you the leader of the Church, brother Thomas?' I answered, 'no.' 'Well then,' said he, '*Why do you not let that alone!*'"[9]

A week later, senior apostle David Patten was fatally wounded in an encounter with the mob near Crooked River. Thus Brigham and Heber Kimball (who had returned late in July from his mission in England) became the senior apostles. This pattern of the two working in harmony and supporting one another had established itself before they had even learned of the restored Church and associated themselves with it. Their confidence in one another's integrity, the intimacy of affection dating to the days when they had lived in the same household together, and the depth of their commitment to the cause rendered them an invincible force for good which would be much needed.

Only a few days later, on October 27, Governor Boggs issued an actual "Extermination Order" which gave clear-cut legal sanction to whatever the mobs cared to do:

> The Mormons must be treated as enemies and must be exterminated or driven from the state, if necessary for the public good. Their outrages are beyond all description. If you can increase your force, you are authorized to do so, to any extent you may think necessary.[10]

The worst result of this inhuman document was in the massacre which took place on October 30 in the little Mormon settlement of Haun's Mill, where men, women and children were killed and abused with impunity and the horrors, reaching the ears of their brethren, struck terror into every heart.

On the morning of the 28th, Brigham had been one of several men to ride out under a white flag to survey the situation and try to deal with the men—troops and mobsters—who were gathering around Far West. These forces grew to an army of over two thousand, camped restlessly only two miles from the homes of the people, and outnumbering the city four to one.

The governor's order, generally unknown to the Saints, was read publicly in the square at Far West on the night of the 29th. Not only were its terms unendurable, but its tone, and the insults delivered by General Clark with undisguised contempt, were nearly more than could be borne:

> You are the best and most orderly people in this State, and have done more to improve it in three years than we have in fifteen. . . .

Brigham amply attested to that as he described for the Saints in Salt Lake the "degraded" conditions in which the Missouri settlers lived, "without schools, orchards or mills, like the brutes almost."

> But we have this to say to you [General Clark continued], No more bishops, no more high councils, and as for your prophet . . . you will never see him again.

Brigham responded with characteristic emotion—for he was, even years later, emotional about the experiences of those days, despite his assertions that "I do not acknowledge that I ever received persecution; my path has been so kind from the Lord I do not consider that I have suffered enough even to mention it." But the injustice of "man's inhumanity to man" was difficult for Brigham's noble spirit to ignore, and the magnificence with which he and the Saints endured and triumphed, by the strength of their spirits—these things were, like victories in battle, not altogether unpleasant to think upon or recall.

I will see you in hell first [Brigham countered to General Clark].
Renounce my religion? No, sir, . . . it is my all, all I have on this earth.
What is this world worth as it is now? Nothing. It is like a morning
shadow; it is like the dew before the sun, like the grass before the
scythe, or the flower before the pinching frosts of autumn. No, sir, I
do not renounce my religion. I am looking beyond; my hope is
beyond this vale of tears, and beyond the present life. I have another
life to live, and it is eternal. The organization and intelligence God
has given me are not to perish in nonentity; I have to live, and I cal-
culate to take such a course that my life hereafter will be in a higher
state of existence than the present.[11]

This powerful testimony rings, not only with conviction, but
with the poetry which Brigham's heart lent his unschooled tongue.

October 31 dawned gray and silent. Mormon Lieutenant-
Colonel Hinkle approached the armies under a white flag of
truce, the brethren he had betrayed riding behind him, innocently
believing they were to meet with the enemy to come to some
terms. But the men—Joseph, Sidney Rigdon, Parley Pratt, Lyman
Wight, and George W. Robinson—were surrounded and taken
into camp as prisoners.

The people in their homes in Far West could hear the horrible yelling
and screeching of the mob. Lucy Smith records how she and her husband stood at the door listening, when suddenly they heard the shots
of five or six guns. The Prophet's father cried out, "Oh, my God! my
God! they have killed my son! They have murdered him, and I must
die, for I cannot live without him!" He fell nearly senseless on the bed.
Lucy further records, "No tongue can describe, no heart can imagine
the sensations of our breasts as we listened to those awful screams.
Had the army been composed of so many bloodhounds, wolves and
panthers, they could not have made a sound more terrible."[12]

The following morning, Hyrum Smith and Amasa Lyman
were taken by the mob. That night a court martial was held, with
the verdict that the prisoners were to be shot at eight the following morning in their own town square, as an example to their

friends and families. General Lucas gave the order to Brigadier General Doniphan, who flatly refused to carry it out. "It is cold-blooded murder," he replied boldly. "I will not obey your order, and if you execute those men, I will hold you responsible before an earthly tribunal, so help me God!"[13] Lucas quickly altered his orders, placed the prisoners in General Wilson's care, and instructed that they be marched to Independence.

Meanwhile, the citizens of Far West were required at gunpoint to sign over their property to pay the expenses of going to war against them. They were also required to hand over an additional fifty-six of their leaders for arrest. Both Brigham and Heber, being generally unknown to the mobsters, were overlooked. Lastly, the Saints were required to leave the state:

> Whatever may be your feelings concerning this, or whatever your innocence, it is nothing to me. . . . The character of this state has suffered almost beyond redemption, from the character, conduct, and influence you have exerted . . . you have always been the aggressors— you have brought upon yourselves these difficulties. . . . I am sorry, gentlemen, to see so great a number of apparently intelligent men found in the situation that you are; and oh! that I invoke that Great Spirit, the unknown God . . . to liberate you from these fetters of fanaticism . . . that you no longer worship a man . . . I would advise you to scatter abroad, and never again organize yourselves . . . lest you excite the jealousies of the people, and subject yourselves to the same calamities that have now come upon you.[14]

The many contradictions in General Clark's cruel speech are evident. The realities, nevertheless, remained. He mercifully allowed the stricken people time to gather their corn and prepare, but warned them that "you must not think of staying here another season, or of putting in crops," adding a further promise that "if I am called here again, in case of a non-compliance . . . you need not expect any mercy, but extermination, for I am determined the governor's orders shall be executed."[15]

This was on Tuesday, the 6th of November. The next day the prisoners—leaving wives and children behind who were sick, penniless, some confined in childbed—were marched under heavy guard to Richmond. Thursday there was a terrible snowstorm, dispiriting the Saints, but perhaps also dampening a little the exuberance of the mob who had been plundering houses, attacking innocent women and children, killing animals, trampling fields, and doing all in their power to hurt and destroy.

It was under such wretched, heart-rending conditions that Brigham took over leadership of a people exhausted, terrified, and bereft. A heart less stout, less valiant, would have quailed at the task. But Brigham attacked it with his usual energy, order, and faith.

The Saints, anxious to leave the state as soon as they could, became somewhat scattered and disorganized. Too many lacked means—even a team and animals—to carry them out of the reach of their enemies. And, despite the pledged word of their leaders, the mobsters threatened and harassed the Mormons constantly.

Concerned, Brigham approached Bishop Partridge for help in assisting the poor. In a moment of discouragement the Bishop, who had once been a wealthy man and had beggared himself in the service of the Church, replied, "The poor may take care of themselves, and I will take care of myself." Brigham simply replied, "If you will not help them out, I will."[16]

On the 16th of January, 1839, Joseph wrote from prison a letter of instruction to the Apostles wherein he counseled them to organize the Twelve, ordaining the two men they had nominated, George A. Smith and Lyman Sherman, in place of Orson Hyde and Thomas Marsh. Lyman Sherman died a few days later and so was never sustained. Joseph encouraged them to rejoice, even in the midst of persecution, thinking of the strengths they were developing and the joy which would eventually be theirs. "Pray for us," the Prophet asked, "and cease not till our deliverance comes." Then he counseled, "Let the Elders preach nothing but the first principles of the Gospel, and let them publish our afflictions."[17]

Brigham got straight to work, calling a meeting of all the leading elders who could be found. One of their actions was to appoint a committee whose dual function was to discover and assist destitute families and to prepare an appeal to the citizens of the state for assistance. Brigham, Heber, and John Taylor, all apostles, were appointed to this front-line committee. But Brigham knew he had to obtain commitment from as many as possible. Three days later he drafted a covenant

> that should bind the saints in an agreement to assist each other to the extent of their available property to remove from the State of Missouri. . . . Elder Young secured eighty names . . . the first day, and three hundred the next. The Prophet Joseph, . . . hearing what was going on through those who visited him in prison, from his gloomy dungeon at Liberty, sent the brethren a hundred dollars to assist in removing the Saints.[18]

On February 7 of the new year, 1839, Brigham and Heber traveled to Liberty to visit the Prophet Joseph and the other prisoners. "We had the privilege of going in to see and converse with them," Heber wrote. "Stayed at Liberty over night. Next morning we were permitted to visit the prisoners again while they were at breakfast, and returned during the day to Far West."[19] Communication with Joseph boosted their spirits and resolve, but oh, how difficult it must have been to see him in such a state, to witness his suffering and his concern for the Saints.

It did not take the Missourians long to identify Brigham as one of the Church's new leaders—a threat it would be well worth their trouble to remove. On Thursday, February 14, Brigham recorded: "I left Missouri with my family, leaving my landed property and nearly all my household goods."[20] Heber Kimball wrote:

> I fitted up a small wagon, procured a span of ponies, and sent my wife and three children, in company with Brother Brigham Young and his family, with several others, who left Far West, Feb. 14th. Everything my family took with them out of Missouri could have been packed on the backs of two horses; the mob took all the rest.[21]

Mary Ann leaves us some insight into that terrible journey, undertaken in cold and destitute circumstances, with danger on every side. She started her journey and traveled two days alone, without Brigham's aid, until he met her with a wagon and two yoke of oxen. She had somehow secured a small wagon and persuaded one of the Elders to help her get away from the city:

> She sat on the top of the load of her baggage and bedding with a baby on each arm, and three little children clinging to her skirts. Just as they started out, the wagon ran into a huge rut, and the baby girl was thrown under the wheel. With a groan of dismay the driver picked up the bleeding bundle and laid it on the trembling mother's lap, with the remark that "the poor little thing could not live." Blood was pouring from mouth and nose. "Don't prophecy evil, brother, take the other baby!" cried the mother as she dressed the wounds, praying mightily all the while. Mary lived and grew to be the finest child of the family.[22]

They would travel a short distance under Brigham's care, then he would leave them wherever they might find a little care or shelter and return "with such help as he could get . . . to gather up the poorer and more destitute of the brethren and sisters, the widows and helpless orphans of those who had fallen victims at the hands of the mob." Brigham left his own family eleven separate times in the service of others. Thus, by painful degrees, they reached Quincy on the banks of the Mississippi, having "kept house . . . during the short interval of three months . . . in eleven different places."[23]

The citizens of Illinois were proving to be generous and sympathetic toward the Mormons. Brigham met with the Saints in Quincy in mid-March to discuss appeals for assistance which were still being pressed upon them. He took space in his journal to record the following in detail:

> Though the brethren were poor and stripped of almost everything, yet they manifested a spirit of willingness to do their utmost, offering to sell their hats, coats and shoes to accomplish the object. . . . At the close of the meeting $50 was collected in money, and several teams were subscribed to go and bring the brethren. Among the subscribers was widow Warren Smith, whose husband and son had their brains blown out and another son shot to pieces at the massacre at Haun's Mill. She sent her only team on this charitable mission.[24]

In council on March 18, Brigham advised the brethren to purchase land on Dr. Galland's half-breed tract, and Elders Wilford Woodruff and George A. Smith, a young cousin of the Prophet, were sustained as members of the Twelve.

In the midst of all this, Brigham did not forget or hold lightly the word of the Lord, who had stated in prophecy that the Twelve were to "take leave of my saints in the city of Far West, on the twenty-sixth day of April next, on the building-spot of my house" (Doctrine and Covenants 118:5). Despite sneers and taunts from their enemies to the contrary, Brigham did not agree with some of the brethren who "considered, in our present persecuted and scattered condition, the Lord would not require the Twelve to fulfill his words to the letter, and, under our present circumstances, he would take the will for the deed." This was Brigham at his finest. Persecution had not broken or weakened, but rather honed his qualities and his mastery over himself. Those meeting with him agreed that they ought to fulfill the revelation, "and leave the event in his hands and he would protect us."[25]

Brigham, Wilford, John Taylor, Orson Pratt, George A., and Alpheus Cutler traveled the difficult, dreary journey back to the scenes of their sufferings. Passing through Huntsville, they crossed a long stretch of prairie where the roads were still full of fleeing Saints. More as a means of doing good to a brother than a fulfilling of responsibility, Brigham exhorted John E. Page to go with them, even though they found him with his wagon turned upside down, up to his elbows in soap he was scooping up with his hands. He did not see how he could leave his family, but Brigham assured him his family would be fine. "He asked how much time I would give him to get ready. I answered, five minutes. We assisted in loading his wagon; he drove down the hill and camped, and returned with us. We travelled 30 miles and camped for the night."[26]

Brigham possessed power to stir confidence and resolve in Brother Page, mainly because his own motives were pure and obviously driven by a sincere, unconditional love.

On the morning of the 26th of April, the Twelve found themselves standing on that hallowed ground, with feelings which could not be described. Alpheus Cutler had been master workman of the Lord's house; it fell to him to re-commence laying the foundation, "by rolling up a large stone near the south-east corner." Each of the Twelve prayed vocally, then joined in singing "Adam-ondi-Ahman."

"Thus was the revelation fulfilled," Brigham wrote, "concerning which our enemies had said, if all the other revelations of Joseph Smith were fulfilled, that one should not, as it had day and date to it."[27]

It seemed a mob had collected in several different places to detain them, but when they finally made it to Far West it was only to learn that the Twelve had already been there, and what had been promised had been carried out.

Compassion and commitment were yet uppermost in Brigham's mind. He further recorded:

> We had entered into a covenant to see the poor Saints all moved out of Missouri to Illinois, that they might be delivered out of the hands of such vile persecutors, and *we spared no pains to accomplish this object until the Lord gave us the desires of our hearts.* We had the last company of the poor with us that could be removed. Brothers P. P. Pratt and Morris Phelps were in prison, and we had to leave them for a season. We sent a wagon after brother Yokum, who had been so dreadfully mutilated in the Haun's Mill massacre that he could not be moved.[28]

Another desire of Brigham's heart was realized when, following his return to Quincy, he rode out to Mr. Cleveland's with several of his brethren to see Joseph and Hyrum Smith, who had escaped from their six months' confinement, and had actually been en route to Quincy when the Twelve were heading back to Far West:

> It was one of the most joyous scenes of my life to once more strike hands with the Prophets and behold them free from the hands of their enemies. Joseph conversed with us like a man who had just escaped from a thousand oppressions—and was now free in the midst of his children.[29]

Notes

1. *Journal of Brigham,* p. 13.
2. Ibid., p. 14.
3. Emmeline B. Wells, "Heroines of the Church: Biography of Mary Ann Angell Young," *Juvenile Instructor,* vol. 26 (1 January 1891), p. 19.
4. *HC,* 3:23.
5. "Lucy Walker Kimball," *They Knew the Prophet,* comp. by Hyrum Andrus and Helen Mae Andrus (Salt Lake City: Bookcraft, 1974), pp. 139-40.
6. Ibid., "Jesse W. Crosby," p. 145.
7. *JD,* 10:28, 8:62.
8. *JD,* 5:207.
9. Arrington, *American Moses,* p. 65; italics author's.
10. *HC,* 3:175.
11. *JD,* 14:206.
12. McCloud, *Joseph Smith,* p. 87.
13. Ibid., p. 89.
14. *Journal of Brigham,* p. 16.
15. *HC,* 3:203-4.
16. *HC,* 3:247.
17. Whitney, *Life of Heber C. Kimball,* pp. 237-38.
18. Brigham H. Roberts, *The Missouri Persecutions* (Salt Lake City: Bookcraft, 1965), pp. 263-64.
19. Whitney, *Life of Heber C. Kimball,* p. 239.
20. Journal of Brigham, p. 19.
21. Whitney, *Life of Heber C. Kimball,* p. 239.
22. Gates and Widtsoe, *Life Story,* pp. 19-20.
23. Wells, "Biography of Mary Ann Angell Young," *Juvenile Instructor,* p. 19.
24. *Journal of Brigham,* p. 19.
25. Ibid.
26. Ibid., p. 20.
27. Ibid., p. 18.
28. Ibid., p. 21.
29. Ibid.

Chapter Seven

Extending the Borders of Zion

*Early struggles, healings in Nauvoo – fulfilling a mission
in faith – leadership, growth in Great Britain –
baptism and emigration of British Saints – publications –
organization in British Isles – return home*

What is it that enables our Elders to go forth and preach the Gospel?
The Spirit of the Lord. This is their experience and testimony. What
do they testify when they go forth? That the Gospel, as set forth in
the Old and New Testaments, is true; that the plan of salvation,
revealed by God through his prophets in ancient times, and in modern times through Joseph Smith, is true; and as they are enlightened
and aided by the Spirit of the Lord, error must fall before them. . . .
How easy it is to sustain truth! How easy it is to sustain the doctrines
of the Savior!

Journal of Discourses, 14:75-76

Commerce was a beginning; after the horrors of Missouri, at
least it was that. But it would not yet be home for Brigham, who
was determined to fulfill the mission to which he had been
appointed. He had at this time, in fact, settled his family in one
of the rooms of the old military barracks at Montrose, Iowa, on

the other side of the river from Nauvoo. He and the others began preparing for that mission—more in a spiritual manner than in a physical, for there was very little they could do in their generally destitute state. They met with the Prophet and were instructed by him, inspired and uplifted by his example. One of these meetings was held at Brigham's house, and though his entry is simple— "Brother Joseph taught many important and glorious principles calculated to benefit and bless [us] on [our] mission"[1]—the import behind the statement is powerful. These men—penniless, ill, exhausted by persecution, distress, loss, travel under the most trying of conditions—were yet willing to discipline their minds and spirits to receive the solemnities of heaven. And all for what purpose? To serve God, whom they loved, and to serve their fellow men. Wilford Woodruff, in his wonderfully detailed journal, provides insightful detail of that meeting, stating that the Prophet blessed each man and *his wife* separately. Certainly there was full recognition in this setting of the vital importance of unity between husband and wife, that each must fulfill an incredible role to carry this work forward. "If we were faithful," Wilford wrote, "We had the promise of again returning to the bosoms of our families and being blessed on our missions and having many souls as seals of our ministry."[2] This promise was abundantly fulfilled, as this synopsis of his activities for the one year of 1840 shows:

> I traveled 4,469 miles, held 230 meetings, established 53 places for preaching, and planted 47 churches and jointly organized them. These churches chiefly comprised the two conferences raised up in Herefordshire, consisting of about 1,500 Saints, 28 elders, 110 priests, 24 teachers and 10 deacons. The baptisms of the year were 336 persons under my own hand, and I assisted at the baptism of 86 others. I baptized 57 preachers. . . . I confirmed 420 members. . . . blessed 120 children, and administered to 120 sick, by prayer . . . I assisted in procuring £1,000 for the publication of 3,000 copies of the Hymn Book, 5,000 copies of the Book of Mormon, for the printing of the Millennial Star, and to assist 200 Saints to emigrate to Nauvoo. I wrote 200 letters, and received 112.[3]

The burden of Joseph's advice concerned the importance of love: fellowship, forgiveness, long-suffering, "the principles of mercy," the importance of repenting and confessing their own sins. "Let the Twelve be humble," he counseled, "and . . . beware of pride . . . and not seek to excell one above another . . . and pray constantly for one another before the Lord."[4] Obviously missing from Joseph's remarks was any practical advice on how to preach, how to administer, and how to organize. He knew well the capabilities of these men before him. He understood the necessity of their growth—and he understood the order of the kingdom, which was safely under the direction of God, who was capable of magnifying these men if they followed the counsel he had just given them and kept themselves worthy of light and direction from above.

This was on July 2. Five days later, Brigham, Heber, and some of the others spoke in a meeting of the Saints—their farewell addresses—at which time Brigham "bore testimony in the Spirit."[5] A small phrase, a term familiar to Latter-day Saints, but telling us, nevertheless, of his preparation and worthiness to embark on this work.

The preparations, going in good order, were halted by the malaria which infested the swampy ground along the Mississippi where the Saints' new settlement sat. All of the Twelve were afflicted with the chills and fevers, as were most of their friends and family. Joseph had taken the sick into his home and filled his yard with them, he and Emma administering to the distressed with their own hands, until the Prophet himself was stricken, and lay for some days as helpless as the others.

Then, on July 22, Joseph roused himself, prayed mightily to the Lord, and rose from his own sickbed to go forth in power, administering to his brethren—first those in his own house and yard, then traveling "from house to house and from tent to tent upon the banks of the river," at length crossing to the Iowa side. "He walked into the cabin where I was lying sick," Brigham wrote, "and commanded me, in the name of Jesus Christ, to arise and be made whole. I arose and was healed and followed him and the brethren of the Twelve into the house of Elijah Fordham."[6] In passing Wilford Woodruff's door, Joseph called out simply, "Brother Woodruff, follow me,"[7] which he did. Brother Fordham lay at the point of death, but Joseph, through the power of his priesthood, raised him. "His voice was as the voice of God,"[8] Brigham recorded. "The words of the Prophet were not like the words of man, but like the voice of God," Elder Woodruff wrote. "It seemed to me that the house shook on its foundation."[9]

When Wilford started on his mission early in August, he was extremely ill, traveling with John Taylor, the only one of the quorum who was well. Brigham started on Saturday, September 14, so weak with sickness that he could not walk the thirty rods to the river without help, and so exhausted by his efforts that he collapsed at Heber's house, where he remained sick for four days. He had left his family in a dismal state—all of them ill and unable to move, to assist one another, even to draw water to drink. Mary Ann, sick and weakened by the birth of a baby only ten days before, was able only to wave weakly to him when he stumbled away from her, leaning against the door for support. Yet, hearing of her husband's state, she roused herself and somehow managed to cross the river to be at his side. We have no description of that last bittersweet encounter, but the triumph of physical and spiritual stamina which Mary Ann demonstrated reveals a depth of love, devotion, and selflessness that we cannot help but admire and wish to emulate. The unity between husband and wife was a vital part of the strength of each.

Both Brigham and Heber were a sorry sight when they at last took their leave. Both were without a second suit of clothing, and Brigham was wrapped in a quilt for want of an overcoat. They made it only as far as Quincy before having to stop for several days before they were strong enough to continue again. After their arrival in England, the memory of this day remained so vivid that Heber wrote feelingly to Vilate:

> I will tell you, my Dear, that time will be remembered by me as long as time lasts. Fore no man has ever suffered as much as I did in my

feelings. No more do I wish to while I live on earth. I think if ever one man did, I have left all for the Caus of Christ.[10]

Brigham's first communication to Mary Ann may, in comparison, seem mundane, too practical and unfeeling, as he talks about debts and monies to be paid out, leaving her with the pathetic sum of $2.75. "This is allmost rob[b]ing you, I [k]now," he wrote, "But I doe not now wht elce to doe. Brother Joseph has pledged himself that the wives of the Twelve should have what they wanted . . . I doe feel as thou the Lord would provide for you and me."[11] In this statement again is the quiet, unadorned affirmation of his commitment and faith. He was, especially at this stage of his life, uncomfortable with the overt expression of emotion. Concerning his description of his leaving, his daughter, Susa, wrote that it was "like his own character, devoid of high lights or grewsome details."[12] Brigham, in later years, explained himself in these words: "I am careful to keep my tears to myself."[13] Indeed, this was part of the inner power of the man, which contributed to the eventual genius of his leadership. He did not complain. He went about uplifting, sustaining, making others feel good. "I calculate to carry my own sorrows just as long as I live upon this earth, and when I go to the grave, I expect them all to go there, and sleep with me in eternal silence."[14]

During his stay in Quincy, Brigham had the blessing of visiting his father for the last time. John Young, worn out by the strenuous life he had lived and the persecutions of Missouri, died not long after Brigham left.

Brigham and Heber went from Quincy to Kirtland, stopping at Jacksonville, Terre Haute, Pleasant Garden, and other places along the way, preaching to the Saints and obtaining gifts, sustenance, and encouragement from many hands. But sickness and difficulty plagued their steps. Brigham at first was more ill and weak than his faithful companion, Heber. But when Heber was given a dose of morphine by a drunken doctor, he nearly died. "When I came to," he wrote, "Brother Brigham was attending to me with a fatherly care, and manifesting much anxiety in my behalf."[15] Yet, not many days later, he was nursing Brigham through a relapse. George A. Smith was laboring in the same vicinity. Although but twenty-two years old, he became so sick that his eyesight was severely affected, so "that I had to wait on him while travelling, and select his food and put it on his plate, as he could not tell one dish from another," Brigham wrote. He was also unable to resist the following, which he added: "While I was settling our bill, I heard some gentlemen conversing, who said, 'Do you know that old gentleman who came in the stage?' He was answered, 'No.' 'Do you know that young man who waits on him?' 'No.'"[16] This was humor such as Brigham took delight in, and a little compliment to himself, which was well appreciated.

The brethren sustained and assisted each other, and were gratified to realize that they were receiving divine assistance as well. Heber C. Kimball tells the story best:

> We proceeded to Kirtland and arrived the same evening. . . . Brother Brigham had one York shilling left, and on looking over our expenses we found we had paid out over $87.00 out of the $13.50 we had at Pleasant Garden, which is all the money we had to pay our passages with. . . . Brother Brigham often suspected that I had put the money in his trunk, or clothes; thinking that I had a purse of money which I had not acquainted him with, but this was not so; the money could only have been put in his trunk by some heavenly messenger, who thus administered to our necessities daily as he knew we needed.[17]

On Friday, November 22, they took a lake steamer to New York, where a storm in the night became so severe that Brigham decided to take action:

> I went up on deck and I felt impres[sed] in spirit to pray to the Father in the name of Jesus, for a forgiveness of all my sins, and then I felt to command the winds to cease, and let us go safe on our journey. The winds abated, and I felt to give the glory and honor and praise to that God who rules all things.[18]

The three important elements here, and their order, are significant. There was no real pride in Brigham; his first impulse was to humble himself before the Lord. But then, understanding his right to call upon that Power to which he had submitted, he felt no hesitation in calling the elements into submission. And, when such came to pass, his natural, heartfelt impulse again was to remember and acknowledge in gratitude "God who rules all things." This lends insight to the very real confidence he felt in placing the care and welfare of his beloved family into the hands of his Heavenly Father.

En route to New York, Brigham met with some of his cousins of the Phinehas Brigham family, whose surname was, in fact, the source of his own given name. They were still as unyielding against the gospel as they had been years before. He tried his best, bore his testimony with great power, then left them alone. But he had tried. He never closed the door on anyone, nor did he cease giving people an opportunity to alter and grow.

The brethren did not arrive in New York until the end of January, and Brigham's health was "feeble." Two days later, he met with an accident which tried him yet more:

> Passing from Brooklyn to New York, I jumped on to the ferryboat with my left arm extended, meaning to catch hold of the stanchion, but I fell on a large iron ring on the deck, which put my shoulder out of joint. I asked brother Hedlock to roll me over on my back, which he did; I directed brothers Kimball and Hedlock to lay hold of my body, and brother Pratt to take hold of my hand and pull, putting his foot against my side, while I guided the bone with my right hand back to its place. The brethren wound my hand-kerchief round my shoulder and helped me up. When I came to a fire I fainted, and was not able to dress myself for several days.[19]

Despite this, he spent five active weeks in the city, baptizing, preaching, attempting to raise much-needed funds—a task Brigham did not relish:

> At the last meeting I held, I told the people I was on a mission to England with my brethren; I had never asked for a dime in all my preaching, but we had not sufficient means to proceed, and if any one wished to contribute to help us, I would thankfully receive it. After meeting, $19.50 was put in my hands.[20]

When he had paid for his fare of $18.00 aboard the ship *Patrick,* with an additional dollar to the cook, he had only 50 cents left. But the sisters sewed and filled ticks and pillows for the departing missionaries, and the members in New York provided them with the food they would need for the journey.

The excitement of an ocean journey was somewhat dulled by Brigham's seasickness, which plagued him nearly all of the way. The ship arrived in Liverpool on April 6, a day which was sacred to the young apostles, and which marked the tenth anniversary of the organization of the Church. Although he was pale and emaciated, Brigham was filled with the spirit of his calling: "When we landed on the shore I gave a loud shout of hosannah. . . . I felt that the chains were broken, and the bands that were upon me were burst asunder."[21]

The first thing they did after finding a room at No. 8 Union Street was to hold a meeting, administer the sacrament, and appeal to God to open the way before them. The brethren looked "thin and weather-beaten" as Joseph Fielding described them, and Brigham was so pale and reduced that his cousin, Willard Richards, meeting him three days later, did not even recognize him. Yet this did not prevent them from setting to work with all the energy of their souls.

They traveled to Preston, because this was where Heber Kimball, Orson Hyde, Willard Richards, and Joseph Fielding had met with such success in 1837. Their hearts must have been warmed by the large gathering of Saints who came to welcome them. John Taylor, Wilford Woodruff, and Theodore Turley, who had arrived in January, joined Brigham, Heber, Orson and Parley Pratt, and George A. Smith in conference, calling it "the first Council of the Twelve among the Nations." Brigham was acknowledged as the "Standing President of the Twelve," and took charge with both ease and energy. Willard Richards was ordained to the apostleship, making a total of eight apostles in England together.

Wasting no time, Brigham called a general conference, which nearly sixteen hundred Saints attended. His first concern was to obtain approval and support for his rather ambitious publication proposal: the Book of Mormon, a hymn book, and the *Latter-day*

Saints' Millennial Star, to be a monthly periodical. Brigham recognized the importance of unity of belief in forging these converts from varying backgrounds into Latter-day Saints who believed alike and understood the tenets of the kingdom. Many of these came from the Primitive Methodists and United Brethren, who attracted simple people seeking for some depth of religious meaning in their lives. From the very beginning, the Twelve encouraged the British members to emigrate to the States. And from the very beginning, Brigham was aware of the needs of the poor, insisting that no one "that has money" go to America "without assisting the poor according to our council."[22]

Brigham's skills as an observer of human nature were honed during this missionary experience. "Almost without exception it is the poor that receive the gospel," he wrote to the Prophet Joseph. For them, he said, "simple testimony is enough."[23] To George A. Smith he observed,

> I have had an intervue with a Priest, one a Baptist, the other a Methodost. But they are jest like the rest of the Priest[s]. They have jest religion enuph to damb them—no inclenation to even inquire after the gospel of Jesus Christ. This [Herefordshire region] is a wicked place but there is a fue that want to be saved.[24]

The success of these powerful and gifted men during this two-year period was phenomenal. Truly "the field was ripe, already to harvest" (D & C 4:4), and the laborers, dedicated in mind and spirit, toiled with all their might.

Brigham, as the ranking apostle, carried several weighty, interwoven responsibilities upon his shoulders. It was his charge to oversee the general proselyting work, which included organizing, assisting, and sustaining the other apostles. By inspiration, Brigham, Willard Richards, and Wilford Woodruff were initially assigned to Herefordshire; Heber Kimball to the branches near Preston he had helped to establish two years before; Parley P. Pratt to Manchester; Orson Pratt to open up Scotland; John Taylor to Liverpool; and George A. Smith to the Pottery district of

Staffordshire. George A., only 22, suffered much with illness, including bleeding from the lungs and a raw sore throat. He attempted to work in the London area, but the fogs and pollution irritated his suffering even more. Orson Pratt, 28, stood upon historic Arthur's Seat above Edinburgh and dedicated the land to the preaching of the gospel, lifting here his prayers of entreaty to heaven in behalf of the people of the city, darkened by prejudice, apathy, and an abundance of false teachers. John Taylor, 31, a native Englishman who was articulate, cultured and sincere, built up a strong organization in the Liverpool area, and also opened up Ireland and the Isle of Man. The most astounding success was achieved in the Herefordshire area by Wilford Woodruff, whose power was increased by his openness and his absolute reliance upon the spirit of the Lord.

Despite the weight of administrative detail which often kept Brigham confined to the Manchester office where the Church was headquartered, he did travel throughout the areas where the missionaries labored, preaching about every three days and baptizing and confirming many converts himself. His labors were mostly concentrated in Manchester and Liverpool, though his first view of the English countryside was in Herefordshire—the Malvern Hills, which he called "the most beautiful range of hills in England, being among the highest and affording the most splendid prospect of the surrounding country for 30 miles."[25] Here he had a brief and blessed opportunity to relax, restore his health, and plan the work he hoped to do. His personal power was evident here as elsewhere. When he preached in the Gadfield Elm chapel—the only Latter-day Saint chapel in the world at that time—he filled it to overflowing, so there was not even standing room in the hall which would normally seat one hundred.

While directing the entire church from his Manchester office, Brigham took it upon himself to uplift and set in order the work in that city. He would not allow himself to get bogged down by the mundane details of the work, but instead responded to the promptings of the Spirit whenever they came:

[I] organized the Priesthood in Manchester to meet every Sabbath morning, and distribute themselves throughout the different parts of the city to preach in the streets. In this way they occupied about forty preaching stations, at each one of which the congregation were notified of our regular meetings in the Carpenter's Hall. This so annoyed the sectaries, particularly the Methodists, that they made complaints to the mayor, who issued an order to have all street preachers arrested. I went to the Priesthood meeting in the morning and felt impressed to tell the brethren to go home. The police, who had been instructed to arrest all street preachers that morning, took up about twenty, who all proved to be Methodists. When the magistrate learned they were not "Mormons," they were dismissed.[26]

At the first Manchester conference, held in July of 1840, an increase of 842 members for the previous three months was recorded. At the second conference, held on the 6th of October, baptisms were recorded at 1,113, and at this time forty-two brethren volunteered to labor as missionaries. At the last conference in the city, held just two weeks before the brethren returned to America, all nine of the apostles were in attendance, including Orson Hyde, who was on his way to Jerusalem. The increase reported for the last quarter was 2,188, with well over 500 priesthood ordinations, including two new patriarchs.

Brigham displayed a sensitivity to the personal needs of his brethren, bearing with their personal idiosyncracies and difficulties, and striving to respond to their needs. To his "beloved Willard Richards," as he often addressed him, Brigham wrote characteristic words of counsel which show both his sense of humor and his humility. "Be careful not to lay this letter with the new testament writings," he wrote at the conclusion of one communication. "If you doe somebody will take it for a text after the [Millennium] and contend about it." At the very closing he added, "Now my Dear Brother you must forgive all my noncense and over look erours."[27] And when Willard's wife, Jenetta, whom he had married soon after his arrival in 1837, was ill, Brigham wrote a lengthy communication which mingled humor with sensitivity:

Now as to the other question about Jennet thus saith the scripter he that provideth not fore his own house has—but perhaps he has no house. Well has he got a family, yes he has got a wife. Then let him see that she is taken care of and her hart comforted. But stop say som why doe you not tak care of your family. I doe when circumstances doe not render it otherwise. There is difference betwen 3 months jorny and a fue ours ride. Now I say to answer my own feelings com as soon as you can leve things there. This is not by revelation nor by commandment so put it not with the anapistles of the new testament but Brigham sayes come and see your wife.[28]

Brigham found benefactors who helped make the publication of his 3,000 copies of the Book of Mormon possible. John Benbow contributed over £200, and Thomas Kington £100, sums that would represent $15,000 or more today. Copies of this first edition, bound in morocco leather and imprinted in gold, were presented to Queen Victoria and Prince Albert.

Parley P. Pratt was the first editor of the *Millennial Star,* which was first issued from Manchester in late May of 1840. He wrote the words of his inspiring hymn, "The Morning Breaks," for the premier number. In characteristic fashion, Brigham told Parley "to go ahead and publish 2,000 copies and he, Brigham, would see that the bill was paid." It became a vital means of communication for the British Saints, including revelations from the Prophet in Nauvoo, letters, instructions and progress reports from apostles and leaders up and down the mission, "doctrinal articles by Brigham Young and other apostles," and regular features called "Questions and Answers for Children."[29]

The gathering of Israel was an ancient theme which was lent new pathos and power, sacrifice and vision, in its modern-day setting. "The depression which racked Britain in 1837-42 has been called 'the grimmest period in the history of the nineteenth century.'"[30] This and the devastations of the Irish potato famine made emigration appear appealing; indeed, at times grimly necessary, to the people of the British Isles. But Joseph had cautioned the missionaries not to preach gathering until they felt the inspiration to do so. Brigham and the apostles began the movement, quietly but surely, soon after their arrival and organization in spring of 1840. Under their leadership and instruction,

> converts began to catch the vision of their own role in fulfilling ancient prophecy and following modern revelation. They began to feel the urgency of preparing for Christ's second coming—and theological reasons then combined with economic and social motives for the gathering, to bring about a significant, continuous religious migration.[31]

The first company of only forty-one Saints set sail on the *Britannia* in June of 1840. On September 5, two hundred Saints sailed under the direction of Elder Theodore Tuttle. Brigham, with other apostles, personally contracted for the ship, provisions, and stores, and appointed an American elder, who was capable of leadership, to head each group. He constantly coordinated efforts so that all the vital areas were properly seen to, and all would run smoothly and successfully as they outfitted each ship. In October he wrote to his brother, Joseph:

> The Saints have got a start for to gether to America and goe they will, and nothing can stop them. . . . They have so much of the spirit of getherin that they would goe if they knew they would die as soon as they got there or if they knew that the mob would be upon them and drive them as so[o]n as they got there. They have the spirit of the times here as well as the Church there.[32]

Within a year, nearly a thousand hopeful Saints left for Zion, following with faith and obedience the counsel the First Presidency had set:

> Let those who can, freely make a sacrifice of their time, their talents, and their property, for the prosperity of the kingdom; and for the love they have to the cause of truth, bid adieu to their homes and pleasant places of abode, and unite with us in the great work of the last days, and share in the tribulation, that they may ultimately share in the glory and triumph.[33]

Margaret Pierce

Margaret Pierce (1823-1907) was married to Brigham in 1846, before the trek. She bore him one son, Brigham Morris. Photo ca. 1851

Brigham Young and Amelia Folsom

Brigham married Harriet Amelia Folsom (1838-1910) in 1863. She was twenty-four, tall, fair of complexion, musically talented, and a general favorite, even among his children, although she bore him none of her own. Photo ca. 1863

Mary Ann Angell Young

Brigham married Mary Ann Angell (1803-1882) in 1834, following the death of his first wife, Miriam Works. She bore him three sons and three daughters, and suffered through all the early challenges and trials by Brigham's side. She lived until 1882, five years after Brigham's death. Photo ca. 1850

Heber C. Kimball
Baptized the day after Brigham, Heber was his closest friend and counselor from 1829 until his death in
1868. His prophetic nature was recognized and
respected by the Saints.

Brigham Young
The earliest known photo of Brigham (age 42) from
a daguerreotype taken in Nauvoo about 1843 and
presented to his third polygamous wife, Clara
Decker.

Brigham Young
Brigham, age 46, as he looked at the time of the trek
in 1847.

A mature Brigham Young—colonizer, president,
prophet, aged 54-55. Ca. 1855-56. Considered by
many to be his best photograph.

As Brigham's skills expanded with each new challenge and each new sphere of responsibility, so did the strengths and perceptions of the inner man. Although the English "brotherin and sisters would pluck out there eyes" for him and his brethren "if it ware nessary," help in the vineyard was still badly needed. "I have not herd who is acoming but I trust they will be good men that will be sent, for [s]churely it requires men of strong mind and determined persistence to due all things right, and then due nothing more."[34] This delicate, but vital balance was one he had mastered, but he understood the maturity of spiritual elements needed to bring it about. In a note to his brother, Joseph, who was senior president of the Seventy, he reiterated his appeal for more elders, but added, "for Heven sake due not send men here that is to[o] big to be counseled."[35] In a report back to the Prophet Joseph he wrote:

> Brethren, our hearts are pained with the poverty and misery of this people, and we have done all we could to help as many off as possible to a land where they may get a morsel of bread, and serve God according to his appointment; and we have done it cheerfully as unto the Lord, and we desire to ask you have we done right? Or is it a right principle, for us to act upon, to involve ourselves, to help the poor Saints to Zion?[36]

Here again is displayed the balance between confident initiative and humble willingness to be directed, enlightened, and led.

> Our motto is go ahead. Go ahead, and ahead we are determined to go till we have conquered every foe. So come life or come death we'll go ahead, but tell us if we are going wrong and we will right it.[37]

In a letter composed by himself and Elder Richards, Brigham's sharp discernment is evident:

> We find the people of this land much more ready to receive the gospel, than those in America, so far they do receive it, for they have not that speculative intelligence, or prejudice, or prepossession, or false learning, call it what you please, which they have there [in America]. Consequently we have not to labor with a people month after month

to break down their old notions, for their priests have taught them but little, and much of that is so foolish as to be detected at a glance. Viewing the subject in this light we find ignorance a blessing, for the more ignorant of false notions the more readily they sense truth.[38]

For two weeks in December of 1840, Brigham labored with Elder Woodruff and Elder Kimball in London, where Heber had complained there was "so much nois that we can neither Sleep nor think," and Willard had observed: "The minds of the people here in London are taken up with everything but the things of God and righteousness. . . . it almost requires a trump to be blown from heaven in order to awaken the attention of the people to the subject of the fulness of the gospel."[39] But Brigham preached to record-sized groups, and extended his personal education by touring the ancient city with his brethren, acutely aware of the cruel contrast between the powerful and wealthy, and the destitute and downtrodden. The Thames, London Bridge, the queen's jewels, the Tower and the government houses were all duly seen, but nothing impressed them more than Westminster Abbey, where British monarchs are crowned and so many great men lie buried beneath monuments raised to their honor. Wilford Woodruff spoke what they all felt, that London had been "as profitable a school to me as any I have ever met with in my travels."[40] In the same letter, published in the *Times and Seasons*, he gave insight into the character of his leader:

> . . . and while the Saints were much edified and their hearts made glad with the teachings and instruction of Elder Young, I also obtained much benefit myself by enjoying his society, sitting under his instructions and sharing in his councils.[41]

While Brigham was working relentlessly in so many capacities ("My labor has been such that I am quite unwell," he confided to Elder Richards, "But I keepe going with all my might"[42]), it could be assumed that he had little time to think of his family and dwell upon what they might be going through. Yet almost the opposite seems to have been the case. He not only thought of his loved ones, but dreamed about them. In his "night vision," as he called it:

I first dremed of being at home in the Stat[e]s. I first saw Elizabeth. I asked her whare her mother was. She said she was about the house. She soon came in. I shook hands [with] her hart[i]ly as I had don with Elizabeth. I embraced her in my arms and kissed [her] 2 or 3 times and asked hir whare my four children was. She and Elizabeth both ansard and said they ware at [s]chool and . . . loved there books. My wife says we feel well but you must provide for your own families for the Church are not able to doe for them.[43]

Haunted by this dream, knowing full well the sufferings his loved ones had already endured, frustrated by his necessary ignorance of their conditions, he wrote poignantly to Mary Ann:

"I thought that I had got to takare of my own famely fore the Church would not be able to doe much for our famelies." He told her of material for "a butiful Calico frock kaften" for her and Vilate Kimball, courtesy of Henry Moon, and said he would like to see her in the frock when he returned. . . . he promised "the Lord being my helper I will doe as much and as fast as posable, for I feel that I with my Brethren will be wonted with our families eare long."[44]

This was shortly after the departure of Brother Moon's company aboard the *Britannia* in early June of 1840. Over six months later, after reading in a letter from her of her sickness and trials, he confided: "I pray for you and the children continually, it is all I can due. I cannot help you about your daly work." The practical Brigham comes out here, yet it is mingled with his very literal faith, as further revealed when he wrote, "If I would give up my mind to think of my famely it would destract me and I should not be fit for the work the Lord has set me about."[45] Despite the inner sorrows, the loneliness he kept locked in his heart, he knew the best way of "caring" for his family right now was to do the work the Lord had set him about, and let the Lord, in turn, do his, which included the care and protection of the apostles' families left behind in Nauvoo. Nothing expresses his conviction better, or gives deeper insight into the man than this excerpt from one of the letters he wrote Mary Ann:

> I understand you have had hard worke to get enny thing for your self and famely to make you comfortable. This I doe not here from you but from others. You may well think that my hart feeles tender toards you, when I relise your patiants and willingness to suffer in poverty and doe everything you can for my children and for me to goe and due the thing the Lord requires of me.

He understood the importance of her role, and the unity which existed between their efforts:

> I pray the Lord to bless you in all things and my children and help us all to be faithful to him and our Bretherin. This will bring [honor] to the name of our Redemer on the Earth also upon our heds and the best of all is we shall have eternal life.[46]

It is interesting that in December, Joseph wrote directing the Twelve to return in the spring, but the delivery of the letter was delayed until late February, and Brigham's correspondence reveals that the same inspiration had come to him. Under date of January 15, 1841, he wrote to Mary Ann:

> On the 6 day of Apriel 1841 we hold Council of the Twelve with the officers of the Church for the purpos of arrangen the affares of the Church so that we can leve. I think we shall start for home then, and make ouer way as fast as we can. I believe this is the feelings of all the Twelve. This is all I can say upon the subject, the will of the Lord be don.[47]

The apostles left Liverpool on April 21, 1841, following an evening of festivity and fellowship where the seven hundred in attendance were served cake and joined in singing hymns and listening to Brigham and William Miller serenade them with "Adieu, my dear brethren." Brigham blessed the assembled Saints:

> May the God of our fathers bless you all with wisdom and grace to act each your part in the great work which lies before you, that the world may be warned, and thousands brought to the knowledge of the truth; and may He bless and preserve you blameless until the day of His coming.

Then he added, "Brethren and sisters, pray for us."[48]

Later, speaking to the Saints in Salt Lake City, he recalled the events and accomplishments of the 376-day mission which he and his brethren fulfilled:

> In these twelve months and sixteen days, under my supervision, between eight and nine thousand persons were baptized, . . . the Churches were organized, the emigration prepared, ships were chartered and companies sailed out, . . . we have printed five thousand copies of the Book of Mormon, three thousand hymn books, and commenced the Millennial Star; over sixty thousand tracts had been printed . . . . Our labor was successful, God blessed us, and when we returned our Book of Mormon was paid for. The gentleman who bound the first Book of Mormon in England binds them to-day [1870] . . . . we have not owed the first farthing . . . but have paid promptly, according to promise . . . In that twelve months I sustained several families . . . and preserved them from starvation and death. . . . I do not recollect of spending more than one penny, needlessly, while in England, and that was for a bunch of grapes while passing through Smithfield market, Manchester. When I took them in my hand I saw women passing through the market who, I knew, were suffering through hunger, and who probably perished and died. I felt that I ought to have given that penny to the poor. Whenever I went from my office, if I neglected to take my pocket full of coppers to give to the poor mendicants which are everywhere to be met with, I would return to the office and take a handfull of coppers from the drawer, and as I walked along would give something to such objects of pity and distress as I met, and pass on without being hindered by them. We organized the Church, we ordained two patriarchs, and from that time on we have been gathering the poor.[49]

The return journey had its fair days and foul; ocean voyages in those days were always rigorous and demanding. In an April entry aboard ship Brigham wrote, "I feel as though I could not endure menny such voiges as I had endured for 2 years . . . and ware it not for the power of God and his tender mercy I should despair."[50]

But he did not despair, even when he found his family living "in a small unfinished log cabin, situated on a low wet lot, so swampy that when the first attempt was made to plow it the oxen mired."⁵¹ Brigham reached Nauvoo on the first day of July, 1841. On the 9th Joseph visited his beloved apostle in his humble home, and there pronounced a special revelation upon his head:

> Dear and well-beloved brother, Brigham Young, verily thus saith the Lord unto you: My servant Brigham, it is no more required at your hand to leave your family as in times past, for your offering is acceptable to me. I have seen your labor and toil in journeyings for my name. I therefore command you to send my word abroad, and take especial care of your family from this time, henceforth and forever. Amen. (D & C 126)

It was enough. The Lord had accepted his offering. He was never to leave his homeland again. It is of significant note that the only entry in either of the two diaries which cover this period was penned in January of 1842 and said simply: "This Evening I am with my love alone by my fireside for the first time for years. We enjoi it and feel to prase the Lord."⁵²

Notes

1. *Journal of Brigham*, p. 22
2. Matthias F. Cowley, *Wilford Woodruff: History of His Life and Labors* (Salt Lake City: Bookcraft, 1964), p. 134; hereafter referred to as *Wilford Woodruff*.
3. Cowley, *Wilford Woodruff*, p. 197.
4. Journal of Wilford Woodruff, typescript, 2 July 1839, Wilford Woodruff Papers, Church Archives.
5. Arrington, *American Moses*, p. 74.
6. *Journal of Brigham*, pp. 22-23.
7. Cowley, *Wilford Woodruff*, p. 104.
8. Journal of Brigham, p. 23.
9. Cowley, *Wilford Woodruff*, p. 105.
10. Arrington, *American Moses*, p. 75.
11. Ibid.
12. Susa Young Gates, "Brigham Young as Missionary," *Juvenile Instructor* 63 (1928), p. 307.
13. *JD*, 1:49.

14. *JD*, 1:31.
15. Whitney, *Life of Heber C. Kimball*, p. 269.
16. *Journal of Brigham*, p. 31.
17. Whitney, *Life of Heber C. Kimball*, p. 273.
18. *Journal of Brigham*, p. 27.
19. Ibid., p. 32.
20. Ibid., p. 33.
21. Ibid.; see also *JD*, 13: 211-12.
22. Arrington, *American Moses*, p. 81.
23. Ibid., p. 83.
24. Ibid.
25. *Journal of Brigham*, p. 34.
26. V. Ben Bloxham, James R. Moss, and Porter, Larry C., eds. *Truth Will Prevail: The Rise of the Church of Jesus Christ of Latter-day Saints in the British Isles 1837-1987* (Cambridge, England: University Press, 1987), p. 148. Published by the Corporation of the President, The Church of Jesus Christ of Latter-day Saints with U.S. distribution by Deseret Book, Salt Lake City, Utah.
27. England, *Brother Brigham*, p. 48.
28. Ibid., pp. 48-49.
29. Arrington, *American Moses*, pp. 84-85.
30. Bloxham et al., *Truth Will Prevail*, p. 166.
31. Ibid., p. 167.
32. Arrington, *American Moses*, p. 94.
33. Bloxham et al., *Truth Will Prevail*, p. 169.
34. Arrington, *American Moses*, p. 90.
35. Ibid.
36. Arrington, *American Moses*, p. 88.
37. Ibid.
38. Brigham Young to Joseph Smith, 7 May 1840, Joseph Smith Papers, Church Archives.
39. England, *Brother Brigham*, p. 52.
40. Letter from Wilford Woodruff to *Times and Seasons*, vol. 2 (1 March 1841), p. 330.
41. Ibid.
42. Arrington, *American Moses*, p. 85.
43. Ibid., pp. 86.
44. Brigham Young to Mary Ann Angell Young, 12 November 1840, Manuscript, University of Utah Library.
45. Arrington, *American Moses*, p. 92.
46. *HC*, 4:347-8.
47. *JD*, 13:212.
48. Brigham Young Historical Papers, entries before and after 5 May 1841,

Church Archives.

49. "History of Brigham Young," *Deseret News,* 10 March 1858, Church Archives.

50. Diary of Brigham Young, 1837-1845, Brigham Young Papers, Church Archives.

51. Ibid.

52. Ibid.

Chapter Eight

Nauvoo, the City Beautiful

*Growth of Nauvoo: charter, Legion, publications,
shifts in organization and function of the Twelve – missions –
Relief Society – plural marriage – martyrdom
of Joseph and Hyrum*

Joseph Smith did not escape death from the hands of his enemies. . . .
Neither did Jesus Christ . . . who died an ignominious death upon the
cross. Why was this? Because God so ordained it, for no testament is
in force, until after the death of the testator . . . All that Joseph Smith
did was to preach the truth—the Gospel as the Lord revealed it to
him—and tell the people how to be saved, and the honest-in-heart
ran together and gathered around him and loved him as they did their
own lives. . . . All who believe and obey the Gospel of Jesus Christ are
his witnesses to the truth of these statements.

Journal of Discourses, 10:326

Nauvoo, the City Beautiful, was a unique place in the history
of the Saints, as it was in the history of the American nation as a
whole. A people who had arrived on the banks of the Mississippi
weak, half-starved, worn-out with persecution, deprived of possessions and means, created a city which, with its surrounding

area, by the summer of 1841 housed some eight to nine thousand people, and within another year had "eclipsed every other Illinois city in size, with the possible exception of Chicago. Almost singlehandedly, the Saints made Hancock County the most populous county in Illinois by the 1845 census."[1] Small businesses were encouraged by an actual Agricultural and Manufacturing Association. There were potteries, tanneries, bakeries, shops, comb and match factories, grist and lumber mills, several brickyards, foundries, a slaughterhouse—and the river provided easy transportation for the goods the Saints made. Building was one of the largest enterprises. "One visitor reported seeing some two thousand homes, of which 'six hundred of them at least were good brick or frame structures. The number . . . made wholly of brick was about five hundred, a goodly proportion of them large and handsome.'"[2] There was a "common school" system in the city, and public halls for the production of plays and concerts and such public amusements as banquets and dances, lectures and exhibits of art. There were several newspapers, among them the *Wasp,* begun in April of 1842, which was a versatile weekly publication treating a range of subjects from agriculture and trade to science, art, and literature. There were also the *Nauvoo Neighbor* and the *Times and Seasons.* There were parades and reviews, festooned by the Nauvoo Legion, and the homey activities of skating and sliding on the ice in winter, picnics, swimming, quilting and husking bees, and competitive racing, pulling sticks, wrestling, and throwing weights in the warmer months.

"When I went to Commerce, I told the people I would build up a city," Joseph reminded his enemies and detractors in January of 1843. ". . . The old inhabitants replied, 'We will be damned if you can.' So I prophesied that I would build up a city, and the inhabitants prophesied that I could not; and we have now about 12,000 inhabitants."[3]

The amazing growth of the Mormon city was threatening to their neighbors, as was the nature of the liberal charter granted by Governor Carlin, certified by the Secretary of State, Stephen A. Douglas, and supported by Illinois legislator Abraham Lincoln.

The charter provided for the establishment of a university, as well as an independent military unit to be called the Nauvoo Legion. The city mayor and aldermen, members of the city council, were also designated as judges in the municipal court. This feature allowed the Saints to place trusted church leaders in key positions, and provided an avenue of escape from illegal and trumped-up arrest by the issuing of writs of habeas corpus. Of course, enemies of the Church chafed against this power as much as the Saints rejoiced in it.

The most distressing factor to the city was disease. Large numbers died from malaria each year, especially during the late summer months. Children, of course, were particularly susceptible, and very few families escaped this horror. But when Heber arrived in Nauvoo in July of 1841, in company with Brigham, he reported positively on the conditions he observed:

> I never saw crops look better than they do in this place at present. The wheat is in general cut, and secured. Provisions are cheaper. . . . The whole country for many miles is cultivated with corn, wheat, potatoes, and all kinds of produce. . . . Most of the Saints have plenty growing to last them for a year, and to spare; and the blessing of God rests on this people.[4]

Under such conditions, Brigham set to work providing for his own:

> Although I had to spend the principal part of my time at the call of Brother Joseph in the service of the Church, the portion of time left me I spent in draining, fencing and cultivating my lot, building a temporary shed for my cow, chinking and otherwise finishing my house, and as the ground was too damp to admit of a cellar underground, I built one with two brick walls about four to six inches apart arched over the brick. Frost never penetrated it, although in summer articles would mildew in it.[5]

On August 10, Joseph inaugurated the next phase of development and authority for the Twelve, who were emerging for the first time as a united body. In the economy of God, he had used these powerful, distinctive men to build up his kingdom in Great Britain, at the same time providing them with a field of experience which would serve to forge and unify them. Now the Prophet announced that the Twelve were to assume "the burthen of the business of the church in Nauvoo, and especially as pertaining to the church lands, settling of the Saints after their arrival, and selling church lands,"[6] and he called a special conference to have his action ratified by the members of the Church. It was vital that the Saints have full knowledge of what he was doing, for Joseph knew he would not be long with them and was fully aware of the need of securing proper, ordained leadership once he was gone.

In September Brigham was elected to the Nauvoo City Council, extending his personal influence yet farther, and was also inducted into the Masonic lodge. The Twelve took under their supervision the collection of tithes and contributions toward the construction of the Nauvoo House hotel, as well as the construction of the temple. It was general practice for the brethren to donate one day in every ten to work on temple construction. And it was in part to facilitate their cooperative efforts toward this project that the women of Nauvoo became organized, under the hand of the Prophet, into "The Female Relief Society of Nauvoo." When baptisms for the dead were instituted by revelation so that those who died without hearing the gospel could receive this ordinance by proxy, a font was quickly completed and dedicated, and the very first baptisms were performed on November 21, with Brigham as one of the initial participants:

> [Monday, November 8] I attended the dedication of the baptismal font in the Lord's House. President Smith called upon me to offer the dedicatory prayer. This is the first font erected and dedicated for the baptism for the dead in this dispensation.

> [Sunday, November 21] Brothers Hyrum Smith and John Taylor preached. At 4 p.m., brothers Kimball, Taylor and I baptized about forty persons in the font, for the dead; brothers Richards, Woodruff and George A. Smith confirming. These were the first baptisms for the dead in the font.[7]

Filling missions and absences from his family were inevitable considering Brigham's role in the Church. In the autumn of 1842, Brigham, Heber, George A., and Amasa Lyman returned to Illinois to preach in defense of Joseph Smith and the Saints. Powerful non-Mormons, jealous of the Prophet, were intent on slandering his name and engendering fear in others. Thomas Sharp, editor of the *Warsaw Signal*, was foremost among these detractors. As was often and sadly the case, he received his greatest support from dissenters within the kingdom. John C. Bennett, a general in the Legion and mayor of Nauvoo, charged Joseph with seducing women under the guise of polygamy, while in truth, he was attempting to cover his own base practices. He published a scathing expose and went on a speaking tour to promulgate his abuses, stirring up the minds of people against Joseph and the Mormons to such a degree that both candidates for the governorship of Illinois favored repeal of the Nauvoo Charter.

When an attempt was made upon the life of Govenor Boggs, who had issued the order exterminating the Saints from Missouri, it was a perfect opportunity for his enemies to lay the deed at Joseph's door. They accused Porter Rockwell, bodyguard and close boyhood friend of the Prophet, of the deed; Joseph with foreknowledge and complexity. While Joseph was forced into hiding, his apostles publicly and boldly proclaimed his innocence and defended the integrity of the people called Latter-day Saints.

Despite the awesome weight he and his brethren carried, Brigham found it possible to apply humor, as when he allayed the tensions of a spirited debate amongst his brethren. In arguing the question: "Is the prosperity of any religious denomination a positive evidence that they are right?" Brigham lightened the mood with the following:

I told them I was reminded of the anecdote of the negro's attempt at shooting a squirrel. His master having occasion to be absent from home, charged him to be sure and not meddle with his guns and ammunition; but no sooner had the master got fairly out of the way, when the negro's curiosity prompted him to try one of the master's guns. He accordingly took one down which had been loaded for some time, and went into the woods. He soon saw a squirrel, and crept up a hill behind a log and fired. But the gun, being heavily charged, knocked the negro over, and he rolled down the hill. Upon gaining his equilibrium and realizing his defeat, he looked up from the ground where he lay, and seeing the squirrel jumping from tree to tree as if conscious of victory, cried, "Well, well, cuffy, if you had been at the other end of the gun you would have known more about it."

Then he laughingly concluded "that the prosperity of any people was not positive evidence of their being right."[8]

Quite apart from the heinous lies and cruel accusations, there was yet more to endure—a truth which took incredible stamina of heart and mind to accept. The practice of plural marriage, as part of the restoration of all things, was being taught by Joseph Smith to his closest friends as an eternal principle which God would expect them to embrace. Joseph himself demurred, postponing the terrible confrontation as long as he dared. Brigham's finer sensitivities were appalled at the thought, and he later spoke feelingly of that time:

> Some of these my brethren know what my feelings were at the time Joseph revealed the doctrine; I was not desirous of shrinking from any duty, nor of failing in the least to do as I was commanded [these words ring with the authority of a sincerity and dedication already countless times proved]—but it was the first time in my life that I had desired the grave, and I could hardly get over it for a long time. And when I saw a funeral, I felt to envy the corpse its situation, and to regret that I was not in the coffin, knowing the toil and labor that my body would have to undergo; and I have had to examine myself, from that day to this, and watch my faith, and carefully meditate, lest I should be found desiring the grave more than I ought to do.[9]

Because of his nature, it was essential for Brigham to reason the thing out for himself, explore every aspect and feature, then make an informed, intelligent, dedicated decision, from which he would never retreat. An opportunity came soon after the adoption of the practice for him to debate the issue with a professor from a southern university. Drawing the man out, questioning him to establish his point, Brigham said:

> We see in this life, that amongst Christians, ministers and all classes of men, a man will marry a wife, and have children by her; she dies, and he marries another, and another, until men have had as many as six wives, and each of them bear children. This is considered all right by the Christian world, inasmuch as a man has but one at a time. Now, in the resurrection this man and all his wives and children are raised from the dead; what will be done with those women and children, and who will they belong to? and if the man is to have but one, which one in the lot shall he have?

His listener realized the efficacy of his argument, so Brigham continued:

> "Very well," said I, "you consider that to be a pure, holy place in the presence of God, angels, and celestial beings, would the Lord permit a thing to exist in his presence in heaven which is evil? And if it is right for a man to have several wives and children in heaven at the same time, is it not a consistent doctrine that a man should have several wives, and children by those wives at the same time, here in this life, as was the case with Abraham and many of the old Prophets? Or is it any more sinful to have several wives at a time than at different times?[10]

This reasoning satisfied the minister, and it satisfied Brigham as well. Besides, the essence of the thing lay deeper; its foundation lay in his conviction of truth and his faith in the prophet who had conveyed it:

> I did not embrace Mormonism because I hoped it was true, but because I knew it was that principle that would save all the human family that would obey it. . . . Joseph Smith has laid the foundation of the kingdom of God in the last days; . . . I know that he was called of God, and this I know by the revelation of Jesus Christ to me, and by the testimony of the Holy Ghost.[11]

Brigham loved Joseph. But beyond Joseph, the man, were these unassailable eternal principles and priesthood powers, which magnified the bearer, from Joseph to Brigham, to any worthy and desirous man. Thus, his loyalty to the Prophet could be unquestioned:

> . . . It was not for me to question whether Joseph was dictated by the Lord at all times and under all circumstances or not. I never had the feeling for one moment, to believe that any man or set of men or beings upon the face of the whole earth had anything to do with him, for he was superior to them all, and held keys of salvation over them. Had I not thoroughly understood this and believed it, I much doubt whether I should ever have embraced what is called "Mormonism."'
> . . . It was not my prerogative to call him in question with regard to any act of his life. He was God's servant, and not mine. . . . That was my faith, and it is my faith still.[12]

Joseph Smith said, concerning this doctrine,

> I have had no dark revelations. . . Happiness is the object and design of our existence, and will be the end thereof, if we pursue the path that leads to it; and this path is virtue, uprightness, faithfulness, holiness, and keeping all the commandments of God.[13]

Echoing this statement, Brigham told the Saints:

> Plurality of wives is not designed to afflict you nor me, but is purposed for our exaltation in the kingdom of God. If any man had asked me what was my choice when Joseph revealed that doctrine, provided that it would not diminish my glory, I would have said, "Let me have but one wife."[14]

Plural marriage was the spiritual ideal. In order to "endure" it, the Saints had to raise their sights, their understandings, their affections and desires to a higher, purer plain. Helen Mar Kimball, youngest of the Prophet's wives, argued in favor of the institution, as the majority of women involved in polygamous marriages (despite difficulties, and even heartaches) did:

> It is the plan of the Almighty to make of His noble daughters queens instead of serfs, that woman may reign in the sphere for which she was created. The celestial order of marriage was introduced for this purpose, and God commanded His servants to enter into that holy

order preparatory to the day, which is at our doors, when noble and virtuous women, now blinded by prejudice and priestcraft, will be glad to unite themselves to men equally noble and pure.[15]

Parley P. Pratt clothed in eloquent language the extent of this principle as it was taught in its purity by Joseph Smith:

In Philadelphia I had the happiness of once more meeting with President Smith . . . he taught me many great and glorious principles concerning God and the heavenly order of eternity. It was at this time that I received from him the first idea of eternal family organization, and the eternal union of the sexes in those inexpressibly endearing relationships which none but the highly intellectual, the refined and pure in heart, know how to prize, and which are at the very foundation of everything worthy to be called happiness.

Till then I had learned to esteem kindred affections and sympathies as appertaining solely to this transitory state, as something from which the heart must be entirely weaned, in order to be fitted for its heavenly state. It was Joseph Smith who taught me how to prize the endearing relationships of father and mother, husband and wife; of brother and sister, son and daughter. It was from him that I learned that the wife of my bosom might be secured to me for time and all eternity; and that the refined sympathies and affections which endeared us to each other emanated from the fountain of divine eternal love. It was from him that I learned that we might cultivate these affections, and grow and increase in the same to all eternity . . .

It was from him that I learned the true dignity and destiny of a son of God, clothed with an eternal priesthood, as the patriarch and sovereign of his countless offspring. It was from him that I learned that the highest dignity of womanhood was, to stand as a queen and priestess to her husband, and to reign for ever and ever as the queen mother of her numerous and still increasing offspring. I had loved before, but I knew not why. But now I loved—with a pureness—an intensity of elevated, exalted feeling, which would lift my soul from the transitory things of this grovelling sphere and expand it as the ocean. I felt that God was my heavenly Father indeed; that Jesus was my brother, and that the wife of my bosom was an immortal, eternal companion; a kind of ministering angel, given to me as a comfort, and a crown of glory for ever and ever. In short, I could now love with the spirit and with the understanding also.[16]

It is evident that Brigham understood the majesty and magnitude of this matter as completely as did Parley or any of his fellow apostles. At one time, in preaching to the Saints, he said:

> But the whole subject of the marriage relation is not in my reach, nor in any other man's reach on this earth. It is without beginning of days or end of years; it is a hard matter to reach. We can tell some things with regard to it; it lays the foundation for worlds, for angels, and for the Gods; for intelligent beings to be crowned with glory, immortality, and eternal lives. In fact, it is the thread which runs from the beginning to the end of the holy Gospel of Salvation—of the Gospel of the Son of God; it is from eternity to eternity.[17]

Brigham married his first plural wife in June 1842. Lucy Ann Decker Seeley was born in New York of Dutch and English parents who joined with the Church after moving to Ohio in 1833. Although she was but twenty when she married Brigham, she had been married before. William Seeley, also a Latter-day Saint, had abused, then abandoned her. She had suffered the death of a stillborn, and brought a small son and daughter into the union with her. She and Brigham became the parents of seven children, their first son, Brigham Heber, being the first or one of the first born into polygamy. Their son Feramorz attended the Naval Academy at Annapolis; their youngest daughter, Clarissa, in her book about life in Brigham Young's home told of the tender, unwavering love and devotion her mother felt for her father.

At this time Joseph Smith also introduced "the ancient order of things," and Brigham recorded on Wednesday, May 4, that "I received my washings, anointings and endowments."[18] He and his brethren received further instructions at the hands of the Prophet in priesthood matters, and he was sealed to his parents, and his children were sealed to him. To be thus eternally bound with the mother who had been lost to him since his youth, must have been a source of great joy to Brigham, and increased the sense of peace and rightness which the gospel had brought into his life.

Two months after his marriage to Lucy, Brigham served a short mission, and only weeks after his return had an unexpected brush with death. He described the experience in vivid detail:

> November 26, 1842. I was suddenly attacked with a slight fit of apoplexy. Next morning I felt quite comfortable; but in the evening, at the same hour that I had the fit the day before, I was attacked with the most violent fever I have ever experienced. The Prophet Joseph and Elder Willard Richards visited and administered unto me; the Prophet prophesied that I should live and recover from my sickness. He sat by me for six hours, and directed my attendants what to do for me.[19]

It is pleasant to picture the tender efforts of the Prophet as he worked for the safety and well-being of his devoted friend. In our day we do not often think of men, especially those who hold powerful executive and leadership positions, in the role of nurses and ministers of mercy. Yet Joseph filled that role often and willingly, setting an example in this, as in all else, for those who looked to him. The Prophet's mother, Lucy, recorded that in the summer of 1843 she became extremely ill and "brought nigh unto death":

> For five nights Emma never left me, but stood at my bedside all the night long, at the end of which time she was overcome with fatigue and taken sick herself. Joseph then took her place and watched with me the five succeeding nights, as faithfully as Emma had done."[20]

Now, after Brigham had suffered thirty hours with the fever, the skin began to peel from his body, and he entreated them to allow him to be baptized in the river. But not until the fourteenth day of his illness would Joseph allow him to be "showered with cold water, when my fever began to break, and it left me on the 18th day." The burning fever immuned him to the conditions of the "rather open" log house where he lay, "so cold that Isaac Decker, his attendant, froze his fingers and toes while fanning him. Decker was clad in greatcoat, boots and mittens, while Brigham, burning with fever, was shielded from the fire by a blanket."[21] Brigham's own account continues: "I laid upon my back, and was not turned upon my side for eighteen days." Then a singular thing happened:

> I was bolstered up in my chair, but was so near gone that I could not close my eyes, which were set in my head—my chin dropped down and my breath stopped. My wife [Mary Ann], seeing my situation, threw some cold water in my face, that having no effect, she dashed a handful of strong camphor in to my face and eyes, which I did not feel in the least, neither did I move a muscle. She then held my nostrils between her thumb and finger, and placing her mouth directly over mine, blew into my lungs until she filled them with air. This set my lungs in motion, and I again began to breathe. While this was going on I was perfectly conscious of all that was passing around me; my spirit was as vivid as it ever was in my life, but I had no feeling in my body.[22]

Perhaps Brigham realized how Mary Ann's instinctive act saved his life. He spent the next two weeks recuperating, but as the cold winter set in his weakness persisted, and at the end of the following summer he still recorded that he was not "wholly recovered from my last winter's illness."[23]

Despite this, he was able to build a new home for Mary Ann that summer—a task which was long overdue. A relieved gratitude is evident in his journal entry of May 31, 1843: "I moved out of my log cabin into my new brick house, which was 22 feet by 16, two stories high, and a good cellar under it, and felt thankful to God for the privilege of having a comfortable, though small habitation."[24] He was not disgruntled or resentful that the Lord's work took so much of his time and his means, but was, in a simple, humble way, grateful for what he had.

Meanwhile, his family was shifting and altering. His seventeen-year-old daughter, Elizabeth, had been married in February, while he was still recovering from his illness, the ceremony being performed by his brother, Joseph Young. Twelve-year-old Vilate was in Salem, Massachusetts, studying music. And, six weeks after his marriage to Lucy, Mary Ann gave birth to a daughter, whom they named Luna Carolina, so there was now a toddler in the house. During the next summer Brigham would construct wings one story high on either side of the house, one serving as bedroom, the other, with an outside entrance, as an office for him. Throughout this period Lucy Ann lived in the house she had shared with her first husband, which stood some five blocks from Brigham's new house.

Brigham's responsibilities were heavy, and the affairs surrounding the Prophet's life so crucial at this time that, of necessity, these valiant women were expected to largely maintain themselves. They did not resent this, nor shirk from the form of duty which fell upon them. Later, Mary Ann recalled the joint feeling she and her husband shared that Brigham was doing right to labor for the good of "the kingdom."[25] Certainly she and her valiant sisters understood Milton's sentiment when he wrote, "They also serve who only stand and wait,"[26] for they clearly understood the nobility and necessity of their supporting role. Despite the most trying of circumstances, as detailed in Mary Ann's letter to Brigham in August 1843, when the children were all ill with scarlet fever, Vilate appearing "nigh unto death," Mary Ann "much worn down with standing over them by day and by night and hearing their cries of pain and distress," she could humbly say, "I feel to thank my heavenly father there is prospect of health returning to us again," and apologize for burdening him: "I do not want to say things to you to trouble you. You must excuse me for saying so much about the distress we have passed through." And she could end her letter: "May the Lord bless you and make you an instrument of doing much good you have all our prairs. I am yours in the bonds of the everlasting gospel. Mary A. Young to Brigham Young."[27]

Nor should we make the error of assuming that the men were always anxious to leave the more mundane tasks of the household to their wives and sally forth in work they considered more vital. One tender communication from Brigham to Mary Ann in the early summer of 1844 will suffice: "I feel lonsom. Oh that I had you with me this somer I think I should be happy. Well I am now [happy] because I am in my cauling and duing my duty, but [the] older I grow the more I desire to stay at my own home instead of traveling."[28]

Brigham's journals often contained such comments as "rode out with the Prophet," "met in council with the Prophet," "the Twelve, according to directions from the Prophet . . . ," and these were consistent entries. On Sunday, 31 July, 1842, he recorded: "In the month of July I attended Councils, waited upon the immigrants; and as President Joseph Smith kept concealed from his enemies, I had continual calls from the brethren for counsel, which occupied much of my time." And on Sunday, 10 December, 1843: "I attended prayer-meeting in the Assembly Room. President Joseph Smith being absent, I presided and instructed the brethren upon the necessity of following our file leader, and our Savior, in all his laws and commandments, without asking any questions why they were so."[29]

The growth and maturity in Brigham's leadership is evident, as well as his simple, humble obedience. And, obviously, these conditions did not go unnoticed:

> Brigham became generally known as "President Young" and seems to have gradually become more close in counsel to Joseph; . . . and was in every practical sense the second in command (except for Hyrum's role as close advisor and defender on spiritual and doctrinal matters).[30]

The rare relationship which Joseph and Brigham shared was built upon an almost perfect harmony of thought, feeling, desire, and dedication, tempered and exalted by the influence of the Spirit. Part of Brigham's calling seemed to be to define, comprehend, and preserve the Prophet Joseph's teachings. That he understood this is evident, as revealed in the statement he made in August of 1868:

> In the days of the Prophet Joseph, such moments were more precious to me than all the wealth of all the world. No matter how great my poverty—if I had to borrow meal to feed my wife and children, I never let an opportunity pass of learning what the Prophet had to impart.[31]

Nothing could be more powerful, except, perhaps, this tender admission: "I used to think, while Joseph was living, that his life compared well with the history of the Saviour."[32]

The months from January to June of 1843 represented a period of comparative peace, during which Joseph introduced new doctrine and organized the "Anointed Quorum" or "Holy Order," which included some of the Twelve and their wives, as well as other leaders of the Church, and women such as Fanny Young Murray, Brigham's widowed sister. They met regularly for prayers, ordinances, and instructions from the Prophet's hand. Nauvoo continued to grow. The town plat was extended, and ten wards were formed. That summer Joseph and his family moved into the twenty-two-room Mansion House, part of which was soon opened as a hotel.

In June, while Joseph and Emma were visiting her sister near Dixon—about two hundred miles north of Nauvoo— two officers from Missouri, Reynolds and Wilson, arrested him illegally, not even informing him of the charges against him. With threats and abuse they dragged him away at once, not even allowing Emma to bring out a change of clothing for him. He was taken to Dixon, where the citizens did their best to assist him. He and his captors spent one night in the village of PawPaw Grove. When the people expressed a desire to hear him preach, Sheriff Reynolds rudely refused. Then "an elderly man arose and shouted angrily, 'You damned infernal Puke, we'll learn you to come here and interrupt gentlemen! Sit down there and don't open your head till General Smith gets through talking. If you never learned manners in Missouri, we'll teach you that you can't kidnap men here.' The threats were enough; Joseph spoke for an hour and a half."[33]

The Prophet was at length granted a writ of habeas corpus, to be taken to the nearest authorized court—which happened to be in Nauvoo! The Missourians, by a twist of fate, were now in custody of the man they had abused, and were terrified to be taken back into the midst of the Mormons, many of whom would remember their names and faces, and the part they had played in the persecutions of the Saints. Joseph and Emma, however, set the standard of Christlike behavior. The men were treated with deference, sat down to a meal at Joseph's table, and were waited upon by Emma herself. That afternoon, when hundreds gathered to hear Joseph speak, he told his people, "I have had the privilege of rewarding them good for evil."[34] Brigham continued this tradition of noble graciousness many times in the Salt Lake Valley, when armies and corrupted officials were sent to irritate, misrepresent and distress his people. The spirit of the gospel of Christ lived in his daily actions, as it did in those of the man after whom he modeled his life.

In Brigham's account of the incident he wrote:

> Sunday, June 25—Two p.m., brother William Clayton having brought news of President Smith's arrest at Dixon, brother Hyrum Smith went to the stand and requested the brethren to meet him in half an hour at the Masonic Hall, when three hundred volunteered to go in pursuit of President Joseph Smith and prevent his being taken to Missouri, out of which number several companies were selected to go. The companies agreed to meet in the evening at William Law's, which they did, when Hyrum reported he could not raise means. Wilson Law said, if means were not raised he would not go. I told the brethren to get in readiness and the money would be forthcoming, although at the time I knew not from whence, but in two hours I succeeded in borrowing $700 to defray the expenses of the expedition.[35]

This is typical of Brigham: decisive, filled with a practical, unquestioning faith—doing all in his power to aid that faith by his efforts, and trusting quite literally to God for the rest. Of the Prophet's return into the city he wrote:

> Friday, June 30—Brother Joseph returned to Nauvoo with the brethren who were sent after him. On his entrance into the city, multitudes of the brethren and sisters turned out to meet and greet him, witnessing the devotion and good feelings in the hearts of the Saints towards their Prophet.

And the following day:

> Hyrum Smith, Parley P. Pratt, Lyman Wight, Sidney Rigdon and myself were duly sworn before the municipal court, and gave in our testimony as witnesses in the case of Joseph Smith . . . We embodied in our testimony an account of the persecutions of Joseph Smith and the Saints . . . It was certainly a rehearsal of the most heartrending

scenes that ever saluted the ears of any tribunal in a civilized government on earth; it would have been a disgrace to Arabs, cannibals, or
the most brutal savages. Not only theft, arson, burglary, imprison-
ment, chains, expulsion, rape and murder were practiced on the Saints
without any redress, but even the Prophet, Joseph Smith, with his
companions in prison, were loaded with chains, were fed a portion of
the time on the flesh of their murdered brethren, which was cooked
and given them to eat by their inhuman persecutors. The recital of
this part of the testimony was sufficient to curdle the blood in the
veins of all who heard it; even the lawyers were shocked to the soul,
and at the close of the testimony, in their speeches, before the Court,
exhorted the Saints to maintain their rights, "stand or fall, sink or
swim, live or die." This testimony of the unparalleled persecutions of
the State of Missouri against the Saints of God in the last days, will
stand on history's page to future generations.[36]

A week later, Brigham started on his mission of preaching and
good will, defending the name of the Prophet and explaining the
tenets of Mormonism.

In mid-August, he wrote woefully from New Jersey of bedbugs
that George A. Smith claimed "had danced to the music at the
battle of Trenton, as their heads were perfectly grey. We took our
blankets and retreated to the further end of the room, and, as the
bugs followed us, I lit a candle, and as they approached, caught
them and burnt them in the candle, and thus spent the night."[37]
Under date of Sunday, August 27, Brigham recorded, "Attended
Conference. The Twelve continued to occupy the time in preaching, morning, afternoon and evening. We blessed several children
and administered to the sick. My health was feeble, never having
wholly recovered from my last winter's illness."[38]

It was at this time that he and Mary Ann were weighted down
by the death of their beloved, gentle little daughter, Mary Ann, the
six-year-old twin of Brigham, Jr., who died of "dropsy and
canker." Neither left any account of their feelings at the time of
this tragedy, but Brigham did write to his wife and confide:

When I was so sick I thought if I could only be at home, I should be
thankful. There is no place like home to me. . . . *You and I must take*

*some masurs to recover our helth or we shall not last a grate meny years
yet and due much good on the earth.*[39]

In March of 1844 Joseph organized a Council of Fifty, whose
initial composition included some non-Mormons, as well as leaders of the Church. Among the tasks placed upon them was to
work for redress of Church losses and to investigate places for settlement and manners in which a moving of the people might take
place. Later that month, on the 26th, Joseph addressed a memor-
ial to the United States Congress asking for authority to raise a
large group of men to open up unexplored areas in the West. On
that same day he called the Twelve together, in a mood and spirit
which led many to believe that he had presentiments concerning
his own death and the shortness of the time which was left to him.
He charged them to "bear off the Kingdom," and told them
"some important scene is near to take place." He made it clear
that, if his life was taken, the Twelve had to be in possession of all
the keys and powers which he alone could confer upon them.
"Then, if God wills," he told them, "I can go with all pleasure and
satisfaction, knowing that my work is done, and the foundation
laid on which the kingdom of God is to be reared." Dramatically,
with great feeling,

> he walked the floor and threw back the collar of his coat upon his
> shoulders, "I roll the burthen and responsibility of leading this
> Church off from my shoulders on to yours. Now, round up your
> shoulders and stand under it like men; for the Lord is going to let me
> rest for awhile." . . . After he had thus spoken, he continued to walk
> the floor, saying: "Since I have rolled the burthen off from my shoul-
> ders I feel as light as a cork. I feel that I am free. I thank my God for
> this deliverance."[40]

Parley Pratt "wrote a proclamation six months after the
death of the Prophet." His description of the meetings when
these keys and authorities were conferred upon Brigham and
the Twelve match in every detail the descriptions, diary entries,
and explanations left by others who were involved. "If they kill

me," Parley wrote, "I have finished the work which was laid upon me, by committing to you all things for the building of the Kingdom according to the heavenly vision, and the pattern shown me from Heaven."[41] The intent of the Prophet's mind was clearly evident.

As Congressional elections drew near, the Saints suffered the usual political pressures and intrigues. As it came time for the Presidential campaign, they questioned each candidate on his feelings toward the Mormons and their rights. Only two of the five, Calhoun and Clay, sent replies, and they were far from promising. The Prophet made the determination to offer himself as a candidate, standing for the principles the Saints espoused. Many of his political ideas were before their time and were favorably received by a curious public. "The *Iowa Democrat* said, 'If superior talent, genius, and intelligence, combined with virtue, integrity and enlarged views, are any guarantee to General Smith's being elected, we think that he will be 'a full team of himself.'"[42] In May, several of the apostles were sent on missions, where they would combine proselyting with campaigning for Joseph's candidacy.

In Nauvoo, conditions grew more and more strained. "Indignation Meetings" held in Carthage were increasingly open in their threats and the means they would employ, if necessary, to eliminate the Mormons. Excommunicated apostates conspired openly to take the Prophet's life. When Joseph returned from the Iowa side of the river and went willingly to Carthage, he knew he was going to his death. "I am going like a lamb to the slaughter," he said boldly, "but I am calm as a summer's morning. I have a conscience void of offense toward God and toward all men. If they take my life I shall die an innocent man, and my blood shall cry from the ground for vengeance, and it shall be said of me, 'He was murdered in cold blood.'" While riding for the last time through Nauvoo in the quiet early morning, Joseph paused by the half-finished temple, then gazed over the city to the broad stretch of the Mississippi below. "This is the loveliest place and the best people under the heavens," he said. "Little do they know the trials that await them."[43]

Late on Thursday afternoon, June 27, 1844, despite the pledged protection of Governor Ford, a mob stormed the jail where Joseph and Hyrum were held, killing both the brothers, severely wounding John Taylor, and leaving Willard Richards, their other companion, virtually unharmed. The Prophet of the Restoration had sealed his testimony and his work with his blood.

The spirit of death and desolation was felt in Nauvoo that night. The dogs howled and the cattle bellowed restlessly in a way the people had never heard before. Many felt a spirit of darkness and depression, of extreme sorrow take possession of their souls. Although the Twelve were scattered, all experienced premonitions and an overwhelming sadness they could not explain. On that day Brigham wrote in his journal:

> Spent the day in Boston with brother Woodruff, who accompanied me to the railway station as I was about to take cars to Salem. In the evening, while sitting in the depot waiting, I felt a heavy depression of Spirit, and so melancholy I could not converse with any degree of pleasure. Not knowing anything concerning the tragedy enacting at the time in Carthage jail, I could not assign my reasons for my peculiar feelings.[44]

It was not until July 9 that rumors of Joseph's assassination began to reach him. What must have been the feelings of his heart? Wilford Woodruff described the state of the brethren at that time:

> Elder Brigham Young arrived in Boston this morning. I walked with him to 57 Temple Street, and called upon Sister Vose. Brother Young took the bed and gave vent to his feelings in tears. I took the big chair, and veiled my face, and for the first time gave vent to my grief and mourning for the Prophet.[45]

Many of the Saints lamented the fact that Joseph had returned and given himself up to the unrighteous authorities who were seeking his life, although some, including Emma, reproached him for desertion and entreated his return. Many believed as one of Brigham's biographers expressed:

. . . had Brigham Young been home he never would have permitted that return. He would have thundered indignation upon the craven heads of those who thus devoted their Prophet to almost certain death. Rather would he have sent a thousand elders to guard him to the mountains, for none loved Joseph better than did Brigham Young.[46]

Yet Brigham understood the duty which that very love and devotion imposed upon him. Under date of Tuesday, July 16, he wrote:

. . . heard a letter read . . . giving particulars of the murder of Joseph and Hyrum. The first thing which I thought of was, whether Joseph had taken the keys of the kingdom with him from the earth; brother Orson Pratt sat on my left; we were both leaning back on our chairs. Bringing my hand down on my knee, I said the keys of the kingdom are right here with the Church.[47]

"'I could do so much more for my friends if I were on the other side of the veil," the Prophet had confided to friends near the end. He had told Benjamin Johnson, 'I would not be far from you, and if on the other side, I would still be working with you, and with a power greatly increased to roll on this kingdom.'"[48]

This is what Brigham would remember, believe, and respond to when he returned to Nauvoo.

Notes

1. Richard Neitzel Holzapfel and L. Jeffrey Cottle, *Old Mormon Nauvoo and Southeastern Iowa: Historic Photographs and Guide* (Santa Ana, CA: Fieldbrook Productions, Inc., 1990), p. 13.
2. Janath R. Cannon, *Nauvoo Panorama* (Nauvoo: Nauvoo Restoration, Inc., 1991), p. 29.
3. Ibid., p. 25.
4. Whitney, *Life of Heber C. Kimball,* p. 315.
5. Preston Nibley, *Brigham Young,* pp. 37-38.
6. *Journal of Brigham,* p. 46.
7. Ms. History, pp. 144-45.

8. *JD*, 3:266.
9. Ms. History, pp. 134-36.
10. *JD*, 9:364-5.
11. *JD*, 4:297-8.
12. *HC*, 5:134-5.
13. *JD*, 3:266.
14. Helen Marr Kimball, "Why We Practice Plural Marriage," pamphlet issued 1884, Salt Lake City, Church Archives.
15. Parley P. Pratt, *Autobiography*, pp. 259-60.
16. *JD*, 2:90.
17. *Journal of Brigham*, p. 50.
18. Ms. History, pp. 124-25.
19. Lucy Mack Smith, *History of Joseph Smith by His Mother* (Salt Lake City: Bookcraft,1993), p. 319.
20. S. DilworthYoung, *Here Is Brigham*, p. 322.
21. Ms. History, pp. 124-25.
22. Ibid., p. 126.
23. *Journal of Brigham*, p. 56.
24. Emmeline B. Wells, "Heroines of the Church: Biography of Mary Ann Angell Young," *Juvenile Instructor*, vol. 26 (1 January 1891), pp. 56-58.
25. John Milton, "Sonnet on His Blindness," *101 Famous Poems* (The Reilley & Lee Co., Chicago, 1958), p. 91.
26. S. Dilworth Young, *Here Is Brigham*, pp. 232-33.
27. Arrington, *American Moses*, p. 110.
28. *Journal of Brigham*, pp. 51-65.
29. England, *Brother Brigham*, p. 67.
30. *JD*, 12:270.
31. *JD*, 5:96.
32. McCloud, *Joseph Smith*, p. 122.
33. Ibid.
34. *Journal of Brigham*, pp. 56-57.
35. Ibid. p. 57.
36. Ibid., p. 62.
37. Ibid.
38. Arrington, *American Moses*, p. 108.
39. Ibid., pp. 109-110.
40. S. Dilworth Young, *Here Is Brigham*, p. 346.
41. McCloud, *Joseph Smith*, p. 125.
42. *HC*, 6:554-55.
43. *Journal of Brigham*, p. 71.
44. N. B. Lundwall, *The Fate of the Persecutors of the Prophet Joseph Smith* (Salt Lake City: Bookcraft,1952), p. 144.

45. *HC,* 7:195.
46. *Journal of Brigham,* p. 71.
47. McCloud, *Joseph Smith,* p. 143.
48. *They Knew the Prophet,* p. 97.

Chapter Nine

A Father to All

The Twelve, Brigham, and "the mantle of Joseph" –
finishing the temple – preparing for the trek –
leaving the City of Joseph

We shall live as long as the Lord wants us to. They may lie and write
lies . . . but if they do not stop their devilish conduct they will be overtaken. . . . We do not ask any odds of them, nor of hell, nor of the
world. We only ask favors of our God; and He is the Being we serve:
to Him we go . . . We serve the living and true God . . . and the
wicked may help themselves the best they can.

Journal of Discourses, 5:58

The Saints were stunned at the deaths of Joseph and Hyrum.
Many had believed the Prophet was invincible; there had been so
many threats made on his life, and yet he had always escaped, as
powerful and vibrant as ever. It was difficult for the people to dis-
tinguish between "Joseph" and "the Church." Now, amid the confusion, the sense of loss, and the perceived lack of direction, it was
vital that the Prophet's own design for the future of the kingdom
be put into place.

"When we landed in the city," wrote Wilford Woodruff, who arrived August 6 with Brigham and others of the Twelve, "a deep gloom seemed to rest over Nauvoo such as we had never before experienced."[1] Sidney Rigdon had crept back from Pittsburgh to make his claim as guardian of the Church, despite the fact that Joseph had wished to release him from his place in the Presidency, and had only acquiesced to the vote of the October 1843 conference to allow him to remain. In a meeting held on August 7, when Rigdon first presented his claim, Brigham replied in a no-nonsense manner:

> I do not care who leads the Church, even though it were Ann Lee; but one thing I must know, and that is what God says about it. *I have the keys and the means of obtaining the mind of God on the subject.* . . . Joseph conferred upon our heads all the keys and powers belonging to the Apostleship which he himself held before he was taken away, and no man or set of men can get between Joseph and the Twelve.[2]

On the following day, at ten in the morning, a vast congregation of Saints gathered around a temporary platform near the temple. Sidney spoke for over an hour and a half, but the people did not respond to either his rhetoric or his harangues. When Brigham rose to speak to the people his presence was dynamic, and the testifying power of the Spirit permeated his words:

> For the first time in my life, for the first time in your lives, for the first time in the kingdom of God in the 19th century, without a Prophet at our head, do I step forth to act in my calling in connection with the Quorum of the Twelve, as Apostles of Jesus Christ . . . whom God has called by revelation through the Prophet Joseph. . . . This people have hitherto walked by sight and not by faith . . . you have had a Prophet as the mouth of the Lord to speak to you, but he has sealed his testimony with his blood, and now, for the first time, are you called to walk by faith, not by sight. . . . When I came to this stand I had peculiar feelings and impressions. The faces of the people seem to say, we want a shepherd to guide and lead us through this world. *All that want to draw away a party from the church after them, let them do it if they can, but they will not prosper.* . . . What do the people want? I feel as though I wanted the privilege to weep and mourn for thirty days at

least, then rise up, shake myself, and tell the people what the Lord
wants of them . . . I feel compelled this day to step forth in the discharge of those duties God has placed upon me.

Brigham's heart was tender, but his mind was sure. He spoke
but briefly in the morning meeting, and about two hours in the
afternoon. He spoke with power and compassion, with logic and
persuasion:

> You cannot fill the office of a prophet, seer and revelator: God must
> do that. . . . The Twelve are appointed by the finger of God. Here is
> Brigham, have his knees ever faltered? Have his lips ever quivered?
> Here is Heber and the rest of the Twelve, an independent body who
> have the keys of the priesthood—the keys of the kingdom of God to
> deliver to all the world: this is true, so help me God.[3]

As Brigham bore this powerful witness, not only his words
stirred the people. Many testified that, as they looked upon him,
in voice, bearing, and appearance he was transformed; it was as if
the Prophet Joseph himself stood again in their midst. Benjamin
F. Johnson recorded his experience:

> . . . suddenly, as from Heaven, I heard the voice of the Prophet Joseph
> that thrilled my whole being, and quickly turning around I saw in the
> transfiguration of Brigham Young, the tall, straight, and portly form
> of the Prophet Joseph Smith, clothed in a sheen of light, covering him
> to his feet; and I heard the real and perfect voice of the Prophet, even
> to the whistle . . caused by the loss of a tooth . . . broken out by the
> mob at Hiram. This view, or vision, although but for seconds, was to
> me as vivid and real as the glare of lightning or the voice of thunder
> from the heavens, and so deeply was I impressed . . . that for years I
> dared not tell what was given me of the Lord to see. But when in later
> years I did publicly bear this testimony, I found that others had testi-
> fied to having seen and heard the same. But to what proportion of the
> congregation that were present, I could never know. But I do know
> that this, my testimony, is true.[4]

When Brigham presented it to the people for a vote—did they
want Rigdon as their leader or spokesman, or did they desire to

"sustain the Twelve as the First Presidency of this people"?—there was not one dissenting hand raised in opposition to the Twelve. In his journal of that evening, Brigham wrote:

> This day is long to be remembered by me . . . I arose and spoke to the people, *my heart was swollen with compassion toward them and by the power of the Holy Ghost, even the spirit of the prophets I was enabled to comfort the hearts of the Saints.* . . . The church was of one heart and one mind, they wanted the Twelve to lead the church as Brother Joseph had done in his day.[5]

Brigham was forty-three years old, in the prime of his life. "For over twelve years he had . . . labored and sacrificed and given his all for the cause of the Saints. . . . Now he was fit to command."[6] To his fellow Saints at this time he said:

> I have traveled these many years, in the midst of poverty and tribulation, and that, too, with blood in my shoes, month after month, to sustain and preach this Gospel and build up this Kingdom, and God forbid that I should now turn around, and seek to destroy that which I have been laboring to build up.[7]

Recent history offers certain parallels to Brigham's experience. When Winston Churchill at last was offered the position, and power, of Prime Minister in May 1940, in the midst of danger and struggles which most shrank from in horror and dismay, he said:

> . . . as I went to bed at about 3 a.m., I was conscious of a profound sense of relief. At last I had the authority to give directions over the whole scene. *I felt as if I were walking with destiny, and that all my past life had been but a preparation for this hour and for this trial.*[8]

So it was with Brigham Young. The Lord had prepared him, and he knew it. He gloried in the truth; with every fiber of his being he was dedicated to the work and the welfare of the Saints. The future of the kingdom was held in his capable hands.

It was clear to Brigham, and he made it clear to the Saints, that they would "carry out all the measures of Joseph."

> You did not know who you had amongst you. Joseph so loved this people that he gave his life for them; Hyrum loved his brother and this people unto death. Joseph and Hyrum have given their lives for the church. But very few knew Joseph's character; . . . he was in your midst, but you did not know it until after his death . . . Brother Joseph has laid the foundation for a great work, and we will build upon it; you have never seen the quorums built one upon another. . . . The Twelve have the power now—the seventies, the elders, and all of you have power to go and build up the kingdom in the name of Israel's God. Nauvoo will not hold all the people that will come into the kingdom.[9]

The prophetic vision was with him, and the unassailable dedication which could make him say, "I have spared no pains to learn my lesson of the kingdom in this world and in the eternal worlds; and if it were not so, I could go and live in peace; *but for the gospel and your sakes I shall stand in my place."*[10]

And the first business in filling that place was to complete the Nauvoo Temple. "We want to build the Temple . . . ," he said, "if we have to build it as the Jews . . . in Jerusalem, with a sword in one hand and the trowel in the other."[11] He not only organized and supervised the work, but, as he wrote in his journal under date of September 17, "In company with Elders Kimball, Woodruff, and others, I went on to the Temple walls, viewed the country and encouraged the workmen."[12] It was his self-appointed task to build up, inspire, and encourage. Two days later his journal said, "At home waiting upon my wife who was sick. The saints called upon me for counsel and direction." And, the following day: "Attending to ordinances in behalf of the Saints, and laying hands on the sick. The Lord is with me continually."[13] Joseph's example was deeply imbued in his soul, and he was practicing in private—as he would do his whole life—those principles he espoused in public. In fact, it is of great import to note that there are only fifty of Joseph Smith's known 250 discourses recorded, and that imperfectly, while 800 of Brigham's were carefully transcribed, and usually reviewed and verified by President Young himself. Thus, it is through him "that one grasps the real scope of Joseph's thinking":

> Brigham was the conscious and true inheritor of Joseph's vision, carefully trained and taught by him for twelve years. . . Again and again Brigham testified that he taught and did only what he knew from Joseph, and the Apostles who knew both of them testified it was true. Just a few months before his own death President Young again insisted: "From the first time I saw the Prophet Joseph I never lost a word that came from him concerning the kingdom. And this is the key of knowledge that I have today, that I did hearken to the words of Joseph and treasured them up in my heart, laid them away, asking my Father in the name of his Son Jesus to bring them to mind when needed."[14]

At the October conference the Twelve were sustained as the First Presidency of the Church, and the work of the kingdom went forward, despite uncertainty and change, and the growing threat of persecution. Eighty-five men were chosen to preside over various mission districts, with Wilford Woodruff as head of the European mission. That fall the limestone blocks for the second story of the temple were laid, and the first sunstone placed. Construction of the Seventies Hall, the Nauvoo House, and a concert hall were also underway. Brigham counseled the Saints to plow, sow and build, assuring them that one plowshare would do more to drive off the mob than two guns. "In that way all may enjoy plenty, and our infant city may grow and flourish, and be strengthened an hundred fold."[15]

Brigham and the brethren avoided political issues and did all they could to assuage the tempers of their enemies. But the hue and cry everywhere was to strip the Mormons of their power. The Nauvoo Charter was revoked on January 24, 1845, leaving an entire community without support of organized law. But Brigham merely extended and redirected the incredible organization of the priesthood to function in civic capacities. One of his measures was to organize a militia or police force comprised of "'quorums' of twelve men acting as 'deacons' under the supervision of 'bishops' who patrolled the streets day and night and served as bodyguards to the apostles and other church authorities."[16] The boys' brigade, of some two hundred and fifty boys, often referred to as the "whistling and whittling brigade," "kept a good watch and were directed to keep an eye on the 'Black Ducks' (any suspects)." We really tried to do our duty," wrote Mosiah Hancock, who had been a member of the group, "and we succeeded in bagging some game."[17]

Brigham gave a new name to his newly formed government, and Nauvoo became known as "The City of Joseph," a title which must have irked their enemies, but was used with tender respect by the Saints.

Brigham and the Quorum pored over government reports, newspaper articles written by Western travelers, even journals of fur trappers, seeking all the information they could gather concerning a move to the West. As early as the winter of 1844-45 the Bear River Valley, or valley of the Great Salt Lake, was being considered, and "by mid-1845 Brigham and the Twelve had definitely decided on the Salt Lake Valley as the most suitable site for settlement."[18]

The October 1845 conference of the Church—the last to be held in Nauvoo—took place in the temple, with 4,000 Saints in attendance. Plans for the proposed move West were discussed. Brigham spoke in bold strokes of verbal color, as was his wont:

> We want to take you to a land where a white man's foot never trod, nor a lion's whelps, nor the devil's; and there we can enjoy it, with no one to molest and make us afraid; and we will bid all the nations welcome, whether Pagans, Catholics, or Protestants.

He could say this, while in the same speech talking of the inhuman persecution heaped upon them by their non-Mormon neighbors. His offer was not mere rhetoric, but a bold avowal of the principles of the gospel of love.

> I had rather live with the buffalo in the wilderness; and I mean to go if the Lord will let me, and spare my life. *Let us become passive as clay in the hands of the potter; if we don't we will be cut from the wheel and thrown back in the mill again.*[19]

His focus was always on dependence upon God and his will, and the necessity of obedience and humility.

During this conference, Mother Lucy Mack Smith rose and spoke to the congregated Saints, expressing her love for them and reviewing, in part, the history of her family and of her prophet sons. "I feel that the Lord will let Brother Brigham take the people away," she said. "Here, in this city, lay my dead; my husband and children; and if so be the rest of my children go with you (and would to God they may all go), they will not go without me; and if I go, I want my bones brought back in case I die away, and deposited with my husband and children." Brigham's response to the Prophet's mother has a note of tragic tenderness to it:

> Mother Smith proposes a thing which rejoices my heart; she will go with us . . . We want her and her children . . . and I pledge myself in behalf of the authorities of the church, that while we have anything, they shall share with us . . . I say in the name of the Latter-day Saints, we will supply her wants; and I want the people to take anything they have for her to her, and let her do with it as she pleases. I have never asked her to go for she told me she would not; but now she has offered it.[20]

Relations with Joseph's widow, Emma, and some of the other members of the Smith family were not so straightforward and warm. In this same conference, Brigham makes magnanimous reference to Joseph's brother, William: "When William came here we furnished him a span of horses and a carriage and a house and Brother Kimball became responsible for the rent of it. He has run away in a time of trouble; but I suppose will come back when it is peace, and we mean to have him with us yet."[21] But in his journal, under date of Sunday, October 19, Brigham recorded: "William Smith who has published a pamphlet against the Twelve was excommunicated from the church by unanimous vote."[22] This could not have served to improve already strained relations. William had always been a source of anguish and trouble to Joseph and the brethren. Did they wait until the Prophet's death to take this painful action which, in some respects, was long overdue?

In his speech before the gathered Saints, Brigham boldly stated:

> We are determined also to use every means in our power to do all that Joseph told us. And we will petition Sister Emma in the name of Israel's God, to let us deposit the remains of Joseph according as he commanded us. And if she will not consent to it, our garments are clear. Then when he awakes in the morning of the resurrection, he shall talk with them, not with me; the sin shall be upon her head, not ours.[23]

This was pretty powerful language, and could not help but offend and anger Emma. Brigham was a busy man with many responsibilities following the death of Joseph, but he did at times—knowingly or unknowingly—slight and offend the woman whom he thought had not behaved in a manner worthy of her dead husband. Both were deeply emotional, opinionated people, perhaps alienated by the very depths of their devotion to the Prophet and their differing methods of demonstrating it. Perhaps Brigham did not take into account the delicate state of Emma's health, both physical and emotional, and the insecurity she must have been experiencing. She did not live up to his expectations; therefore, he did not know how to deal with her. There are references in his diary to business dealings with Emma over properties of Joseph's and their rightful disposal; in this, as in most things, there was usually a lack of agreement between the two. Perhaps this is the single instance in which it might be construed that Brigham had failed, or at least disappointed, his beloved Prophet; kindness and forbearance toward the volatile Emma would have been Joseph's gentle counsel to his headstrong apostle. Given different circumstances and less pressing demands, the strained relations between the two might not have existed to such an unhappy extent.

As the city of Nauvoo was turned into a veritable beehive in preparation for the exodus—George A.'s wife, Bathsheba, described the city as "one vast mechanic shop," with her own parlor being transformed into a paint shop for wagons[24]—persecutions increased, and so did work in the temple. In his journal

Brigham tells of the poisoning of Joshua Smith and Joseph Brackenbury, whose murderers later boasted "that Mormon elders had not faith enough to stand poison." Brackenbury's body, dug up by some of the mob, was saved from desecration by a dream Joel H. Johnson had on the night after Brother Brackenbury's burial which prompted the brethren to venture forth in the midst of a heavy snowstorm and surprise the diggers at the grave.[25]

Now and then, Brigham's journal contains a more personal note: "Dr. Richards and I visited Stephen Markham who was cutting and sawing wagon spokes, at his place in the woods. We helped him to cut and saw a while, and then took his rifle and shot at a mark, with my second shot I cut the pin that fastened the two-inch paper mark to the tree."[26]

As early as November of 1845, Brigham was organizing the Emigrating Companies according to the plan Joseph used on a smaller scale with Zion's Camp. He listed in his journal 3,285 families organized, 1,508 wagons on hand, with 1,892 begun. "Teams are sent to all parts of the country to purchase iron," he recorded, "blacksmiths are at work day and night and all hands are busily engaged getting ready for our departure westward as soon as possible."[27]

Once endowment work in the temple was begun, the response was overwhelming. As early as December, Brigham's journal is peppered with such statements as: "I officiated in the Temple until midnight" . . . "I retired to bed about midnight" . . . "officiated in the Temple during the night until three-thirty a.m." . . . and "tarried in the temple all night" . . . "my son, Joseph A., remained with me in the Temple all night." At one point when Brigham suggested taking a Saturday off to wash the robes and garments used in the ceremonies, the workers became very distressed and offered to wash clothes during the night that the work might not cease.[28] By the beginning of the new year, Brigham was recording:

> One hundred and forty-three persons received their endowments in the Temple. I officiated at the altar. Such has been the anxiety mani-

fested by the saints to receive the ordinances, and such the anxiety on our part to administer to them, that I have given myself up entirely to the work of the Lord in the Temple night and day, not taking more than four hours sleep, upon an average, per day, and going home but once a week.[29]

There were instances of the Lord's help and divine protection, such as the time when Brigham was informed that state troops accompanied by federal officers from Springfield were in the city, intent on arresting the Twelve. When they reached the temple, intent on searching it, Brigham's coachman, George D. Grant, drove the carriage up to the door, as if in wait for Brigham, and William Miller, wearing Brigham's cap and Heber Kimball's cloak, went down. He was immediately arrested, and despite his protests and pleas for counsel, etc, he was taken off to Carthage where at last, to the chagrin of many, it was ascertained that they had the wrong man—this was not Brigham Young, though those professing to know him had pointed Miller out to be the man.[30]

As the pressure of persecution increased, the temple seemed the only place of refuge left the Saints. On more than one occasion they gathered there to praise the Lord in song and dance, enjoying the sweet fellowship such activities offered. "The spirit of dancing increased," Brigham wrote, "until the whole floor was covered with dancers, and while we danced before the Lord, we shook the dust from off our feet as a testimony against this nation."[31]

While the Saints were making physical preparations for the journey, Brigham kept them reminded of the necessity of spiritual preparation as well:

There is too much covetousness in the church, and too much disposition . . . to seek after power . . . in consequence of such feelings Joseph left the people in the dark on many subjects of importance and they still remain in the dark. We have got to rid such principles from our hearts. . . . There is no law to prevent any man from obtaining all the blessings of the priesthood if he will walk according to the commandments, pay his tithes and seek after salvation, *but he may deprive himself of them.* . . . the way to grow and thrive [is] to serve the Lord in all we [do] . . . If Joseph Smith had been living, we should have already been in some other country, and we would go where we would be "the old settlers," and build larger Temples than this.[32]

By the end of January, 2,000 people were prepared to go. The Saints had agreed to leave in April, but their enemies were pressing them, and rumors circulated of federal troops in St. Louis who planned to intercept and destroy them. Brigham wrote in indignation:

We intend to start a company of young men and some few families perhaps within a few weeks. This company will travel until they can find a good location beyond the settlements, and there stop and put in a summer crop, that we may have something to subsist upon, and a portion of us remain there until we can make further discoveries.

We are forced to this policy by those who are in authority. I find no fault with the Constitution or laws of our country . . . it is the abuse of those laws which I despise, and which God, good men and angels abhor.[33]

In late January, the Saints were still scrambling to totally finish the temple building. On Monday, February 9, the temple was set afire by enemies of the Church. "I saw the flames from a distance," Brigham wrote, "but it was out of my power to get there in time to do any good towards putting out the fire, and I said if it is the will of the Lord that the Temple be burned, instead of being defiled by the Gentiles, Amen to it."[34]

The official decision to move out was made on February 2. Brigham counseled the brethren to get boats in readiness, and to have things in such order that "when a family is called to go, everything necessary may be put into the wagon within four hours . . . for if we are here many more days, our way will be hedged up."[35]

Selling property for a fair return was nearly an impossibility. One woman who owned a lot and twenty acres, all fenced, was offered ten dollars, with the stipulation that her furniture also be included. Ten dollars would ferry her over the river; for that she was expected to be grateful. Parley Pratt left a house and lot worth $7,000, and another lot to be sold by the church trustees for whatever they could get. Parley directed them to distribute the proceeds among the poor. Despite these cruel realities, and all else, Brigham refused to see their situation as a calamity, but rather a part of the "merciful design in our Heavenly Father toward all such as patiently endure these afflictions until He advises them that the day of their deliverance has come."[36]

Later, in the valley, discussing with the Saints the experiences they had shared, in an effort to instruct and enlighten them, Brigham revealed the extent of his understanding of God's dealings with the people when he said:

> Some may ask why did we not tarry at the centre stake of Zion when the Lord planted our feet there? We had eyes, but we did not see; we had ears, but we did not hear; we had hearts that were devoid of what the Lord required of his people; consequently, we could not abide what the Lord revealed unto us. We had to go from there to gain an experience. Can you understand this?[37]

On another occasion he remarked, "I never attributed the driving of the Saints from Jackson county to anything but that it was necessary to chasten them and prepare them to build up Zion."[38]

> Wake up, wake up, dear brethren . . . to the present glorious emergency in which the God of heaven has placed you to prove your faith.[39]

Building up Zion was a "glorious emergency"—the most glorious effort and opportunity Brigham could conceive of. He understood, if many of his people did not, and his faith was sufficient for many to lean upon as they honed and developed their own.

The first families crossed the river on February 4th, with hundreds to follow over the next few days. Nor did their enemies, even in their leaving, allow them any peace. In his journal Brigham records how "a wicked man" spit tobacco juice into the eyes of one of Brother Grover's oxen, who plunged into the river, dragging the flatboat on which they traveled and all else with him. The men were fished out of the river, wet and exhausted, but two of the oxen were drowned, the boat sank to the bottom, and many precious goods were damaged or destroyed.[40] The crossing was overseen by the new police force under the direction of Hosea Stout, whose men were at work night and day assisting the Saints.

Brigham, yielding to the entreaties of his people, remained behind to administer endowments, and did not cross the river with his family until Sunday, February 15, leaving his own brother, Joseph, in charge of Nauvoo. The night before, the temperature had dropped to twelve below zero, freezing the broad sweep of the Mississippi and making it possible for the great, heavy caravans of wagons and animals to walk dry-shod over the ice. Brigham's family unit at this time consisted of fifty people fit into fifteen wagons. Although little is recorded of his personal affairs during this period, it is known that by the time of the Prophet Joseph's death he had married Lucy Ann's sister, Clarissa Decker, Harriett Cook, and Augusta Adams Cobb. By the time of the exodus he had been sealed to four additional women: Clarissa Ross, Margaret Maria Alley, Emmeline Free, and Margaret Pierce. He had also, in Old Testament fashion, offered himself to Joseph Smith's widowed plural wives (possibly with the intention of raising up seed to the Prophet), eight of whom were sealed to him for the remainder of their earth lives only. Five of these had the status of "name only" marriages, with Eliza R. Snow, prophetess-poet and sister to Lorenzo Snow, being the most prominent of these. The other three later bore children by Brigham: Louisa Beaman (five), Emily Dow Partridge (seven), and Zina D. Huntington Jacobs (one). At the time of his leaving Nauvoo, Brigham's children numbered nine, as well as several foster children.[41]

By nightfall, Brigham and those traveling with him reached Sugar Creek on the Iowa side, where many of the Saints were camped. The task before him of organizing, disciplining, and caring for hundreds of displaced families seemed daunting, even to Brigham. In his journal he confided:

> I wish the brethren to stop running to Nauvoo, hunting, fishing, roasting their shins, idling away their time, and fix nosebaskets for

their horses, and save their corn, and fix comfortable places for their wives and children to ride, and never borrow without asking leave, and be sure and return what was borrowed, lest your brother be vexed with you and in his anger curse you . . . That all dogs in the camp should be killed, if the owners would not tie them up; and any man who would keep a horse in camp, that had the horse distemper [because it was rife in the camp and contagious] ought to forfeit all his horses. We will have no laws we cannot keep, but we will have order in the camp. If any want to live in peace when we have left this, they must toe the mark.[42]

Brigham's task would take all the fortitude and faith he could muster, but he was the one man who possessed the capabilities to carry it through. His entry for Monday, February 16, gives us much insight into the source of his power and the reasons for his success:

Ten a.m. I walked up the valley with Amasa Lyman and Willard Richards where we united in prayer, and I read to them a communication received two days previously, then *returned to camp and continued the organization, acting the part of a father to everybody.*[43]

Notes

1. Cowley, *Wilford Woodruff*, p. 210.
2. *HC,* 7:230.
3. *HC,* 7:232-33.
4. S. Dilworth Young, *Here Is Brigham,* p. 359.
5. Ibid., p. 366.
6. Preston Nibley, *Brigham Young,* p. 58.
7. *HC,* 5:100.
8. Martin Gilbert, *Churchill: A Photobiographic Portrait* (Boston: Houghton Mifflin, 1974), p. 245.
9. Minutes of "Special Meeting in Nauvoo," 8 August 1844, Brigham Young Papers, Church Archives, as quoted in England, *Brother Brigham,* p. 73.
10. *HC,* 7:233-34, 239.
11. Ibid., p. 256.
12. Preston Nibley, *Brigham Young,* p. 59.
13. *Journal of Brigham,* p. 78.
14. Eugene England, *Why the Church Is as True as the Gospel: Personal Essays on*

Mormon Experience (Salt Lake City: Bookcraft,1986), p. 94.

15. *HC,* 7:251.

16. Arrington, *American Moses,* p. 122.

17. *HC,* 7:388.

18. Arrington, *American Moses,* p. 124.

19. *HC,* 7:467; italics author's.

20. *HC,* 7: 470-72.

21. *HC,* 7:472.

22. *Journal of Brigham,* p. 102.

23. *HC,* 7:472-73.

24. Kenneth W. Godfrey, Audrey M. Godfrey and Jill Mulvay, *Women's Voices: An Untold History of the Latter-day Saints, 1830-1900* (Salt Lake City: Deseret Book,1982), p. 120.

25. *Journal of Brigham,* p. 106-107.

26. Ibid., p. 108-109.

27. Ibid.

28. Ibid., p. 110-15.

29. Ibid., p. 123-4.

30. *JD,* 14: 218-19.

31. *Journal of Brigham,* p. 119.

32. Ibid., p. 113-14, 122; italics author's.

33. Ibid., p. 125.

34. Ibid., p. 129.

35. Journal of Joseph, p. 128.

36. *HC,* 7:479.

37. *JD,* 11:102.

38. *JD,* 13:148.

39. Arrington, *American Moses,* p. 126; italics author's.

40. *Journal of Brigham,* p. 130.

41. Arrington, *American Moses,* p. 121.

42. *Journal of Brigham,* p. 130-31.

43. Journal History, 16 February 1846.

Chapter Ten

Camp of Israel

*Sugar Creek – Winter Quarters – Mormon Battalion –
the first pioneers – reaching the Salt Lake Valley*

We wish strangers to understand that we did not come here out of
choice, but because we were obliged to go somewhere, and this was
the best place we could find. . . . It is a first-rate place to raise Latter-
day Saints, and we shall be blessed in living here, and shall yet make
it like the Garden of Eden; and the Lord Almighty will hedge about
his Saints and will defend and preserve them if they will do his will.
The only fear I have is that we will not do right; if we do we will be
like a city set on a hill, our light will not be hid.

Journal of Discourses, 14:121

The Camp of Israel, lofty though the term may have been,
consisted at first of a conglomerate of people with various degrees
of dedication, both to the gospel and to the extremity at hand.
That Brigham was able to mould them into an effective and cooperative unit, at times even approaching the ideal, speaks forcefully
of his extraordinary leadership skills.

Brigham stayed at the Sugar Creek encampment for fifteen days. The temperature of twelve degrees below zero was severe. "I was so afflicted with the rheumatism," he wrote, "it was with difficulty I could walk."[1] Yet he worked all that day without complaint in helping to build a log house. As Saints scattered throughout Iowa joined the Camp, it swelled to five hundred in number, and Brigham wished to remove to a location further from Nauvoo. They traveled through snow, mud, and freezing rain, along nearly impassible roads, from March 1 through the 24th of April, when they reached Garden Grove on the Grand River, 150 miles from Nauvoo. On Monday, April 6, Brigham recorded that he was "in the rain all day, arranging the wagons, pitching tents, chopping wood until all were comfortable"—again demonstrating that the highest among them should be servant to all. The conditions the people endured would be difficult to imagine. Brigham himself makes mention of a Sister Stewart, who, after her labor pains started, walked two miles through the cold dark and crossed the creek on a log so that she could get out of the storm and into the shelter of a vacant house to give birth to her child.[2]

They stayed here for two weeks, during which time Parley Pratt records a chastisement he received from Brigham which he felt he did not deserve. The rebuke was administered to others as well as himself, for drawing ahead of the main camp and possessing a "spirit of dissension and insubordination." Parley concluded, however, that the reproof came of the Spirit, for others of the group, unable to take counsel, had left and gone their own way. "Although my own motives were pure, so far as I could know my own heart, yet I thank God for this timely chastisement; I profited by it, and it caused me to be more watchful and careful ever after."[3] Brigham, with the instincts of a natural leader, knew that discipline and compliance beyond the ordinary would be required of all, that strong-minded, hitherto independent men would have to learn to follow a will outside their own, if the whole was to operate in harmony. He also understood that real offenders would at times be unable to bear a "singling-out," and therefore a kind of group discipline would be kinder and wiser. Such discipline would try the sincerely humble and obedient; but, by the very nature of that trial, it would make of them better men.

It was Parley who first came upon the beautiful location which he named Mount Pisgah, set amid grassy slopes with groves and forests. Here they stayed several days and built a bridge by which they could cross the Grand River.

Late in May, Brigham recorded that "eight hundred men reported themselves without a fortnight's provisions." He himself had initially possessed a year's provisions for his entire family, but had "fed it all out,"[4] and the reader can sense his frustrated concern over how to feed and provide for so many, as well as the pressing necessity of moving, moving, until they found a true resting place. By mid-June they reached the Missouri River, in the lands of the Potawatomi Indian tribe, where they established Council Bluffs, which they called Kanesville, on the east bank, and Winter Quarters (at what is now called Florence, near Omaha, Nebraska) on the west.

Although Brigham's desire was to send a group west before the year ended, he realized such a move would be unfeasible; the people were in no wise ready or prepared. Random journal entries for May and June bear this out:

> At noon the horn sounded for the saints to assemble, but few came out . . . I want to know whether those that have recently arrived here will be united and work for the general good, and not desire to separate themselves . . . I told the saints they were hedging up their own way by the course they were pursuing.[5]

Also, with the sudden outbreak of war between the United States and Mexico, an opportunity was presented to the Saints—one which would require great discipline and sacrifice, as most of the Saints' opportunities seemed to do, but which would assure them government permission to camp on Indian lands and use the timber and grazing they would require, as well as provide them with greatly needed cash funds. The opportunity was for four to five hundred men to be mustered into a battalion, and the Saints responded. On July 20, the Mormon Battalion headed out on what would become a 2,000 mile march on foot, one of the longest infantry marches in American history. Brigham spoke to the young men before their departure, giving them timely and wise counsel, touched with the tenderness of a father:

> I instructed the captains to be fathers to their companies, and manage their affairs by the power and influence of their priesthood . . . I told them I would not be afraid to pledge my right hand that every man will return alive, if they perform their duties faithfully . . . and go in the name of the Lord . . . A private soldier is as honorable as an officer, if he behaves as well. No one is distinguished as being better flesh and blood than another . . . keep neat and clean, teach chastity . . . insult no man; never trespass on the rights of others; when the Father has proved that a man will be his friend under all circumstances, he will give to that man abundantly, and withhold no good thing from him.[6]

Now the task remained of organizing the gathered Saints whose number would be increased before winter to 12,000 people, huddling in tents and wagons, facing a bitter winter and the necessity of sustaining themselves and their animals. It was Brigham Young's constant encouragement and example which convinced them they could survive and go on.

Joseph Fielding's diary described the animals he lost, the absence of sufficient food, the difficulty in building houses for himself and his sisters (Mercy Thompson and Mary Fielding Smith, Hyrum's widow), and his children wearing out their clothing, with no means of obtaining more. Yet he could say, "we have had our health in general, and I have felt no disposition to complain."[7] The fortitude and faith of such men and their women made Brigham's overwhelming task possible.

By the new year, Brigham was reporting to the brethren in England that they had upwards of seven hundred houses, some a little makeshift in nature, but adequate for protection. There was an effective mail system and a grist mill in the building. He had divided the camp into 22 wards, each with a bishop and two counselors, and he was instructing the people that "in the

Government of this Church, in business transactions, every man should have a voice in the matter, as if the whole responsibility were on his shoulders."[8] The Saints who could were paying tithing to be used in relief of the poor, and each company was instructed to take an equal number of widows and orphans. The previous October, when the last destitute Saints had been driven from Nauvoo and made a miserable camp on the opposite bank of the Mississippi, flocks of quails descended upon them, so that even the ill and feeble were able to catch them with their hands, and thus the Lord saved them from despair and starvation.[9]

There were yet run-ins and misunderstandings, suffering and deaths (one of Brigham's wives, Mary Pierce, died March 17 of consumption), but the spirit of unity and brotherhood increased, and the Saints danced and sang and made merry one with another. Brigham comprehended the deeper elements involved:

> The Lord said he wanted His saints to praise Him in all things. It was enjoined on Miriam and the daughters of Israel to dance and celebrate the name of the Almighty, and to praise Him on the destruction of Pharaoh and his host.

> For some weeks past I could not wake up at any time of the night but I heard the axes at work. Some were building for the destitute and the widow; and now my feelings are, dance all night, if you desire to do so, for there is no harm in it.[10]

In February, Brigham related to his brethren of the Twelve a dream he had:

> While sick and asleep about noonday on the 17th, I dreamed that I went to [see] Joseph . . . I took hold of his right hand and kissed him many times, and said to him: "Why is it that we cannot be together as we used to be. You have been from us a long time, and we want your society and I do not like to be separated from you." Joseph rising from his chair and looking at me with his usual, earnest, expressive and pleasing countenance replied, "It is all right." I said, "I do not like to be away from you."

Certainly here is revealed Brigham's exhausted need—whatever uncertainty existed within him, whatever desire to lay down the burden, would be naturally directed toward the man who had been his guidance and his strength.

> Joseph said, "It is all right; we cannot be together yet; we shall be by and by; but you will have to do without me a while, and then we shall be together again."

The counsel Joseph gave him could be summed up in the phrase which was repeated in the dream: "Tell the people to be sure to keep the Spirit of the Lord and follow it, and it will lead them just right."[11]

By early April, the plans and the dreams solidified into reality. On Sunday, April 4, one of the last acts of the Twelve before Brigham's departure was to write "a lengthy letter to Mrs. Lucy Smith, mother of the Prophet Joseph, inquiring after her whereabouts and circumstances, and offering to convey her westward if she desired to join the body of the Church."[12]

The first group of pioneers had been organized to include 148 people, at first intended to be all men. But Brigham gave in to his brother Lorenzo's entreaties that his asthmatic wife, Harriet, be allowed to accompany him. Lorenzo's six-year-old son and a stepson were also included, then Clara Decker, Brigham's wife and Harriet's daughter by her first husband, and Ellen Sanders, one of Heber's wives.

On Monday, April 5, Heber started out with six of his teams, traveled about four miles, and formed an encampment with others of his division. He then returned to Winter Quarters for conference, and took the opportunity to bless the members of his family. Parley P. Pratt, en route to his mission to England, returned from Leavenworth with between five and six thousand dollars sent by members of the Mormon Battalion, whom he had met with there. On the 9th the Twelve started again, Heber riding in President Young's wagon, according to Brigham's arrangement. The camp was strictly organized, with the bugle blown at five every morning and prayers the first order of the day. Travel began at seven, and the men were to carry guns that were loaded and ready. There would be only half an hour for dinner, and when the camp halted for the night the wagons were to be drawn into a circle. The horn would blow again at half past eight, and bedtime was at nine o'clock sharp, except for those on guard duty.

During the first weeks of travel, William Clayton suggested to Orson Pratt, who possessed a fine scientific turn of mind, that a system be devised to measure the turning of the wagon wheels and the distance they traveled each day. It took a month of prodding, but eventually Orson designed a roadometer and Appleton Harmon built it. And, as the brethren traveled, they took note of conditions and began to map out a precise set of instructions for those who would follow, outlining the places where grazing was plentiful and water available, identifying areas of possible danger and privation. They also worked out a system of leaving periodic and frequent messages enclosed in boxes and attached to high poles. This came to mark the Mormon Pioneer Trail as entirely unique. It was a permanent roadway for travelers who were not simply wayfarers, but part of a tightly knit community whose means of communication and cooperation were highly developed and enviable.

There was the tedium of travel and daily tasks to be performed over and over again: "[Heber recording] President Young and myself both volunteered and stood the first part of the night, till one o'clock. It was very cold indeed, and about the middle of the night it rained again."[13] But every stretch of the journey was a new experience which brought its own challenges and gifts.

April saw their first encounter with Indians (a large body of Pawnee), the Platte river to be navigated, and the discovery of nature's substitute when there were wood shortages: "buffalo chips" (dried buffalo dung), which were plentifully available and made a good fire.

May started out cold, and the first day of May marked their first sight of buffalo. "The buffaloes that our eyes beheld," Wilford Woodruff recorded on May 8,

> were most astonishing. Thousands upon thousands would crowd together as they came from the bluffs to the bottom-land to go to the

river and sloughs to drink, until the river and land on both sides of it looked as though the face of the earth was alive and moving like the waves of the sea.[14]

The brethren would in time experience the chilling thrill of the chase and the succulent flavor of buffalo meat cooked over the fire. Sometimes the buffalo walked right alongside the wagons, and the brethren could shoot them with no effort at all.

Brigham took time to complete a letter he had begun earlier to Mary Ann in which he called her his "dear companion partner in tribulation" and wrote that "I due think the Lord has blest me with one of [the] best famelyes that eney man ever had on the earth." Now he told her,

> I pray for you continualy . . . I am glad you are not a going to come on this sumer for I want to be with my famely when they come this jorney. . . I want the brethren to help my famely whils I am gon and not supress them. Joseph and Brigham be good boys and mind your mother and Ales [Alice], Caroline, little Johne and finely all my children and famely be you blest for ever and ever.[15]

After a time, Brigham felt it expedient to challenge the brethren to a higher level of behavior. He expressed his disgust and disappointment in strong terms and descried the spirit of the camp, the playing of cards and checkers, the "folly and wickedness." This journey was meant to serve as an inspiration for generations to come. He declared he would not go one step further with them under such conditions. But then, according to the Lord's counsel in the Doctrine and Covenants, he concluded his rebuke by "very feelingly and tenderly blessing the brethren. . . ."[16] They responded, and a general reformation seemed to take place. "No loud laughter was heard," Heber reported,

> no swearing, no quarreling, no profane language, no hard speeches to man or beast, and it truly seemed as though the cloud had burst, and we had emerged into a new element, a new atmosphere, a new society and a new world.[17]

Wilford Woodruff described the effect the experience had upon him:

> In the morning I shaved, cleansed my body, put on clean clothing, etc., read a chapter in the Book of Mormon, humbled myself before the Lord, and poured out my soul in prayer before Him, and His spirit descended upon me and I was blessed and prepared for the service of the day.[18]

On the 2nd of June, the pioneers camped across from Fort Laramie. In seven weeks they had traveled 543 miles from Winter Quarters, leaving the low, even country of Nebraska behind. After they crossed the Platte, opposite the Fort, they would be traveling through Wyoming and gradually ascending the great eastern plateau of the Rocky Mountains.

Several of the brethren crossed the river and met the Frenchman, Mr. Burdoe, who superintended the fort. He received them in a kindly manner, but astonished them by saying that Governor Boggs of Missouri and his men had come through,

> and had much to say against the Mormons and cautioned him to take care of his horses and cattle, etc., lest they should steal them. He tried to prejudice him all he could against us. Burdoe said that Boggs' company were quarreling all the time, and most of them had deserted him. He finally told Boggs and company to let the Mormons be what they might, they could not be worse than he and his men.[19]

At the fort, members of Brigham's camp were surprised to be joined by a small company of Saints from Mississippi who, under the direction of Brother Crow, were in search of the main body of the Church. They remained with Brigham's company for the rest of the journey.

The going began to get rough. It took them seven days to cross the Platte river, and a small party Brigham had sent ahead ferried a group of emigrants across at the price of $1.50 for each wagon and load, paid in foodstuffs. Wilford Woodruff recorded:

In the evening the flour, meal, and bacon which had been earned from the Missouri company for ferrying them over were distributed through the camp equally. It amounted to five and one-half pounds of flour, two pounds of meal and a small piece of bacon for each individual in the camp. It looked as much of a miracle to me to see our flour and meal bags replenished in the midst of the Black Hills as it did to have the Children of Israel fed with manna in the wilderness; but the Lord has been truly with us on our journey and wonderfully preserved and blessed us.[20]

In the Black Hills, Heber discovered a beautiful spring of water, bubbling up clear and cold. He named the spot "Kimball's Spring," perhaps wondering if he might, indeed, be the first white man to have discovered its charms.

The crude, quarrelsome nature of the Missourians who traveled near the Saints irritated the brethren. Once six of these men, ridiculously disguising themselves as Indians, came upon Heber and Ezra T. Benson as they were riding ahead of the company to scout out a camping ground. The Missourians sprang up suddenly from the grass at the side of the road and mounted quickly, hoping to frighten the two men. When the brethren failed to respond, one of the party motioned dramatically for the two to go back. As they kept on, ignoring their would-be tormentors, the men scampered off and disappeared, though Heber and Ezra, on reaching the summit, observed them racing into camp to brag of their exploit. Indignant, but dignified, the two men let the incident go.[21]

The company reached Independence Rock on the 21st of June, and beheld the magnificence of South Pass on the 26th, with the stretching vistas of the Rocky Mountains outlined at a great distance before them, gray with the gauntness of bare rock, softened by the mottled purple of shadow. "I went to the north end, which is the highest point of Independence Rock," Wilford Woodruff recorded.

There is an opening or cavern that would contain thirty or forty persons and a rock standing upon the highest peak of about three tons

weight. Upon this rock we climbed to the highest point and offered
up our prayers according to the order of the priesthood, praying
earnestly for the blessing of God to rest upon President Young and his
brethren the Twelve and the whole Pioneer Camp.[22]

During the trek, Brigham's company had a number of interesting visitors. Moses "Black" Harris, who had lived nearly a quarter of a century west of the Rockies, was not optimistic about the
possibilities of the Great Basin. Jim Bridger, the famed "Mountain
Man," didn't seem to think that grain could be grown there, stating a bit flamboyantly that he would give a thousand dollars for
the first bushel of corn grown in the Great Basin. On the heels of
these visitors came Samuel Brannan, whom Brigham had sent to
colonize California. He and two companions had come overland
from San Francisco, and it was his intent to persuade Brigham to
settle the Saints in the favorable climate of the coast. In
California, all things seemed possible and promise seemed to
whisper in the very breath of the ocean-blessed air.

Brigham had other, more crucial considerations in mind:

I do not wish men to understand that I had anything to do with our
being moved here, that was the providence of the Almighty. It was the
power of God that wrought out salvation for this people, I never
could have devised such a plan . . . We had to have faith to come here.
When we met Mr. Bridger on the Big Sandy River, said he, "Mr.
Young, I would give a thousand dollars if I knew an ear of corn could
be ripened in the Great Basin." Said I, "Wait eighteen months and I
will show you many of them." Did I say this from knowledge? No, it
was my faith . . . . Why did we not go to San Francisco? Because the
Lord told me not: "For there are lions in the way, and they will devour
the lambs, if you take them there."[23]

On the Fourth of July, "just another hot, dusty, mosquito-rid-
den day of traveling,"[24] five volunteers (including Brigham's brother
Phinehas), headed back to meet the second group of pioneers and
guide them in their journey. Three days later the company reached
Fort Bridger, where they took two days to make much-needed
repairs, shoe horses, and prepare for the last leg of their journey.

On July 12, Brigham was struck with a fever, now identified as Colorado tick fever. He immediately became very ill, "raving and insensible." "He experienced excruciating headaches, high fever, and severe aches and pains in his back and joints. He was, as he described himself, 'almost mad with pain.'"[25] The situation was so severe that at times the brethren paused to pray and fast for his recovery. Brigham was to remain sick and bedridden for the remainder of the journey.

Orson Pratt, Erastus Snow, and others were sent from Bear River ahead of the general group to break a road through the canyons. This group reached the valley on July 20. On July 22, the main camp caught their first view of the valley—"the Salt Lake in the distance with its bold hills on its Islands towering up in bold relief behind the Silvery Lake," wrote Thomas Bullock.

> The sky is very clear, the air delightful and all together looks glorious, the only drawback appearing to be the absence of timber. But there is an ocean of stone in the mountains to build stone houses and walls for fencing. If we can only find a bed of coal we can do well and be hidden up in the mountains unto the Lord.[26]

Lorenzo's wife, Harriet, was not so enthusiastic in her assessment. As she gazed over the barren valley she said to her husband, "We have traveled fifteen hundred miles to get here, and I would willingly travel a thousand miles farther to get where it looked as though a white man could live."[27] Lorenzo seemed to partake of the same spirit of discouragement and exhaustion, for he wrote: "This day we arrived in the valley of the great Salt Lake. My feelings were such as I cannot describe. Everything looked gloomy and I felt heartsick."[28]

Brigham, however, recorded on July 23,

> I ascended and crossed over the Big Mountain, when on its summit I directed Elder Woodruff, who had kindly tendered me the use of his carriage, to turn the same halfway round so that I could have a view of a portion of the Salt Lake valley. The spirit of light rested upon me and hovered over the valley, and I felt that there the Saints would find protection and safety.[29]

It took only hours for the Saints to begin settling in. "There were no idlers in the camp, all were busy as bees," Wilford Woodruff recorded. "They dammed up one creek, and before night had spread the water over a large tract and irrigated the parched ground. This was the beginning of irrigation in the Salt Lake Valley, July 24, 1847."[30]

That same day, Brigham and Heber crossed Emigration Creek the necessary eighteen times and went down into the Salt Lake Valley together—as they had been since the Lord first placed his hand on their lives. That evening the Lord sent a beautiful thundershower, and a gentle rain washed the entire valley as a benediction on that first Pioneer Day. The Camp of Israel, weary and grateful, had come home to the place which the God of Israel had prepared for his Saints.

Notes

1. *Journal of Brigham,* p. 134.
2. Ibid., p. 148.
3. Parley P. Pratt, *Autobiography,* p. 306-307.
4. *Journal of Brigham,* p. 159.
5. Ibid., p. 160-61.
6. Ibid., p. 171.
7. Diary of Joseph Fielding Smith, Book 5, p. 144, Church Archives.
8. *Journal of Brigham,* p. 206.
9. Richard Neitzel Holzapfel and Jeni Broberg Holzapfel, *Women of Nauvoo* (Salt Lake City: Bookcraft,1992), p. 177.
10. *Journal of Brigham,* p. 207.
11. Ibid., p. 208-209.
12. Ibid., p. 214.
13. Whitney, *Life of Heber C. Kimball,* p. 368.
14. Cowley, *Wilford Woodruff,* p. 279.
15. Arrington, *American Moses,* p. 134, 137.
16. Whitney, *Life of Heber C. Kimball,* p. 369.
17. Ibid.
18. Cowley, *Wilford Woodruff,* p. 292.
19. Ibid., p. 294.
20. Ibid., p. 299.

21. Whitney, *Life of Heber C. Kimball,* p. 371.
22. Ibid., p. 303-304.
23. John A. Widtsoe, *Discourses of Brigham Young* (Salt Lake City: Deseret Book,1954), p. 481-82.
24. Arrington, *American Moses,* p. 142.
25. Ibid., p. 143.
26. Ibid., p. 145.
27. Ibid., p. 145.
28. Ibid., p. 146.
29. *Journal of Brigham,* p. 221.
30. Cowley, *Wilford Woodruff,* p. 315.

Chapter Eleven

Great Salt Lake City

*City laid out, stake organized – Brigham returns to
Winter Quarters, sustained as President of Church –
second journey west – sustained by Saints in Salt Lake Valley*

No man will gain influence in this Kingdom, save what he gains by
the influence and power of the Holy One that has called him to truth,
holiness, and virtue. That is all the influence I have, and I pray God
that I may never have any different influence.

Journal of Discourses, 7:140

"The City of the Great Salt Lake," named thus in conference
on Sunday, August 15, was laid out in blocks of ten acres, each
divided into eight equal-sized lots of one and a quarter acres.
Brigham thought the houses ought to be built in the center of the
lots, so that an outbreak of fire in one location would not endanger another. The lots were designed to be an inheritance to all the
people, preventing land speculation and personal aggrandizement
to those who had happened to come first. The farming land,
placed outside the city limits,

was parceled out in five acre plats, joining them a little further out into ten acres, and outside of these, twenty acre fields. This arrangement prevented any one man from holding a large tract near the city, and by so doing prevented speculation by the individual to the detriment of the whole community.[1]

On Monday, July 26, Brigham and the Twelve climbed the high peak a little north of the city. Here they raised the American flag, the "Ensign of Liberty." Although they were, at the time, technically standing on Mexican soil, this was a symbol of their love and faith, their loyalty to the government which had abused and abandoned them, but which they believed, nevertheless, to have been divinely inspired of God. Brigham named the place "Ensign Peak."

George A. Smith, speaking in Salt Lake City in later years, told the people:

> After the death of Joseph Smith, when it seemed as if every trouble and calamity had come upon the Saints, Brigham Young who was President of the Twelve, then the presiding quorum . . . sought the Lord to know what they should do, and where they should lead the people for safety, and while they were fasting and praying daily on this subject, President Young had a vision of Joseph Smith, who showed him the mountain that we now call Ensign Peak . . . and there was an ensign fell upon that peak, and Joseph said, "Build under the point where the colors fall and you will prosper and have peace." The pioneers had no pilot or guide, none among them had ever been in the country or knew anything about it. However, they travelled under the direction of President Young until they reached this valley. When they entered it President Young pointed to that peak, and, said he, "I want to go there." He went up to that point and said, "This is Ensign Peak."[2]

Brigham himself often reminded the Saints that "in the days of Joseph we have sat many hours at a time conversing about this very country. Joseph has often said, 'If I were only in the Rocky Mountains with a hundred faithful men, I would then be happy, and ask no odds of mobocrats.'"[3]

On July 28, Brigham, in company with the Twelve, "walked to about the center between the two creeks," waved his hand and said, "Here is the forty acres for the Temple. The city can be laid out perfectly square, north and south, east and west."[4]

The brethren also bathed in the Great Salt Lake, fascinated that a man would not sink in it, but could sit comfortably, cradled in the water's warmth. Brigham set the members of the Battalion, who came into the valley late on Thursday the 29th, to building a bowery on the temple block where meetings could be held. By Sunday, Heber Kimball recorded:

> Brother Markham says that there are already about fifty-three acres of land plowed and most of it planted with corn, beans, garden seeds, etc., There have been thirteen plows and three drags at work nearly all the week. At ten o'clock we assembled for meetings in the bowery. It was decided to build a stockade of adobes, and adobie houses, and a number of men were selected to commence making adobies tomorrow.[5]

Within three weeks a wall was constructed around a fort that contained twenty-nine log houses with willow bough roofs and adobe chimneys, four of them built by Brigham Young. Clara, the wife who had come with him, moved into one, where she would later be joined by Eliza R. Snow.

On the 7th of August, at Brigham's suggestion, the members of the camp were re-baptized, that they might pledge a re-dedication to their Covenants. Brigham baptized the Twelve and sealed their apostleship upon them anew, then Heber baptized and confirmed Brigham.

At a conference held the 22nd of August, a stake of Zion was formed with Father John Smith as president. The city received its name, as well as the stream running west which they called "City Creek," the two streams from the mountains on the east to be called "Great Canyon Creek" and "Little Canyon Creek," and the river on the west to be known as "Western Jordan," distinguishing it from the river with the same name in Palestine.

Heber Kimball spoke with prophetic power at this conference, and his words stir emotion, even in the reader of today:

Brother Brigham is going to be greater than he was; he will be greater
in strength, in beauty, and in glory. . . . I want you, Brother Brigham,
[addressing him directly] to save yourself, for you are wearing down.
I feel tender towards you, to live, and if I and my brethren do wrong,
tell us of it, and we will repent.[6]

Brother Brigham, after only a month in the valley, set his face
back along the trail, to see to the task of gathering his waiting and
anxious people.

As they retraced their steps, Brigham and his company met
several groups of Saints en route to the city. One camp was under
the direction of Parley P. Pratt, and Brigham took occasion to call
Brother Pratt severely to task for failing to keep to the established
rules and regulations for organizing and superintending the trek.
The fact that Parley responded to being "severely reproved and
chastened" with a spirit of patient acceptance is illuminated by
Brother Bullock's report of the incident:

Prest. Young reproved P.P.P. very strongly for disorganizing all the
Winter's work of the Quorum of Twelve. He at first manifested a con-
tra Spirit, but afterwards repented—the Spirit and power of God was
poured out—much instruction was given—and it proved a most glorious meeting to all.[7]

The Spirit of God could not have been poured out if Brigham
himself had been markedly out of tune. Parley sincerely recorded a
statement which appears more than once in his autobiography:
"This school of experience made me more humble and careful in
future, and I think it was the means of making me a wiser and better man ever after."[8] Brigham, on the other hand, was not unaware
of his own failings; he was not a leader after the fashion of the world
where, if the power resided in him, he would use it however he
desired, and woe to the offender. "Never in the days of my life have
I hurt a man with the palm of my hand," he told the Saints. "I never
have hurt a person any other way except with this unruly member,
my tongue."[9] He constantly struggled for the control he desired. On
another occasion he taught: "Now I charge you again, and I charge

myself not to get angry. Never let anger arise in your hearts. No, Brigham, never let anger arise in your heart, never, never!"[10]

The eastward return trip was difficult and harrowing, mainly due to the stealing of many horses by the Indians. Yet it took less time, and in some ways seemed easier, perhaps because the way was known, and they were not constantly beset by concern over the mysteries and possible dangers of each step ahead. On September 7, Brigham's party pressed some fourteen miles through a snowstorm to meet with John Taylor's company on the Sweetwater. There was a sumptuous supper prepared of "roast and boiled beef, veal, pies, cakes, biscuits, butter, peaches with coffee, tea, sugar, cream and a variety of the good things of life." About sixty found room to eat at the first sitting, the remainder waiting till the second round, and they spent the rest of the evening dancing off the effects of the meal, tripping "the light fantastic toe . . . until about 10 or 11 o'clock."[11]

Shortly thereafter, Brigham encountered the last two companies of Saints, one led by Jedediah M. Grant in which two of his wives, Margaret Pierce and Eliza R. Snow, were traveling. Eliza, who had driven her own team all the way to Winter Quarters and who was traveling with the Markham family, with no real place of her own, felt gratified to meet with her leader-husband on Friday, September 10. Although the general tone of their private conversation was "light," she took occasion to ask him who was to be her counselor during the year to come. "He said, 'Eliza R. Snow.' I said, 'She is not capable.' He said, 'I have appointed her president.'"[12] Then he blessed her, knowing full well her capabilities, her power not only to care for herself, but to labor and serve as a blessing to all. Her lightly spoken protest couched real fears and a loneliness he could not be aware of. Yet the very tenor of their interchange served to maintain the spirit of hope, the quiet awareness that *what was* had to be dealt with, and a spirit of bitterness or self-pity would be the first thing to disintegrate their finely held strengths and resolves.

The last few days of the trip seemed drawn out, weary with cold and a sense of impatience to reach family and friends waiting in Winter Quarters. On Saturday, October 30, a group of friends bringing food and cheer arrived to spend the last night with the pioneers. The following day:

> We drove into the town in order, about an hour before sunset. The streets were crowded with people to shake hands as we passed through the lines; we were truly rejoiced to once more behold our wives, children and friends after an absence of over six months, having traveled over 2000 miles, sought out a location for the saints to dwell [in] peace, and accomplished the most interesting mission in this last dispensation.[13]

Might Brigham have remembered that dark 31st of October, Halloween day, when Joseph and Hyrum were in custody of the mob and their enemies, set loose on Far West, were howling for the blood of the Saints? Truly, peace seemed to have been taken from the earth during those nightmarish days. Brigham's heart must have rejoiced to see the contrast and to contemplate the possibilities that lay ahead of him and his people in the mountain fastnesses where God had led them.

But business was the first order of the day—councils and conferences to tie up loose ends and determine the immediate future. Through discussions and prayer sessions with the Twelve, it was agreed that Brigham, as President of the Church, had the right to select his counselors, who would then be sustained by the Twelve. Wilford Woodruff's journal recorded his interchange with Brigham, in which he expressed his conviction that "a quorum appointed by revelation . . . would require a revelation to change. . . . *[But] whatever the Lord inspires you to do in this matter, I am with you.*"[14]

The brethren's faith in Brigham's access to revelation and the integrity of his spiritual guidance seemed absolute. Surely the President himself appeared to feel no doubts or qualms. He expressed his conviction that he had for a long time felt the necessity of organizing a First Presidency, which would then free the Twelve to fulfill their missionary efforts throughout the world. He had waited until the Spirit told him that the Church should be so organized. Now he nominated Heber Kimball as his first counselor, Willard Richards as his second. On Monday, December 27, 1847, the body of Saints from Winter Quarters, Kanesville, and Council Bluffs assembled and sustained Brigham Young as President of The Church of Jesus Christ of Latter-day Saints. This action was later ratified by unanimous vote of the Saints in the Salt Lake Valley, and in General Conference held October 8, 1848, when approximately 5,000 people had gathered.

> "The spirit of the Lord at this time rested upon the people in a pow-
> erful manner," Brigham wrote to Orson Spencer in England.
> "Insomuch that the saints' hearts were filled with joy unspeakable;
> every power of their mind and nerve of their bodies was awakened."
> A dead silence reigned in the congregation while the President spoke
> following the vote which had been taken.[15]

Following the benediction, the congregation shouted three times, "Hosannah, Hosannah, Hosannah to God and the Lamb, Amen, Amen and Amen." As explained in the *History of the Church:*

> This shout of "Hosanna" is given only on very great occasions. It is
> usually given three times in immediate succession; and when voiced
> by thousands and sometimes tens of thousands in unison, and at their
> utmost strength, it is most impressive and inspiring. It is impossible
> to stand unmoved on such an occasion. It seems to fill the prairie or
> woodland, mountain wilderness or tabernacle, with mighty waves of
> sound; and the shout of men going into battle cannot be more stir-
> ring. It gives wonderful vent to the religious emotions, and is followed
> by a reverential awe—a sense of oneness with God.[16]

The gathering of the Saints was the first and foremost business at hand. Brigham gave a herald call to the outlying or laggardly Saints to come quickly to the Winter Quarters area and prepare themselves to be able to leave by May. To the converts in the British Isles, he wrote an epistle which sings with eloquence and conviction:

> Let all Saints who love God more than their own dear selves—and no
> one else are Saints—gather without delay to the place appointed,
> bringing their gold, their silver, their copper, their zinc, their tin, and

brass, and iron, and choice steel, and ivory, and precious stones; their curiosities of science, of art, of nature, and everything in their posses-sion or within their reach, to build in strength and stability, to beau-tify, to adorn, to embellish, to delight, and to cast a fragrance over the House of the Lord; with sweet instruments of music and melody and songs and fragrance and sweet odours, and beautiful colours, whether it be in precious jewels, or minerals, or choice ores, or in wisdom and knowledge, or understanding, manifested in carved work; or curious workmanship of the box, the fir and pine tree, or any thing that ever was, or is, or is to be, for the exaltation, glory, honour, and salvation of the living and the dead, for time and for all eternity. Come, then, walking in righteousness before God, and your labour shall be accepted; . . . for the time has come for the Saints to go up to the mountains of the Lord's house, and help to establish it upon the tops of the mountains.[17]

By the time May arrived, two thousand people stood in readi-ness to go. Brigham recorded that he attended meetings each Sunday of the month, and on the 14th "preached at length and blessed the land for the benefit of the saints who should occupy it." On the 26th, his second and last journey across the plains and mountains to the Salt Lake Valley began. "[I left] my houses, mills and the temporary furniture I had acquired during my sojourn there. This was the fifth time I had left my home and property since I embraced the Gospel of Jesus Christ."[18]

Brigham's company was made up of 1,220 souls and 397 wag-ons. Yet, he found ways to "act the part of a father" to all, as is demonstrated in the case of Lucy Groves, who tried to climb out of her wagon while it was in motion—most probably because of the camp rule which prohibited a wagon from stopping out of turn and breaking up the whole train. She slipped and fell, and the front wheel ran over her body, breaking her arm and three ribs. Brigham himself saw to her, both setting her leg and blessing her that she would reach the valley in good condition. But, as fate would have it, just as the leg was healing, her thirteen-year-old daughter stum-bled over it and broke it a second time. The pain was so severe that she could not bear the slightest movement of the oxen. Finally, in desperation, she asked her husband to pull to one side.

When President Young realized what was happening, he refused to give in to her tearful entreaties to leave them behind. He called a halt and made camp on the spot, then sawed the legs of the poster bed on which she had been sleeping so that nothing was left but the framed mattress and springs. He contrived a way to tie these to the wagon bows so the bed swung freely, much like a hammock. He renewed his earlier blessing to her, and he eased her restless suffering by riding beside her for several days to check on her progress and condition. "With his gentle kind manner," wrote one of her grandsons, "he won the love of Lucy and her posterity forever."[19] Such a tale would be impressive even if it represented isolated instances, but it did not. Brigham's consistently intimate and patient care of his people wove the gentle strands of his power and influence over them. It was the rule, not the exception, for Saints to be granted powerful and lasting testimonies of Brigham and his role as Prophet in the Church.

As an old man, Samuel P. Orton recounted his story for the *Instructor:*

> In 1856 I crossed the plains in Captain Edward Bunker's handcart company. We got along very well until we ran short of flour; our rations being a quarter pound of flour per day without trimmings. Being young and healthy, I became very weak, and I prayed to the Lord that I might die; but my prayers were not answered. One day, about this time, there came an old buffalo past our camp; we killed him and I being very hungry ate some of the meat while it was warm. This nearly killed me, I was so sick I had to leave my cart and walk behind the company. All at once a voice spoke to me and said, "Samuel are you here?" I said, "Yes, I am here," and turned to see who it was that spoke to me, but saw no one. This set me to thinking what I was here for, and what I was going to Utah for. I wanted to know if the Gospel was true, and if the Father and the Son did appear to Joseph Smith and reveal it to him, and if Brigham Young was his lawful successor. If so, I wanted to see when I got to Salt Lake City that halo of light around the head of President Young that we see in pictures around the head of the Savior. While this train of thought was passing through my mind I had caught up with the company, feeling quite well, as my sickness had left me. We soon

after met a team from Salt Lake City with some flour for us; so we got along all right during the rest of the journey. We arrived in Salt Lake City on the 5th of October. The next morning, it being Conference, I went to meeting in the old Bowery, and took my seat about the middle of the building. The people were coming in "pretty lively." I was watching to see if there was any one that I knew, but saw no one. Then on looking toward the stand I saw President Young there with the rays of light around his head as I had asked to see while on the plains, and the same rays seemed to faintly encircle the brethren on each side of him. Then the same voice that spoke to me on the plains, said to me plainly: "Now, Samuel if ever you apostatize, here is your condemnation." I looked around me to see if any of the people heard the voice, but I thought they did not. This has ever since been a valuable testimony to me.[20]

Despite the realities of the trail, of over two thousand people traveling together, and despite Brigham's pragmatic approach to the organization of things, he could say, "From the spirit I have seen manifested, I am inclined to think that the peace, love, and union that is in the Camps of Israel will continue to increase." And, knowing what would foster that continuance, he improved every opportunity he had to remind the Saints of the same: ". . . if it was for the riches, honors, glory, comfort, and enjoyment they expect to receive in this world" that they came, they may as well have stayed where they were. In typical fashion he told them forthrightly, "Should any want to return now, I will have you guarded safe back to Winter Quarters."[21] His declaration is reminiscent of Henry V at Agincourt: ". . . he that hath no stomach to this fight, Let him depart, his passport shall be made, And crowns for convoy put into his purse: We would not die in that man's company, That fears his fellowship, to die with us."[22] The straightforward requirement for a Saint was bluntly stated: "But if it is for the reward of immortality and eternal life beyond the veil, then persevere and live so as to obtain it."[23]

As they traveled, the Saints' harmless community amusements of song and dance, accompanied by banjo or violin, even dramatic and humorous plays and readings, were incorporated into the routine, as they had been during the trying days of Nauvoo. Brigham's sharp wisdom, supported in a multitude of ways by psychological findings of today, went right to the heart of the matter:

> I want it distinctly understood, that fiddling and dancing are no part of our worship. The question may be asked, What are they for, then? I answer, that my body may keep pace with my mind. My mind labors like a man logging, all the time; and this is the reason why I am fond of these pastimes—they give me a privilege to throw everything off, and shake myself, that my body may exercise, and my mind rest. What for? To get strength, and be renewed and quickened, and enlivened, and animated, so that my mind may not wear out. Experience tells us that the most of the inhabitants of the earth wear out their bodies without wearing their minds at all, through the suffering they endure from hard labor, with distress, poverty, and want. While on the other hand, a great portion of mankind wear out their bodies without laboring, only in anxiety. But when men are brought to labor entirely in the field of intelligence, there are few minds to be found possessing strength enough to bear all things; the mind becomes overcharged, and when this is the case, it begins to wear upon the body, which will sink for want of the proper exercises. This is the reason why I believe in and practice what I do.[24]

When the pioneer companies, under direction of various of the Twelve, neared the valley, "between September 17 and 19, a 'gathering' apparently took place . . . preparatory to their entry into the Salt Lake Valley. . . ." Brigham and those with him had often stopped as the president offered assistance where it was needed.

> But now, nearing the end of their long march, those ahead of Brigham's group stopped and waited. "This halt," wrote John Pulsipher, "was in honor of President Young, the leader of Israel. The companies that have traveled ahead of him, except a few stragglers, stopped and waited until he passed into the valley in his place, at the head of the joyful multitude."[25]

Brigham recorded simply, "My company arrived in Great Salt Lake valley on and after the 20th and Elder Kimball's a few days later."[26] The leader, the Moses of his people and of this American continent, had, like a true shepherd, brought the people of his beloved Prophet Joseph safely home.

On Sunday, October 8, Brigham Young was sustained by unanimous vote as President of the Church, with Heber C. Kimball and Willard Richards as his counselors. The Quorum of Twelve Apostles was comprised of Orson Hyde, Parley P. Pratt, Orson Pratt, Lyman Wight, Wilford Woodruff, John Taylor, George A. Smith, Amasa Lyman, and Ezra T. Benson. John Smith, brother of the Prophet Joseph's father, was sustained as Patriarch to the people, Newel K. Whitney as Presiding Bishop, and Charles C. Rich as president of the Salt Lake Stake, with John Young and Erastus Snow as his counselors.[27]

Brigham had no doubt that the Saints were where the Lord wanted them to be. He had no doubt that the land would be blessed for their sakes—and he intended to do all in his power to see that it was.

Notes

1. Cowley, *Wilford Woodruff,* p. 317.
2. *JD,* 13:85-86.
3. *JD,* 11:16.
4. Cowley, *Wilford Woodruff,* p. 318.
5. Whitney, *Life of Heber C. Kimball,* p. 379.
6. Ibid., p. 380-81.
7. Journal of Thomas Bullock, 4 September 1847, typescript from holograph, Church Archives.
8. Parley P. Pratt, *Autobiography,* p. 331.
9. *JD,* 1:108.
10. *JD,* 14:146.
11. Journal of Thomas Bullock, 7 September 1847.
12. John J. Stewart, *Brigham Young and His Wives* (Salt Lake City: Mercury Publishing, 1961), p. 90.
13. *HC,* 7:616.
14. Cowley, *Wilford Woodruff,* p. 327; italics author's.
15. *HC,* 7:623.
16. Ibid., p. 624.

17. Arrington, *American Moses,* p. 156.

18. *HC,* 7:625.

19. Arrington, *American Moses,* p. 157-58.

20. N. B. Lundwall, *The Fate of the Persecutors of the Prophet Joseph Smith* (Salt Lake City: Bookcraft,1952), p. 140-41.

21. Arrington, *American Moses,* p. 159.

22. William Shakespeare, *The Complete Works of William Shakespeare* (London: Cambridge University Press, 1980) "King Henry V," Act 4, scene 3, lines 36-40, p. 512.

23. Arrington, *American Moses,* p. 159.

24. *JD,* 1:30.

25. Arrington, *American Moses,* p. 165.

26. *HC,* 7:628.

27. *HC,* 7:629.

Chapter Twelve

Making the Desert Blossom

Early struggles and starvations – gold-seekers, and states'
goods sold in Salt Lake streets according to prophecy – printing money –
organizing wards, schools, Deseret Territory – Perpetual
Emigration Fund – government appointees placed
over the Saints – Bowery constructed and dedicated

I . . . feel to urge upon the Latter-day Saints the necessity of a close
application of the principles of the Gospel in our lives, conduct and
words and all that we do; and it requires the whole man, the whole
life to be devoted to improvement in order to come to knowledge of
the truth as it is in Jesus Christ. Herein is the fulness of perfection.
Journal of Discourses, 12:255

In the middle of nowhere, in a land no one else wanted,
Brigham set about establishing his Zion community,
"Deseret"—a term from the Book of Mormon which means
"honey bee" and which came to stand for thrift, economy, unified hard work, and cooperation among the Saints. Unity was
essential for their very existence. The year 1848 had seen the first
great cricket plague in the valley, when the weak, impoverished
people watched their hopes crushed by the black hoard of insects
which crushed and devoured their crops. Drowning them, bury-

ing them—even fire could not stop their grim, persistent destruction. Only prayer and the saving efforts of flocks of seagulls flying in from the lake brought relief at last. But this was not the last encounter with the nightmare. The following year, John D. Lee wrote that "crickets by the millions marched into [my] farm, but luckily the gulls in numbers sufficient visited the fields and repulsed the Destroyers."[1]

Many of the people were living in wagons, dugouts or brush sheds, and when winter came it was severe, with freezing temperatures and a snowfall of ten inches on December 9. Such conditions could not be helped, and Brigham would never have realized his vision without the quiet, persistent endurance of thousands of people who shared his faith. Perhaps this is why Brigham instituted a renewal of covenants for the people in general, such as he and the Twelve had experienced after their arrival in the valley. This was more than a gesture or a ritual, but a cleansing, empowering act which would release the reserves of strength from within and draw the Saints closer to the Source of their aid.

In the autumn, many of the people were set to making adobes, mud-caked clay bricks that were pressed into forms and dried in the sun, used commonly by the Spanish but dating back to Egyptian times. Isabell Horne, who arrived in the valley in October of 1847, described her early living conditions:

> When we moved into our little two-roomed house there were neither floors nor doors. . . . We had no furniture, so we had to manufacture some the best we could. . . . Our candle was a little grease in a saucer with a twisted rag in it. . . . Segoes and wild parsnips were gathered and used as food . . . Graham gruel without milk or sugar for breakfast and supper. . . . Our house, being covered only with poles, grass and earth, it continued to rain in the house after it was fine outside. Wagon covers were fastened nearly to the roof over the head of the bed, sloping to the foot to shed the water and keep the bed dry. . . . One of the greatest sources of trouble and inconvenience were the mice. The ground was full of them. They ran over us in our beds, ate into our boxes, and destroyed much valuable clothing.[2]

Joseph Fielding, in his diary, wrote of not being able to complete his house before winter, so spreading a tent over the walls to serve as a roof.[3] Thus it was for all alike, and instances of sharing and compassion were far more common than selfishness among the Saints. Through it all, Brigham was not concerned, despite the severe weather, the poor harvest, loss of cattle, and low rations, strained always further by the arrival of new settlers as well as the disbanded Mormon Battalion members. His attitude toward it all is well summed up in this advice given the Saints in 1853:

> When I cannot feed myself through the means God has placed in my power, it is then time enough for Him to exercise His providence in an unusual manner to administer to my wants. But while we can help ourselves, it is our duty to do so. . . . While we have a rich soil in this valley, and seed to put in the ground, we need not ask God to feed us, nor follow us around with a loaf of bread begging us to eat it. He will not do it, neither would I, were I the Lord. We can feed ourselves here; and if we are ever placed in circumstances where we cannot, it will then be time enough for the Lord to work a miracle to sustain us.[4]

As part of his call to duty and proving oneself by one's works, Brigham was bold in denouncing the lure of the gold fields and those Saints who might be tempted to seek such obvious earthly treasures:

> The true use of gold is for paving streets, covering houses and making culinary dishes; and when the saints shall have preached the gospel, raised grain, and built up cities enough, the Lord will open up the way for a supply of gold to the perfect satisfaction of his people; until then, let them not be overanxious for the treasures of the earth are in the Lord's storehouse, and he will open the doors thereof when and where he pleases.[5]

In the midst of such finely drawn contrasts and dismal realities of near-famine conditions, Heber C. Kimball, speaking in a public meeting, was moved upon by the spirit of prophecy to promise the Saints that, "within a short time, 'States goods' would be sold in the streets of Great Salt Lake City cheaper than in New York and that the people should be abundantly supplied with food and clothing." His listeners were astonished at his words, but so was he, wondering in disbelief what had prompted him to speak them. "On resuming his seat, he remarked to the brethren that he was afraid he 'had missed it this time.' But they were not his own words, and He who had inspired them knew how to fulfill."[6]

Not long afterward, as the gold-seekers reached Salt Lake City on their mad progress toward California, they were forced to lighten their loads or exchange choice stock for mules and provisions which were suited to the primitive conditions of the gold fields. Thus Heber's prediction became literally fulfilled, as choice valuables were "sold for a song" in the greed or expediency of the moment:

> For a light Yankee wagon, sometimes three or four great heavy ones would be offered in exchange, and a yoke of oxen thrown in at that. Common domestic sheeting sold from five to ten cents per yard by the bolt. The best of spades and shovels for fifty cents each . . . full chests of joiners' tools that would cost $150 in the east, were sold in that place for $25. Indeed, almost every article, except sugar and coffee, is selling on an average, fifty per cent below wholesale prices in the eastern cities.[7]

Nevertheless, gold dust was becoming one of the largest mediums of exchange in the West. It was impractical, and loss was often incurred in inaccurate weighing. There was no national currency until after the Civil War, so in 1848 the Municipal Council of Salt Lake authorized the issuance of paper currency against gold dust deposited until the dust could be coined. These "Valley Notes" or "Treasury Notes" were issued in 25 cent, 50 cent, $1, $2, and $3 denominations, hand-written at first by Thomas B. Marsh. "On January 1, 1849, the first printed bills were issued— the first printing of any kind done in Salt Lake City. In September, after coins became available, Valley Notes were redeemed in coin and were immediately destroyed." In 1849, Brigham established a gold mint, and coins in values of $2.50, $5, $10, and $20 were minted until 1861, when Governor

Cummings forbade further minting in Utah. "Engraved on one side of these coins was an eye surmounted by a miter and surrounded by the legend: 'Holiness to the Lord.' On the reverse side were two hands clasped and the legend: 'G.S.L.C.P.G.' ('Great Salt Lake City, Pure Gold)'"[8]

Establishing a workable system of exchange was one of Brigham's greatest challenges, for the people dealt largely in "in kind" barter and tithing contributions brought in to local bishops' storehouses or sent to the large central one in Salt Lake. The internal church structure existing in the various communities enabled the system to operate, albeit awkwardly. But, despite a careful keeping of receipts, "how did one transform contributions of calves, lambs, and pigs into fare for ocean voyages, the purchase of oxen for the hauling of emigrants across the Plains, the acquisition of machinery for the manufacture of wool?"[9] Brigham suffered great frustration with the system, and did not mind bluntly saying so:

> Walk into the storehouse, and examine for yourselves. To be sure there was an old silk dress put in for $40, that had been lying for years rotting in the chest: this is a specimen of the rest. What are such things worth to our workmen? Why, nothing at all.[10]

Not much, in this regard as in others, escaped Brigham's eye:

> If one hundred dollars in cash are paid into the hands of a Bishop, in many instances he will smuggle it, and turn into the Tithing Office old, ring-boned, spavined horses, instead of the money. I am inquiring after such conduct, and will continue until I cleanse the inside of the platter.[11]

And yet, with the correct elements in place, the system could work to perfection. William Rydalch tells of a time in the spring of 1860 when—upon request—he gave his $500 of hard-earned, carefully hoarded cash to Heber C. Kimball, who promised the unhappy man that in less than three months the amount would double in his hands. Through being repaid in kind by President Kimball—a choice span of mules, a harness, running gear, a prize horse and a shawl valued at over $50, tendered with other goods against a cash amount remaining of $30—this, plus trading and selling some of the payment-in-kind goods to advantage, resulted in the fulfillment of the prediction in less than two months.[12]

Brigham received, and has continued to receive, a steady stream of criticism for his seemingly "loose" distinction between personal and church funds. In defense of himself, he told the people:

> Some may think that my personal business is so mixed up and com-
> bined with public [church] business that I cannot keep them separate.
> This is not the case. . . . Hiram B. Clawson, John T. Caine, and Thomas
> Ellerbeck are the clerks who keep the books of my private business; and
> the Trustee-in-Trust has his clerks, of whom David O. Calder is the
> chief. . . . If brother Calder wishes one hundred or a thousand dollars,
> if I have it, he borrows it of Hiram B. Clawson and pays it back; and so
> also brother Clawson borrows of him and returns it. . . . Brigham Young
> and the Trustee-in-Trust are two persons in business. . . . If you want to
> know anything about the money, item by item, how it has been
> obtained and how expended, our books are open.[13]

Undue concern over money and ownership, pettiness and per-
sonal greed were abhorrent to Brigham's way of thinking. In chastising the Saints for their readiness to hate or condemn a brother who owed them money, he attempted to explain the more expansive principle by which he lived:

> The doctrine of brother Joseph is that not one dollar you possess is
> your own; and if the Lord wants it to use, let it go, and it is none of
> your business what He does with it. . . . The money was not yours,
> but the Lord Almighty put it into your hands to see what you would
> do with it. . . . Should it be laid out to pamper the lazy? No; but you
> can see those who have been out on missions, working in the
> kanyons, and traversing the country right and left, trying to get a liv-
> ing by the work of their own hands. . . . The gold, the silver, the
> wheat, the fine flour, the buffalo, the deer, and the cattle on a thou-
> sand hills, are all His, and He turns them withersoever He will.[14]

Remembering his own young manhood when he was destitute, vulnerable, and in need of means, and a wise older man

showed him the dignity and self-reliance of earning his way by the work of his hands rather than becoming indebted to another, Brigham defended some of his actions to the Saints:

> Some have wished me to explain why we built an adobe wall around the city. Are there any Saints who stumble at such things? Oh, slow of heart to understand and believe, I build walls, dig ditches, make bridges, and do a great amount and variety of labor that is of but little consequence only to provide ways and means for sustaining and preserving the destitute. I annually expend hundreds and thousands of dollars almost solely to furnish employment to those in want of labor. Why? I have potatoes, flour, beef, and other articles of food, which I wish my brethren to have; and it is better for them to labor for those articles, so far as they are able and have opportunity, than to have them given to them. They work, and I deal out provisions, often when the work does not profit me.[15]

B. F. Grant, son of Brigham's beloved friend Jedediah Grant, recorded many of his boyhood experiences with President Young when he returned to the valley years after his father's death, and needed both friendship and assistance. Throwing light upon Brigham's financial methods, he said:

> During the holidays and cold winters, many a time I was sent with my team to President Young's store where my wagon was loaded with cloth, flour, coal and vegetables. Then I was given a list of widowed women and told to deliver the goods to these women with President Young's blessing and kind remembrance. At times when his storehouse was depleted, I was sent to the general tithing office where I obtained such supplies as they had in the way of vegetables and other food stuffs and delivered them to these widowed mothers and their families. Some people . . . lacking proper information, made the remark that President Young was kind to the widows, but it was with the general tithing fund that did not belong to him. I desire, out of respect for this good man and the sympathy in his heart for widows and orphans, to say that never, during the time that I lived with him, did I ever receive one single, solitary article from the tithing office without getting a memorandum of all goods I received, and this ticket was delivered by me in the business office of President Young to be checked with the one coming from the general tithing office.[16]

Brigham could organize the kingdom according to the power accorded him by the Lord and by the Saints, and the less interference from the outside, the better. On July 28, only four days after entering the valley, he said:

> We do not intend to have any trade or commerce with the gentile world, for so long as we buy of them we are in a degree dependent upon them. The Kingdom of God cannot rise independent of the gentile nations until we produce, manufacture, and make every article of use, convenience, or necessity among our people . . . I am determined to cut every thread of this kind and live free and independent, untrammeled by any of their detestable customs and practices.[17]

In February of 1849, Brigham organized the city into nineteen wards with a bishop over each, a stake presidency for the valley and a local high council, and ward structures for the outlying communities as well. He made plans for the building of a Council House, a bowery suitable for large meetings on the temple block, and a bridge across the River Jordan. Then, with audacious confidence he sent missionaries to such far flung-places as India, Malta, Chile, and Hong Kong. In March, he appointed a committee to draft a constitution for a provisional government. Parley P. Pratt, a member of the committee, noted in his autobiography that three days after the appointment "The committee reported, and the Convention unanimously adopted the constitution." He had also recorded a few days previously: "We met with the Presidency almost daily."[18] The work to be done was varied, and may have seemed overwhelming; but all of it was vital, destined to have long-range effects upon life in the valleys of the Saints. Deseret—the state Brigham envisioned—would have encompassed "all the area from the Rockies to the Sierra—all of present-day Utah and Nevada, southeastern Idaho and southwestern Wyoming, western Colorado and New Mexico, northern Arizona, southeastern California, and southeastern Oregon," as well as "the Pacific Ocean port of San Diego in order to provide an entry place for emigrants . . . by way of the Isthmus of Panama,"[19] in an area of about 265,000 square miles. Ambitious?

Perhaps. But Brigham knew beyond question how much more stable, resourceful and industrious his people would prove in building up such a vast region as opposed to any other settlers who might wish to claim it.

With the Mexican cession of the Great Basin to the United States, Brigham was hopeful that Congress would create a Mormon state. Brigham's friend, Colonel Thomas Kane, who had supported and defended the Mormons since 1846, and had been nursed through malaria by Brigham during the Council Bluff days, advised his friend to seek statehood status as opposed to that of Territory. But, under the Compromise of 1850, Congress created the Utah Territory, with the same status on slavery as New Mexico: the citizens could decide for themselves. (California was granted statehood with slavery forbidden, even though they had far less population than the Mormon settlements.) The proposed size of the territory was drastically reduced; and, though Brigham was appointed governor, the central government could, and did, appoint non-Mormon officials to man most of its positions.

In the interim, during two years of unhampered existence, the State of Deseret "created a state university, organized and fixed the boundaries of seven counties; regulated the control of streams, timber, and grazing; prohibited the sale of liquor and ammunition to the Indians; incorporated and granted municipal charters to five cities; and incorporated the Church of Jesus Christ of Latter-day Saints."[20] The distinctions between functions of church and state were of no consequence in Brigham's mind: get the job done, and get it done well was the prime consideration. Nauvoo had set an outstanding precedent, and what choice had presented itself at that time?

Of necessity, education was intermingled with religious instruction. Mary Dilworth (Hammond) held school in her tent on the west side of the old Fort as early as October 1847. It was crowded not only with children, but "with youths of all ages. The seats were sawed-off logs, and her desk was a small camp table. During the winter season, Burr Frost opened school in the Fort for the older ones; adult education again."[21] But, as the community expanded, the first centers built for public use were combined schoolhouses and meetinghouses; indeed, Brigham encouraged each bishop to establish a grade school in his ward, supported not only by "in kind" contributions, but by tithing donations as well. Some men with large families, such as Brigham, Heber, and Daniel H. Wells, found it plausible, even convenient to arrange private family schools. Zina D. Young opened school in 1848 in a little adobe house built near Brigham's Log Row, where the children met in her living room, her infant daughter playing around their feet. When the Lion House was finished in 1856, school was held there, with an extended student body which included orphan children, neighbors, or anyone Brigham decided to take under his wing. Later, a separate schoolhouse was constructed.

General educational philosophies during this period were narrow; Brigham's were not. It was a matter of pride, but also of intense, sincere interest which prompted his personal attention to matters most leaders, even most fathers, would consider beneath them. Even the construction of the building came under Brigham's keen scrutiny. He instructed that the windows be placed high enough so that the light would fall indirectly on the desks. "The ceiling was high and had an elliptical roof so that the sound could be carried easily and light was reflected from the softly tinted walls. Green shutters were attached to each window for storm and shade purposes."[22] The desks were also green and designed to fit the backs and feet of the children; in some locations the floors were actually sloped toward the teacher's platform so that every student would be able to see and hear.

Corporal punishment was not allowed, as Brigham's daughter, Susa, explained in her biography of her father:

> One master, whether in ignorance of the rule, or driven to unmindful distraction by the mischievous behavior of two of the Leader's sons, chastised them rather brutally. The whole childish masculine population promptly rose in rebellion and their teacher was roughly handled, much to his disgust and mortification. He was summarily dismissed, which must have been to him a mingled relief and annoyance. But as Brigham Young could usually control his children, or any

one else's children, with one steady look, perhaps it was hard for him to understand why others could not do the same.

Perhaps in that delight which he felt for superiority in any form he had an exaggerated conception of the majesty of what was then called "book-learning." Be that as it may, his own splendidly poised perceptions weighed the "book-learning" of all the ages in the balance, and he found it too often inadequate and rather barren of results. Hence he was a pioneer, one might say, in industrial education. "Book-learning" must be so definitely attached to real life and real problems that there should be no broken links between the school door and the shop, farm, or kitchen. Boys were given that empirical education which comes of summer courses with the hoe and plough. The girls achieved domestic skill under the trained tutelage of their mothers.[23]

Expanding his financial vision and obligation, as well as his sense of fatherhood over his people, in 1849 Brigham established the Perpetual Emigration Fund Company, which was administered independent of the rest of the Church, and through use of the Fund for which it was named financed ocean voyages and cross-country journeys to Salt Lake. It also supervised the gathering and shipping of the Saints from Great Britain and Scandinavia, at the approximate rate of three thousand a year. This meant that "by 1857 there were about thirty-five thousand Saints in the Basin, and by 1869 approximately seventy-five thousand. At Brigham's death in 1877 there were about one hundred twenty-five thousand."[24]

Nothing was neglected or overlooked. Brigham made plans to bring a printing press across country—had he not learned the importance of the printed word to the people both in Great Britain and Nauvoo? Howard Egan, a member of Brigham's first 1847 company of pioneers, had been appointed mail carrier between Salt Lake and Winter Quarters. On August 7, 1849, his three wagons arrived carrying the printing equipment. Horace K. Whitney, who had learned his trade on the *Times and Seasons* in Nauvoo, was to be typesetter. He was the oldest child of Newel K. Whitney, second presiding bishop of the Church.

By Friday afternoon June 14, 1850, type had been set, checked and set in the forms. By 5:20 p.m., short, stocky Brigham H. Young, 25 years old with light brown hair, a nephew of Brigham Young, began clamping the wrought-iron Ramage press. The first pages of *The Deseret News* were being printed.

As the second-oldest daily newspaper west of the Missouri River, it espoused noble ideals for its prospectus: "Truth and Liberty."[25]

Colonization came early, and was considered a "call" nearly as sacred as a mission assignment. Some of the brethren and their families may have cringed as they faced the task of subduing an untamed, often unfriendly land, but Brigham knew from personal experience what willpower and desire can do. He and his brethren had left their families at the point of death in the malaria-ridden swamps of Nauvoo and gone off, weak and ill unto death themselves, to face the unknown, with nothing but their faith to sustain them. This grand adventure of building, which sang with the promise of growth and progress, must have seemed providential in comparison. The Iron County Mission, for example, under direction of Joseph Smith's apostle-cousin, George A. Smith, set out in December of 1850 with 167 people. Their destination was 250 miles south of Salt Lake—an untouched valley clogged with coarse, fragrant sagebrush, seemingly in the middle of nowhere. By the end of January there were houses, canals, roads, a gristmill, a school and a meetinghouse, with fields full of ripening crops. The leaders knew their business; they knew the uniting, maturing power of shared sacrifice and challenge, as Apostle Erastus Snow's statement reveals: "We found a Scotch party, a Wel[s]h party, an English party, and an American party, and we turned Iron Masters and undertook to put all these parties through the furnace, and run out a party of Saints for building up the Kingdom of God."[26]

In the year 1850, Brigham marked the death of his good friend Newell Whitney, who had stood beside him during the days following Joseph's death. Near the end of that same year, the commodious Bath House built over the hot springs of carbonated sulphur was dedicated. These waters, used for medicinal purposes by the local Indians for generations, provided great enjoyment and benefit for the Saints. The dedication was marked by feasting and dancing, quartets, and, of course, speechmaking. Susa relates:

> In front of this Bath House was an adobe cottage for the caretaker, and soon an immense dancing hall, also built of substantial adobe, was added, with a roomy dining-room and equipped with kitchens, all fitted with benches and tables. Public parties and even theatrical entertainments were given here, even after the completion of the Social Hall.[27]

The year 1851 saw Salt Lake formally incorporated, with Jedediah M. Grant as mayor. On February 3, Brigham was sworn in before Justice Daniel H. Wells as governor for a salary of $1,500 a year, and superintendent of Indian Affairs for an extra $1,000. On Sunday, June 1, Brigham celebrated his fiftieth birthday. Certainly life had brought more to him than he had imagined as a man of thirty with an invalid wife and few prospects, eking out a hard-won living and caring for his little ones. Both he and the kingdom had grown to incredible heights, and had not altogether displeased the Master and his Prophet with their efforts. And there was the future—the future in a Zion of their own was pleasant to think upon.

But the world was determined to encroach on Brigham's idyllic society, despite the fact that they had hidden themselves, at the Lord's command, in the mountains and the wilderness. The attacks that would continue for the remainder of the leader's life began to trickle through. In July, the *Buffalo Courier* viciously accused Brigham Young of levying unjust taxes in the city, openly abusing democracy, and "leaguing with the Indians to harass people on the road to California." That such reports were not looked upon as mere rumor or even exaggeration is proved by the fact that President Fillmore took the trouble to write to Brigham Young's friend, Colonel Kane, in Philadelphia, to express his concern and ask for corroboration of the charges. Fortunately, Kane replied strongly and to the point:

The President: My Dear Sir: I have no wish to evade the responsibility of having vouchsafed for the character of Mr. Brigham Young, of
Utah, and his fitness for the station he now occupies. I reiterate without reserve, the statement of his excellent capacity, energy, and
integrity, which I made you prior to his appointment . . . I made no
qualifications when I assured you of his irreproachable moral character because I was able to speak of this from my own intimate personal
knowledge. . . . I am ready to offer you this assurance for publication
in any form you care to indicate, and challenge contradiction from
any respectable authority.[28]

The President was satisfied, for the moment. But in the
future, when supposed provocations occurred, when non-Latter-
day Saints spoke slanderously against Brigham and his people,
neither the chief executive's faith in the known integrity and discernment of Colonel Kane nor a sense of fair play had much effect
upon the decisions he was to make.

By the end of the summer, all of the government-appointed
officials had arrived in Utah. And, though they were treated cordially and kindly by the Saints, friction developed almost at once
and was compounded by their haughty disregard of the rights and
feelings of the people. Judge Brocchus, described by Utah historian Bancroft, as "a vain and ambitious man, full of self-impor-
tance, fond of intrigue, corrupt, revengeful, hypocritical,"[29]
addressed the people in a speech peppered with insults and crude
insinuations, perhaps expecting to overawe the benighted
Mormons. But Brigham responded with his usual fearlessness and
forthrightness, concerned with truth, not possible future conse-
quences. He had defended right in too many tight places to be
cowed by such a small man as this pompous judge. In his own
report of his responding remarks, Brigham said:

Judge Brocchus is either profoundly ignorant or willfully wicked, one
of the two . . . His speech is designed to have political bearing . . . It
is well known to every man in this community, and has become a
matter of history throughout the enlightened world, that the government of the United States looked on the scenes of robbing, driving
and murdering of this people and said nothing about the matter but

by silence gave sanction to the lawless proceedings. Hundreds of women and children have been laid in the tomb prematurely in consequence thereof, and their blood cries to the Father for vengeance against those who have caused or consented to their death. George Washington was not dandled in the cradle of ease, but schooled to a life of hardship in exploring and surveying the mountains and defending the frontier settlers, even in his early youth, from the tomahawk and the scalping knife. It was God that dictated him and enabled him to assert and maintain the independence of the country. It is the same God that leads this people. I love the government and Constitution of the United States, but do not love the damned rascals who administer the government. I am indignant at such corrupt fellows as Judge Brocchus coming here to lecture us on morality and virtue. I could buy a thousand of such men and put them into a bandbox. Ladies and gentlemen, here we learn principle and good manners. It is an insult to this congregation to throw out such insinuations. I say it is an insult, and I will say no more.[30]

Judge Brocchus had thought polygamy a natural avenue through which he could whip and cow the Mormons. He had little to do with independence and devotion to God. He knew at once that he had thoroughly underestimated Brigham Young. Used to having his own way, he found conditions in Utah untenable. Within weeks he and his compatriots departed, returning to spread lies and slanders and elicit sympathy from the people they lived among. They were laughingly referred to in Deseret as the "run-a-way officials," and no one took the situation very seriously. Eliza R. Snow reduced them to treatment in a humorous verse which was sung the following 4th of July.

Early in March, when the Territorial Legislature closed its session, the Saints celebrated with socials in the afternoon and the evening. Part of Brigham's comments to his fellow Saints on this occasion are worth noting:

I love this people so well that I know they love me; they have confidence in me because I have confidence in them. You may scan the history of the whole Church, and look over the whole surface of the matter, and did you ever see this people, when they had the same confidence they have in each other at this day? No, never. And it is on the increase; and this is what will make us a powerful community. But if we lack confidence in each other and become jealous of each other, our peace will be destroyed. If we cultivate the principles of unshaken confidence in each other, our joy will be full.[31]

The first place of worship prepared for the Saints was the Bowery, constructed of poles, with branches and sagebrush overhead. When the first tabernacle was completed and ready for conference on April 6, 1852, it could hold 2,500 people. Half the building was below ground level, but there were large, elegant glass chandeliers hanging from the ceiling that twinkled in the glow of the oil lamps. At the door stood two large brass caldrons filled with cool water and supplied with a dipper, so the people could avail themselves of a cool, pleasant drink. The building boasted a pipe organ run by water power, played at one time by Brigham's daughter, Fanny, who was an accomplished harpist and had the facility of being able to return from a night at the opera and play through the entire score of what she had just heard by memory.

At the first session held in the building, Brigham was enthusiastic:

Now we have a convenient room, the best hall I ever saw in my life, wherein the people could be convened on one floor. I trust we shall renew our strength, meet here to pray and to praise the Lord, and partake of the sacrament, until our feelings are perfectly pure; for we are where we can sit and enjoy the society of each other as long as we please, and there is none to make us afraid.[32]

In the dedicatory prayer, Willard Richards said:

Bless thy servant Brigham, with health and strength, of body and of mind, with long life, and peaceful days; may he be endowed with thy Spirit, and the revelations of eternity continually and may thine angels visit and sustain him, and ministering spirits from thy presence attend him, in all his ways. Guard him, O Lord, from the malicious designs of wicked men; turn aside every shaft that is aimed for his injury; fit and prepare him with every necessary qualification to lead and guide thy people; may his strength and ability be according to his duties, and the burden he is required to bear; may the rich blessings of heaven and earth be poured out upon him.[33]

The Saints' confidence resided in Brigham; they had just raised their hands and sustained him as prophet and leader again. They were willing to learn, to follow, to acknowledge his worthiness to guide them aright.

The Scottish philosopher Carlyle made a statement which applies in perfection to Brigham Young:

> Find in any country the ablest man that exists there; raise him to the supreme place, and loyally reverence him; you have a perfect government . . . it is in the man; the truest-hearted, justest, the noblest man; what he tells us to do must be precisely the wisest, fittest, that we could anywhere or anyhow, learn.[34]

Notes

1. England, *Brother Brigham*, p. 148.
2. *Faith-Promoting Stories,* comp. by Preston Nibley (Salt Lake City: Bookcraft,1977), p. 69-70.
3. Diary of Joseph Fielding, Book 5, p. 150, Church Archives.
4. *JD*, 1:108.
5. B. H. Roberts, *A Comprehensive History of the Church of Jesus Christ of Latter-day Saints,* 6 vols. (Provo, UT: Brigham Young University Press, 1965) 3:352; cited hereafter as *CCH*).
6. Whitney, *Life of Heber C. Kimball,* p. 389-90.
7. *CCH,* 3:352.
8. *Pioneer,* Summer 1995, A Publication of the National Society of the Sons of Utah Pioneers (Salt Lake City: Western Standard Co., 1995), p. 15.
9. Arrington, *American Moses,* p. 181.
10. *JD,* 1:52.
11. *JD,* 8:317.
12. *Faith-Promoting Stories,* p. 159-62.
13. *JD,* 8:201-202.
14. *JD,* 1:340-31.
15. Journal History of Brigham Young, 4 March 1860, Church Archives.
16. *Faith-Promoting Stories,* p. 151-52.
17. England, *Brother Brigham,* p. 161.

18. Parley P. Pratt, *Autobiography*, p. 336.
19. Arrington, *American Moses*, p. 224.
20. Gates and Widtsoe, *Life Story*, p. 284.
21. Ibid., p. 285.
22. Ibid., p. 285-6.
23. Arrington, *American Moses*, p. 172.
24. *Pioneer*, Summer 1995, p. 27.
25. England, *Brother Brigham*, p. 163.
26. Gates and Widtsoe, *Life Story*, p. 262.
27. Preston Nibley, *Brigham Young*, p. 164-65.
28. Ibid., p. 187.
29. Journal History of Brigham Young, 8 September 1851, Church Archives.
30. Preston Nibley, *Brigham Young*, p. 175-76.
31. Journal History of Brigham Young, 4 March 1852, Church Archives.
32. Preston Nibley, *Brigham Young*, p. 177-78.
33. Ibid.
34. Ibid.

Chapter Thirteen

Improving, Serving, Enduring

*Cornerstone laid for Salt Lake Temple – Indian policies
and uprisings – Beehive House completed – Endowment House –
1856: famine and hardship – handcarts to Zion*

Let us train our minds until we delight in that which is good, lovely
and holy, seeking continually after that intelligence which will enable
us effectually to build up Zion, which consists in building houses,
tabernacles, temples, streets, and every convenience and necessity to
embellish and beautify, seeking to do the will of the Lord all the days
of our lives, improving our minds in all scientific and mechanical
knowledge, seeking diligently to understand the great design and plan
of all created things, that we may know what to do with our lives and
how to improve upon the facilities placed within our reach.
Journal of Discourses, 10:77

From the very beginning, even amidst their weakness and
poverty, the Lord had required of his people a House wherein he
might visit and bless them. On Monday morning, February 14,
1853, the Saints assembled on the Temple Block. Snow covered
the ground, but the day was clear and sunny. President Young

stood in a small buggy and addressed the people:

> The Lord wished us to gather in this place. He wished us to cultivate
> the earth, and make these valleys like the Garden of Eden, and make
> all the improvements in our power, and build a Temple as soon as cir-
> cumstances would permit.

> Seven years ago tomorrow, about 11 o'clock, I crossed the Mississippi
> River with my brethren, from this place, not knowing at that time
> whither we were going, but firmly believing that the Lord had in
> reserve for us a good place in the mountains, and that he would lead
> us directly to it. It is but seven years since we left Nauvoo, and we are
> now ready to build another temple.[1]

Heber C. Kimball offered a consecrating prayer full of eloquence and faith:

> Thy servants, Brigham and his council, have laid the corner stone of
> a holy house, which we are about to erect unto Thy name. We desire
> to do it with clean hands and pure hearts before Thee . . . We ask Thee
> to help us so to conduct ourselves that all the holy Prophets, the
> angels of heaven, with Thee and Thy son, may be engaged continu-
> ally for our welfare, in the work of salvation and eternal lives. Bless us
> in this attempt to glorify Thee. . . .[2]

After President Kimball's prayer, Brigham lifted the first spade
full of earth, then blessed the people before dismissing them.

The following April, on the anniversary of the founding of the
Church, the cornerstones of the temple were laid; the building
would take forty years to complete at the cost of four million dollars. On this beautiful spring morning, the Saints pouring in from
the valley settlements felt nothing but a spirit of gratitude,
promise, and joy. Brigham addressed the assembled thousands in
solemn and eloquent terms:

> This morning we have assembled on one of the most solemn, inter-
> esting, joyful and glorious occasions that ever has transpired, or will
> transpire among the children of men, while the earth continues in its
> present organization and is occupied for its present purposes. . . .

At Nauvoo Joseph dedicated another Temple . . . Before the Nauvoo Temple was completed, Joseph was murdered—murdered at sunlight, under the protection of the most noble government that then existed, and that now exists, on our earth. Has his blood been atoned for? No! And why! A martyr's blood to true religion was never atoned for on our earth. No man, or nation of men, without the priesthood, has power to make atonement for such sins. The souls of all such, since the days of Jesus, are "under the altar," and are crying to God day and night, for vengeance. And shall they cry in vain? God forbid! He had promised He will hear them in His own due time, and recompense a righteous reward.

Clearly, Joseph was still a very real part of the fabric of the kingdom; they were carrying out the work he had set them to do. He yet lived in the cells and sinews of Brigham's faith, of all that Brigham, the man, had become as he set out to be a Saint.

Of our journey hither, we need say nothing, only, God led us. Of the sufferings of those who were compelled, to, and did leave Nauvoo in the winter of 1846, we need say nothing. Those who experienced it know it, and those who did not, to tell them of it would be like exhibiting a beautiful painting to a blind man . . . While these things were transpiring with the Saints in the wilderness, the Temple of Nauvoo passed into the hands of the enemy, who polluted it to that extent the Lord not only ceased to occupy it, but he loathed to have it called by his name, and permitted the wrath of its possessors to purify it by fire, as a token of what will speedily fall on them and their habitations unless they repent . . . But, what are we here for, this day? To celebrate the birthday of our religion! To lay the foundation of a Temple to the Most High God, so that when his Son, our Elder Brother, shall again appear, he may have a place where he can lay his head, and not only spend a night or a day, but a place of peace, where he may stay till he can say, I am satisfied. . . .

We dedicate this, the southeast corner stone of this Temple, to the Most High God. May it remain in peace till it has done its work, and until he who has inspired our hearts to fulfill the prophecies of his holy prophets, that the House of the Lord should be reared in the "tops of the mountains," shall be satisfied, and say, it is enough.[3]

The vision had become a reality.

Brigham's policy with his Indian neighbors was one of kindness and forbearance. He sought to understand their nature and their point of view, and urged the people settling communities on what used to be Indian land to take caution and prudence in protecting themselves, to raise their forts quickly, "to give an inch or even a foot, to lose a dime or even a dollar rather than endanger their property or lives."[4] Beginning in the fall of 1851, he instituted various programs to teach the Indians to farm. "'Let the millions of acres of land now lying waste be given to the Indians for cultivation and use,'" he said. "'Let the poor Indians be taught the arts of civilization and to draw their sustenance from the ample and sure resources of Mother Earth, and to follow the peaceful avocations of the tillers of the soil, raising grain and stock for subsistence, instead of pursuing the uncertain chances of war and game for a livelihood.'"[5] But he experienced only indifferent success in this direction. And when in August of 1853, as Superintendent of Indian Affairs, he forbade the trafficking of arms and ammunition with the Indians and revoked all licenses for trade, he had military commanders, as well as natives, unhappy with him. Brigham's policy was always mercy and defensive action only. "'We exhort you,'" he had advised the settlers in Fillmore, "'to feed and clothe them so far as it lies in your power, never turn them away hungry from your door, teach them the arts of husbandry, bear with them in all patience and long suffering, and never consider their lives as equivalent for petty stealing.'"[6]

One of the major sources of friction between the red men and the Mormon settlers was the Indian practice of slavery. The strong Ute tribes would capture children of weaker bands and sell or trade them with parties from New Mexico and Mexico, where the children, and sometimes women, would be used as slaves, with a status little above that of beasts of burden. In 1850, the state assembly enacted a measure to prohibit this and encouraged through legalization the adoption or apprenticeship of Indian children. But the tribes soon took advantage of this, offering children to settlers whose means were sparse, demanding higher and higher prices, so that the concerned Saints, moved to compassion for the little sufferer, would offer all they had to purchase the child. But if it was not enough, the disgruntled Indian would ofttimes brutally kill the prisoner right before their eyes. One such incident is related by Colonel Kane's wife, as she heard it from a Mormon woman firsthand:

> . . . it was a costly purchase that Wah-ker invited them to make; and on this occasion, Decker and his companions bought what the Indians had brought of other wares, such as dressed skins and ponies and Mexican saddles, but declined the human goods. Wah-ker then produced a shivering little four-year-old girl, whom he insisted on their buying. He asked an extravagant price, "because he had brought her so far; away from the Santa Clara country." Her "board" could not have cost the hero much, for he used to picket his little captives "to a stake by a rope around their necks," and for days at a time they had literally nothing to eat more than was affording them by "the run of their teeth" among the undergrowth within the length of their tether.
>
> The Mormons were willing to pay a rifle, and even to throw in a blanket to boot, but explained that they honestly had no more goods with them than were left on the trading-ground. On this, Wah-ker became enraged, and seizing the child by her feet, whirled her in the air, dashed her down, and then, as she lay quivering out her life, he snatched his hatchet from his belt and chopped her into five pieces. "Now, you can have her at no price," he said.[7]

As Clarissa Young Spencer relates:

> In many instances kind-hearted settlers continued to take them rather than see them starved or killed, and there was a time when a great number of these children were living in Mormon homes. One woman bought a ten-month-old girl for a quilt and a shirt. She reared the child as a sister to her own children, and when the girl was grown she married a white man and reared a large family of her own.[8]

Things did not work out so well for Sally, who became a member of the Young household and was raised with all the skills and sensitivities of a white woman. When Chief Kanosh came courting her, she was not easily won, but when she at last gave in to his wooing, some of the Mormons built her a cottage with "real doors and windows, six chairs, a high post bedstead in the corner, and plates and dishes in a press. She had her own cows and made butter, her poultry, eggs, and vegetables, and her lord and master was sent forth proudly in a clean shirt and collar every Sunday."⁹ Perhaps it was inevitable that the chief's two other wives would envy her and dislike her white ways. One day, while out in the hills hunting rabbits together, Betsykin cut Sally's throat, threw her body in the bottom of a wash, and concealed it with brush. When the deed was discovered, she paid the penalty with her own life. Kanosh used the small white man's house for what he considered important occasions. Once, when Brigham stopped on one of his journeys south to visit the chief, Kanosh did not come out to greet him, but replied, when a messenger was sent to inquire, "that when he went to see 'Brigham, Brigham sat still in his house; and what was manners for Brigham was manners for Kanosh.'"¹⁰ Brigham agreed, left his carriage and went in to pay his respects to the chief, whom he found sitting cross-legged in the center of a four-poster bed. Though it was a warm day in May, he wore shiny new, stiff boots, a heavy overcoat buttoned to his chin, and a bright red blanket to top it all off.

By far the greatest antagonist was Chief Walker, who had acquired great power over the tribe and loved to raid and stir things up with his group of young men. What was called "Walker's War" began with an unfortunate incident near Springville when a white man interfered with an Indian who was beating his squaw. When the brave died from the blow he received, Walker and his brother, Arapeen, planned an immediate retaliatory attack. The hostilities spread like wildfire from Iron County in the south to Summit County in the northeast—over two hundred and fifty miles along which the white settlements stretched. One of the tragic events connected with the "war" was the killing of a prominent, well-respected non-Mormon, Captain Gunnison. But the historian, Bancroft, claimed there was no proof to this assertion. "The Gunnison massacre," he wrote, was brought on by Gentiles. It was the direct result of killing of the Pah Ute by California emigrants. As no compensation had been made to the tribe, they avenged themselves, as was their custom, on the first Americans—for thus they termed all white men other than Mormons—whom they found in their territory.[11]

Although hostilities were stemmed, there was no settled peace. And, despite twelve Mormon deaths and much loss of property, Brigham felt that the people had been taught and humbled by the experience. Speaking in the Salt Lake Tabernacle on July 31, he said:

> How many times have I been asked in the past week what I intended to do with Walker. I say let him alone severely. I have not made war on the Indians, nor am I calculating to do it. My policy is to give them presents, and be kind to them. Instead of being Walker's enemy, I have sent him a great pile of tobacco to smoke when he is lonely in the mountains. He is now at war with the only friends he has upon this earth, and I want him to have some tobacco to smoke.[12]

The letter Brigham sent along with the tobacco, under hand of Colonel George A. Smith's command, is worth noting:

> Great Salt Lake City, July 25, 1853 Captain Walker: I send you some tobacco for you to smoke in the mountains when you get lonesome. You are a fool for fighting your best friends, for we are the best friends, and the only friends that you have in the world. Everybody else would kill you if they could get a chance. If you get hungry send some friendly Indians down to the settlements and we will give you some beef-cattle and flour. If you are afraid of the tobacco which I send you, you can let some of your prisoners try it first, and then you will know that it is good. When you get good-natured again, I would like to see you. Don't you think you should be ashamed? You know that I have always been your best friend. Brigham Young[13]

Perhaps this gives insight into the high tribute Peteetneet, brother of Walker, gave Brigham Young when he said: "What the other white men say go in one ear and out the other but what Brigham says goes to the heart and stays there."[14]

During the mid-1850s the paper mill, the sugar and lead, coal and cotton missions were established. Hundreds of stalwart men and women started from scratch again—and again—and again—that the kingdom might grow. They were motivated by the strength of their own inner convictions, and by the allegiance they had willingly given their prophet: where he called, they would go. Despite the disappointments, discouragements, and failures, hundred of communities were planted, commerce and agriculture grew—and so did the men who struggled to establish them. The cotton mission in Utah's Dixie was opened under the inspiring leadership of Erastus Snow, who took literally Brigham's prophecy that "a city would rise on the Virgin with 'spires, towers, and steeples, with homes containing many inhabitants.'" He gathered those men who had been called around him and told them bluntly:

> I feel to speak encouragingly to my brethren, so far as our removal from this to the southern part of the Territory is concerned. I feel to go body and spirit, with my heart and soul, and I sincerely hope that my brethren will endeavor to do the same; for so long as we strive to promote the interests of Zion at home and abroad we shall be happy and prosperous; and what seems to be a temporary leaving and losing of present comforts that we have gathered around us, will be like bread cast upon the waters, which after many days shall be gathered like seed that brings forth much fruit. . . . To you that think you cannot bring your feelings to go upon this mission like men, so far as I am concerned I will vote to release you.[15]

An unnamed member of the company left a record of his experience in his journal:

> Sunday, 19 October, 1862. . . . At the close of the meeting some 250 men were called to go to the cotton country. My name was on the list and was read off the stand. At night I went to a meeting in the Tabernacle of those that had been called. Here I learned a principle that I shant forget in a while. It showed to me that obedience is a great principle in heaven and on earth. Well, here I have worked for the past 7 years through heat and cold, hunger and adverse circumstances and at least have got me a home, a lot with fruit trees just beginning

to bear and look pretty. Well, I must leave it and go and do the will of my Father in Heaven who rules all for the good of them that love and fear him and I pray God to give me strength to accomplish that which is required of me in an acceptable manner before him.[16]

Brigham experimented with the wool industry, the silk worm (which necessitated the importing of mulberry seed from France), the breeding of fine livestock (at one time importing five thousand graded Merino ewes to add to his own flocks), the raising of alfalfa for grazing, the erection of woolen mills, the planting of sugar beets and the erecting of factories for the manufacture of sugar, and the establishment of Zion's Cooperative Mercantile Institute (ZCMI), perhaps the first true department store in America. Nothing was beyond the scope of his curious interest; anything that offered possible good, possible independence, was worth at least a full-hearted try. Insight into Brigham's influence with his people is given in a statement made by his counselor and friend, Jedediah M. Grant:

How is it that brother Brigham is able to comfort and soothe those who are depressed in spirit, and always make those with whom he associates so happy? I will tell you how he makes us feel so happy. He is happy himself, and the man who is happy himself can make others feel so, for the light of God is in him, and others feel the influence, and feel happy in his society.[17]

In 1854, Brigham Young's Beehive House was finished and first occupied by Mary Ann Angell and her children, who moved to what was called the White House in 1860 and was replaced by Lucy Ann Decker, Brigham's first plural wife, who raised her seven children in the home. The Lion House, adjoining the Beehive House by a short hallway, was built in 1856. A little larger than its companion house and three stories in height, it was designed to accommodate polygamous families; at times as many as twelve of Brigham's wives lived here, some of them childless, some with small families, living in the gabled bedroom/sitting rooms upstairs. Between the two houses Brigham also built a one-story

office, where he worked with clerks and secretaries and held inter-
views with members and visitors alike.

In 1855, the Endowment House was completed. Until a temple was built, it served as the place where eternal marriages and
sacred endowments were administered.

Wholesome entertainment balanced the solemn religious duties
and the grueling requirements of subduing the desert. In addition to
frequent performances of dramatic productions throughout the city,
there was a Public Library which offered literary entertainments as
well as newspapers and books. Though hunting for pleasure was not
encouraged, sleighing, skating—both summer and winter—swimming, and picnicking in the mountains were enjoyed by all. Dancing
was a favorite activity of the people, and of Brigham in particular.
"'The world considers it very wicked for a Christian to hear music
and to dance,'" he said on one occasion. "'Music belongs to heaven,
to cheer God, angels and men. . . . Music and dancing are for the
benefit of holy ones, and all those who are not holy and righteous
and who do not worship God, have no right to be here.'"[18]

Captain Stansbury attended a ball in Salt Lake City in April,
1854, and left a vivid description of what he saw:

> A larger collection of fairer and more beautiful women I never saw in
> one room. All of them were dressed in white muslin, some with pink
> and others with blue sashes. Flowers were the only ornaments in the
> hair. The utmost order and strictest decorum prevailed. Polkas and
> waltzes were not danced; country dances, cotillions, quadrilles, etc.,
> were permitted. At the invitation of Governor Young I opened the
> ball with one of his wives. The Governor, with a beautiful partner,
> stood vis-a-vis. An old-fashioned cotillion was danced with much
> grace by the ladies, and the Governor acquitted himself very well on
> the light fantastic toe. After several rounds of dancing, a march was
> played by the band, and a procession was formed; I conducted my
> first partner to the supper room, where I partook of a fine entertain-
> ment at the Governor's table.[19]

During these years, Brigham lost several men who had been
part of the close circle of his associates: Willard Richards, Orson

Spencer, Jedediah Grant, and John Smith all died. "Uncle John," uncle of the Prophet Joseph Smith, was succeeded as presiding patriarch by Hyrum's son, John. Willard Richards had been with Joseph and Hyrum when they were killed at Carthage, and, though he was a large man, not a hair of his head had been hurt. He served very ably as church historian and recorder, as well as Brigham's second counselor. When his death occurred in March, 1854, Jedediah M. Grant was selected to replace him in the presidency. Orson Spencer, a gentle scholar of great promise, died prematurely from malaria at the age of 53. His wife, as refined and accomplished as himself, had died on the plains of Missouri, leaving six motherless children, who were now fatherless as well. Jedediah Grant, a member of Zion's Camp and the first mayor of Salt Lake, served as Brigham's counselor only briefly. He died unexpectedly December 1, 1856, at the age of forty, one week after the birth of his son, Heber Jeddy, who would become a president of the Church. Daniel H. Wells was selected to fill his place. The loss of these men was felt deeply by Brigham, who had leaned on their counsel and support.

About this time, a period of famine and hardship, combined with the efforts of the leaders toward a general reformation, served to humble the Saints and purify both their motives and behavior. In 1853, Heber Kimball had warned the Saints to take care of their grain, which was of more worth to them than silver or gold. In July of 1855, in a conference in Provo, he reminded them of the counsel they had received:

> How many times have you been told to store up your wheat against the hard times? . . . When we first came into these valleys our President told us to lay up stores of all kinds of grain that the earth might rest once in seven years. The earth is determined to rest, and it is right that it should. It only requires a few grasshoppers to make the earth rest, they can soon clear it."[20]

The seventh year fell in 1856. Heber, who had prepared, shared willingly with all, he and Vilate ministering tenderly to friends and strangers in turn. He loaned several hundred bushels of wheat to President Young to help feed his extended group of dependents. The down-to-earth nature of his prophetic gifts revealed itself in one instance when a destitute brother came to him for assistance and received only the terse counsel: "Go and marry a wife." Dismayed, he thought Brother Kimball out of his mind, yet he determined to take the advice so strangely given, and thought upon a widow with several children who might want to marry him. To his surprise, the widow had a six-months' store of provisions laid by. "Meeting President Kimball shortly afterwards, the now prosperous man of family exclaimed: 'Well, Brother Heber, I followed your advice —' 'Yes,' said the man of God, 'and you found bread.'"[21]

Writing to Orson Pratt in England, Brigham explained:

> The Reformation, as it has been called, has begun,—not a change in our religion, nor of the principles revealed from the heavens through Joseph,—but a change in the practices and an arousing of the people from habits of lethargy; and its salutary influences are already perceptible. We have appointed two or more home missionaries to each ward in the city, and drawn up a list of questions to be asked the Latter-day Saints. Those missionaries go from house to house, and examine every individual therein separately; and, as a consequence, we have had this people examining themselves minutely; much honest confession and restitution have been made. The catechism has been as a mirror to the Saints, reflecting themselves in truth.[22]

We gain important insight into the nature of Brigham Young by the tone of this communication. His task, as he perceived it, was not primarily to be a leader of men, a powerful figure remembered for the communities of men and enterprises of business he had established; his work was to succor and perfect the Saints, to prepare a people worthy to do the work of the Lord, and to be called by his name. When he spoke to his brethren and sisters, he revealed the depth of his convictions and feelings:

> . . . The past year was a hard one for us with regard to provisions, but I never had one faltering feeling in reference to this community's suffering, provided all had understood their religion and lived it. . . .

. . . If all our cattle had died through the severity of the past winter, if the insects had cut off all our crops, if we still proved faithful to our God and to our religion, I have confidence to believe that the Lord would send manna and flocks of quails to us. But he will not do this, if we murmur and are neglectful and disunited.[23]

Heber Kimball, in a letter to his son, reveals some frustration with the narrow, immature nature of men and women who, by this time, should have learned better:

Some of the people drop many big tears, but if they cannot learn wisdom by precept, nor by example, they must learn it by what they suffer. . . . I can say in my heart, I wish to God this people would all listen to counsel, and do at the start as they are told, and move as one man, and be one. If this were the case, our enemies would never have any more power over us, our granaries never would be empty, nor would we see sorrow.[24]

Yet, knowing the Saints' weaknesses, Brigham could not refrain from expressing his deep affection for them:

This people is the best people upon the face of the earth, that we have any knowledge of . . . . I hope and trust in the Lord my God that I shall never be left to praise this people, to speak well of them, for the purpose of cheering and comforting them by the art of flattery; to lead them on by smooth speeches day after day, week after week, month after month, and year after year, and let them roll sin as a sweet morsel under their tongues, and be guilty of transgressing the laws of God. I hope I shall never be left to flatter this people, or any people on the earth, in their iniquity, but far rather chasten them for their wickedness and praise them for their goodness.

Brigham here establishes, by his fearless understanding and commitment, his worthiness to be called a prophet among the people.

The Lord praises you and comforts you if you live as you are directed; if you live with your life hid with Christ in God, you do receive, from the fountain head, life, joy, peace, truth, and every good and wholesome principle that the Lord bestows upon this people, and your hearts exalt in it, and your joy is made full . . . The Holy Ghost reveals unto you things past, present, and to come; it makes your minds quick and vivid to understanding the handiwork of the Lord. Your joy is made full in beholding the footsteps of our Father going forth among the inhabitants of the earth; this is invisible to the world but it is made visible to the Saints, and they behold the Lord in his providences, bringing forth the work of the last days.[25]

The Lord could only do so much in bringing forth the work of the last days without fully unqualified assistance from those who called themselves Saints. In this, as in all things, Brigham served as example and led the way.

In the overwhelming work of bringing Saints from all over the world to Zion, the idea was presented, as early as the epistle of 1851, for those without means of securing wagons to attempt a simpler way:

Yes, if you have the same desire, the same faith. . . Families might start from the Missouri river, with cows, handcarts, wheel-barrows, with little flour, and no unnecessaries, and come to this place quicker, and with less fatigue, than by following the heavy trains, with their cumbrous herds, which they are often obliged to drive miles to feed. . . . There is grain and provision enough in the valleys for you to come to; and you need not bring more than enough to sustain you one hundred days, to insure you a supply for the future.[26]

At first the plan, which looked good on paper, seemed to work in reality as well. Three companies came with remarkable speed and ease (taking about sixty-five days), suffering no more than usual for such a journey. Of course, Brigham and the other leaders were both pleased and relieved. "As I gazed upon the scene," Wilford Woodruff wrote, "meditating upon the future results, it looked to me like the first hoisting of the floodgates of deliverance to the oppressed millions. We can now say to the poor and honest in heart, come home to Zion, for the way is prepared."[27]

The trouble came when the Saints, eager to attain what they considered a worthy goal, acted against counsel and expected the

Lord to compensate for their own lack of wisdom and judgment. When Franklin D. Richards and other missionaries, including Brigham's son, Joseph A., reported two companies still on the trail late in the traveling season, Brigham did not indulge in spiritual rhetoric as some of the brethren did; he knew too well the realities. To the Saints assembled in conference he said:

> The text will be—to get them here! I want the brethren who may speak to understand that their text is the people on the Plains, and the subject matter for this community is to send for them and bring them in before the winter sets in.[28]

Brigham asked for sixty or sixty-five teams, twelve to fifteen wagons, and forty young teamsters; among those who rose up and gave him their names were Cyrus Wheelock and Brigham's own son, Joseph A. Young, both returned from their missions to Great Britain no more than forty-eight hours before. They had helped to convert some of those families who were now stranded and in trouble. These young men, newly restored to the joys and comforts of their own families, returned on a mission of rescue and mercy.

Brigham sent out 250 wagons to keep a relay of supplies and fresh animals available; otherwise, the heroic efforts of the vanguard rescuers would have been in vain, since food and blankets in large supply were needed to prevent further deaths. The stories of suffering and loss are many, and laced with an almost eerie sense of futility and stark tragedy. One young woman died in the act of raising a cracker to her mouth, and was buried in a community grave. Elizabeth Jackson, lying in the bitter cold beside her husband, reached over to touch him and realized he was frozen dead. She remained beside him until daylight came and he could be buried with thirteen others who had died; men pulled their carts, with their shivering children in them, by sheer will power alone, "stumbled into camp with their faces drawn and set, and sometimes if they rested a few minutes before putting up the tents they lay down and died without ever knowing how completely exhausted they were."[29]

Patience Loader recounted an experience she had while resting in the thin, brief sunlight:

> A strange man appeared to her. He came and looked into her face earnestly and said, "Are you Patience?" She said, "Yes." He said, "I thought it was you. Travel on, there is help for you. You will come to a good place; there is plenty." With this he was gone . . . "I looked but never saw whare he went this seemed very strange to me. I took this as some one sent to encourage us and give us strength. We traveld on."[30]

Over two hundred members of the Willie and Martin companies died between Florence and the Valley; nearly 150 of these were from Martin's group. On November 2, Brigham spoke feelingly of the situation of the stranded and suffering Saints, revealing the depth of his own personal reactions—a thing one does only in the company of those who are loved and trusted, those one considers intimate, which is how Brigham Young considered his brothers and sisters in the faith:

> We can return home and sit down and warm our feet before the fire, and can eat our bread and butter, etc., but my mind is yonder in the snow, where those immigrating Saints are, and my mind has been with them ever since I had the report of their [late] start . . . I cannot talk about any thing, I cannot go out or come in, but what in every minute or two minutes my mind reverts to them; and the questions—whereabouts are my brethren and sisters who are on the Plains, and what is their condition—force themselves upon me.[31]

On Sunday morning, November 30th, when he heard that survivors of the Martin Company were entering the valley, he extended his instructions to both the bishops and the people:

> The afternoon meeting will be omitted, for I wish the sisters to go home and prepare to give those who have just arrived a mouthful of something to eat, and to wash them and nurse them up . . . Were I in the situation of those persons who have just come in, . . . I would give more for a dish of pudding or a baked potato and salt . . . than I would for all your prayers; though you were to stay here all afternoon

and pray. Prayer is good, but when baked potatoes and milk are needed, prayer will not supply their place.[32]

There were those who were willing to place the blame for the tragedy on the shoulders of the prophet, but Brigham would not have it so. In defending himself, he seemed to shift the blame largely to Franklin D. Richards:

> Are those people in the frost and snow by my doings? No, my skirts are clear of their blood, God knows. If a bird had chirped in brother Franklin's ears in Florence [Nebraska], and the brethren there had held a council, he would have stopped the rear companies there, and we would have been putting in our wheat, etc., instead of going off to the Plains and spending weeks and months to succor our brethren.[33]

Some would claim that Brigham used Richards as a scapegoat and was cruel in his denunciation of the leader. But, knowing Brigham's manner of rebuke, his dealings with Brother Richards were mild in comparison to some. Eugene England, a biographer of Brigham, suggests an interpretation just as plausible and more in keeping, really, with what is known of President Young and his ways. In possible defense of Elder Richards, Brigham stated: "'Here is brother Franklin D. Richards who has but little knowledge of business . . . and here is brother Daniel Spencer . . . and I do not know that I will attach blame to either one of them.'"[34] As a man, as a human being, Brigham, contemplating the cost in terms of human suffering, could momentarily be consumed with frustration and anger at the lack of wisdom and discernment his brethren had shown. As a leader, he could lament but forgive it, making allowance for the capacities of those involved. Heber Kimball told the people bluntly:

> Some find fault with and blame Brother Brigham and his counsel, because of the sufferings they have heard that our brethren are enduring on the plains. . . . But let me tell you most emphatically that if all who were entrusted with the care and management of this year's immigration had done as they were counseled and dictated by the First Presidency of this Church, the sufferings and hardships now

endured by the companies on their way here would have been avoided.[35]

All things considered, a certain amount of defensiveness on Brigham's part was natural; this was a failure of sorts and, as prophet, all failures came to a degree under his stewardship.

> Here was where his stewardship touched human lives and where his old abhorrence of violence and unneeded, unredemptive suffering came to the fore—and he wanted very much not to feel responsible. He was right most of the time and wanted to be right all the time.[36]

His capacity for anguish and pity at the suffering of others is no better shown than in the experience at this time, related by Mary Ann Goble, as she remembered it:

> We traveled from 15 to 25 miles a day . . . till we got to the Platte River. . . . We caught up with the handcart companies that day. We watched them cross the river. There were great lumps of ice floating down the river. It was bitter cold. The next morning there were four-teen dead. . . . We went back to camp and had our prayers, [and] . . . sang "Come, Come, Ye Saints, No Toil Nor Labor Fear." I wondered what made my mother cry [that night]. . . . The next morning my little sister was born. It was the 23rd of September. We named her Edith. She lived six weeks and died. . . . [She was buried at the last crossing of the Sweetwater]. . . [We ran into heavy snow. I became lost in the snow]. My feet and legs were frozen. . . . The men rubbed me with snow. They put my feet in a bucket of water. The pain was terrible. . . . When we arrived at Devils Gate it was bitter cold. We left many of our number there. . . . My brother James . . . was as well as he ever was when he went to bed [that night]. In the morning he was dead. . . . My feet were frozen; also my brother's and sister's. It was nothing but snow [snow everywhere and the bitter Wyoming wind]. We could not drive the pegs in our tents. . . . We did not know what would become of us . . . [Then] one night a man came to our camp and told us. . . . Brigham Young had sent men and teams to help us. . . . We sang songs, some danced and some cried. . . . My mother had never got well. . . . She died between the Little and Big Mountains. . . . She was 43 years of age. . . . We arrived in Salt Lake City nine o'clock at night the 11th of December 1856. Three out of

four that were living were frozen. My mother was dead in the wagon. . . . Early next morning Brigham Young came. . . . When he saw our condition, our feet frozen and our mother dead, tears rolled down his cheeks. . . . The doctor amputated my toes . . . [while the sisters were dressing mother for her grave]. When my feet were fixed they [carried] . . . us in to see our mother for the last time. Oh, how did we stand it? That afternoon she was buried. . . . I have thought often of my mother's words before we left England. "Polly, I want to go to Zion while my children are small, so they can be raised in the Gospel of Christ, for I know this is the true church."[37]

These were his people, his children—he had long considered himself a father to all, and had administered often in that capacity. As such, Brigham reached his most Christlike heights.

Notes

1. Journal History of Brigham Young, 14 February 1853, Church Archives.
2. Whitney, *Life of Heber C. Kimball,* p. 394-95.
3. Journal History of Brigham Young, 6 April 1853, Church Archives.
4. Ms. History, p. 6.
5. Mrs. Thomas L. Kane, *Twelve Mormon Homes* (William Wood: Philadelphia, 1874), p. 14-15.
6. Spencer and Harmer, *Brigham Young at Home,* p. 122.
7. Ibid., p. 124-25.
8. Ibid., p. 123.
9. Ibid.
10. Gustive O. Larson, *Prelude to the Kingdom* (Francestown, NH: Marshall Jones, 1947), p. 470.
11. Spencer and Harmer, *Brigham Young at Home,* p. 132.
12. *CCH,* 4:49.
13. Larson, *Prelude to the Kingdom,* p. 185-86.
14. *JD,* 3:12.
15. Gates and Widtsoe, *Life Story,* p. 263.
16. Ibid., p. 263-64.
17. Ibid.
18. Whitney, *Life of Heber C. Kimball,* p. 400.
19. Ibid., p. 303-304.
20. Preston Nibley, *Brigham Young,* p. 269.
21. Journal History of Brigham Young, 17 August 1856, Church Archives.

22. England, *Brother Brigham,* p. 195.
23. Whitney, *Life of Heber C. Kimball,* p. 406.
24. Journal History of Brigham Young, 17 August 1856, Church Archives.
25. *Millennial Star* 14, p. 23.
26. Ibid., p. 18, p. 794-95.
27. *JD,* 4:113.
28. Wallace Stegner, *The Gathering of Zion: The Story of the Mormon Trail,* (Lincoln and London (University of Nebraska Press, 1964), p. 245.
29. Ibid., p. 253-53.
30. *JD,* 4:62.
31. England, *Brother Brigham,* p. 175.
32. *JD,* 4:69.
33. England, *Brother Brigham,* p. 173.
34. Ibid., p. 174.
35. Whitney, *Life of Heber C. Kimball,* p. 414.
36. England, *Brother Brigham,* p. 174.
37. *The Mormon Pioneers,* LDS Church Seminary System (Corporation of the President, 1977), p. 1-2.

Chapter Fourteen

In the Hands of the Lord

Johnston's Army and the "Utah War" –
Mountain Meadows Massacre – Governor Cummings
enters Salt Lake City

Many may inquire, "How long shall we stay here?" We shall stay here just as long as we ought to. "Shall we be driven, when we go?" If we will so live as to be satisfied with ourselves, and will not drive ourselves from our homes, we shall never be driven from them . . . I have asked the Lord to mete out justice to those who have oppressed us, and the Lord will take His own time and way for doing this. It is in His hands, and not mine, and I am glad of it, for I could not deal with the wicked as they should be dealt with.

Journal of Discourses, 10:297

In February 1857, the U.S. mail contract was awarded to the Church agent, Hiram Kimball. With pleasurable interest Brigham selected sites for the way stations, planning them in his mind as future settlements, and soliciting the ever-necessary contributions of both money and materials. In this, as in all else, the spiritual element of the work was stressed; Brigham set apart the "express missionaries" and counseled them to view their work as "religious duty and live accordingly—including treating their teams with kindness."[1] By the middle of February the mail was being carried along designated routes, and by July many of the stations were nearing completion.

On July 22, a pilgrimage of 2,5487 people, 468 carriages and wagons, 1,028 horses and mules, and 382 oxen and cows headed up Cottonwood canyon to the Silver Lake resort to celebrate Pioneer Day—ten years since the pioneers had entered the valley. Three boweries had been prepared, with plank floors for dancing. There were five different bands, and numerous choirs to help the Saints celebrate the joy and growth of Deseret. But with dramatic irony, more cruel in life than in the greatest fiction, at high noon the cheerful, hopeful revelry was interrupted by four solemn messengers—travel-worn horsemen who had ridden long and hard: A. O. Smoot, Porter Rockwell, Judson Stoddard, and Elias Smith. They brought news that an army of twenty-five hundred were marching toward the territory, even as they spoke, by order of President Buchanan himself. The American Stars and Stripes rose and fell on the breeze while the Mormons learned that Republicans in Congress were bent to do their sworn duty to "prohibit in the Territories those twin relics of barbarism—Polygamy and Slavery."[2] Slavery could not be struck at so easily, but polygamy was much more vulnerable. Wild charges were circulated that Governor Young, in a state of rebellious dictatorship, was destroying court records and threatening the authority of the United States.

Without investigating either the charges or the character of the accusers (mainly the infamous Judge Drummond, who had deserted his family and brought his mistress to Utah, actually allowing her to sit on the court bench beside him), and without bothering to notify the Mormons themselves, the President cancelled the mail contract, appointed a new governor, and sent him to Utah with the force of twenty-five hundred soldiers to back him. It is conjectured that John B. Floyd, a rank secessionist and secretary of war at the time, contrived this as a way to aid his own cause, employing a large portion of the Union forces in this inaccessible region, leaving Governmental arsenals and military stores unprotected in many Southern states. It has also been suggested that there were probably some money-grabbing contractors who used their influence to have the army on the march. Whatever the causes, the venture was destined to cost the Government somewhere between fifteen and twenty million dollars and to go down in history as "Buchanan's blunder."[3]

Brigham saw his first task as that of keeping the armed forces beyond his borders until he might attempt to communicate with Washington himself. But he did not underestimate the possibilities or motives behind what had been done. He took the precaution of calling back missionaries, at first only from the East and Canada, later from all foreign lands, as well as calling in the outpost settlements and mobilizing the Nauvoo Legion.

On August 19, thousands of Saints, meeting in the tabernacle, pledged their support to the presidency and whatever course they decided to take. On August 20, Brigham recorded the irony of the dealings of God and man with the Saints:

> The Day I entered Salt Lake Valley 24 July 1847 I remarked—if the devil will let us alone for 10 years—we will bid them defiance. July 24 1857—10 years to a day—first heard of the intended expedition to Utah under Genl. Harney. I feel the same now. I defy all the powers of darkness.[4]

These are bold words for a leader. The lonely burden behind them must have weighed heavily on Brigham's heart: so many endangered, so many dependent upon him—so many memories of cruelty and injustice, suffering, trial, and pain. Only with the aid of a power beyond his own could he have faced this return of "the powers of darkness" bent upon the destruction of the Saints.

In declaring the Territory under martial law, Brigham proclaimed:

> Citizens of Utah: We are invaded by a hostile force who are evidently assailing us to accomplish our overthrow and destruction. For the last

twenty-five years we have trusted officials of the Government, from Constables and Justices to Judges, Governors, and Presidents, only to be scorned, held in derision, insulted, and betrayed. Our houses have been plundered and then burned, our fields laid waste, our principle men butchered while under the pledged faith of the government for their safety, and our families driven from their homes to find that shelter in the barren wilderness and that protection among hostile savages which were denied them in the boasted abodes of Christianity and civilization.

The Constitution of our common country guarantees unto us all that we do now or have ever claimed. If the Constitutional rights which pertain unto us as American citizens were extended to Utah, according to the spirit and meaning thereof, and fairly and impartially administered, it is all that we could ask, all that we have ever asked.[5]

As events transpired, Brigham Young proved himself able to back up his words with his actions. Brigham's directions to General Wells, commander of the Nauvoo Legion, were to engage in delaying tactics: burn forage, even set fire to their trains, stampede their animals, destroy the river fords and blockade the roads—but, absolutely, take no lives.

The army was under command of Colonel Albert S. Johnston, but a Captain Van Vliet was sent ahead to purchase provisions and convey the troops' peaceful intent. He was received most cordially by the governor, who assured him there was an abundance of the things he would need, but none would be sold to him. The colonel tried to warn them that any form of resistance would be met with greater numbers of troops being sent in the future, but he was met with a consistently calm determination on the part of the Saints to stand their ground. In a meeting in the tabernacle, four thousand Saints raised their hands to support Elder Taylor's statement that troops coming to Utah would find a desert; "every house burned to the ground, every tree cut down, every field laid waste."[6]

During this tense and vital period of "negotiation with the enemy," a messenger arrived from Southern Utah with news of an impending disaster of tragic proportions. Certainly Brigham must have felt that his cup of anguish was full.

A group of emigrants passing through Utah to California had been irritated by the Saints' reluctance to sell them food. Attached to this company were a band of Missourians who boasted of their participation in the murder and rape of Mormons back in 1838; indeed, they went so far as to threaten more of the same. There were run-ins with Indians, and the rumored possibility that the travelers had poisoned an ox, resulting in the deaths of some Indians; one Mormon also allegedly died. Then things became messy. The disgruntled emigrants had destroyed property in Cedar City and threatened to return with troops and wipe the Mormons out. This was perceived as no idle threat, no matter how it may have been intended; many of the Mormons had memories which were painful and long, and was not the general government rising up against them again? The Indians, resentful and spoiling for a fight with the "Mericats," attacked on September 7 at a place called Mountain Meadows in southern Utah. Meanwhile, a rider had been dispatched the 250 miles north to Salt Lake for the prophet's advice.

Three of the frightened emigrants who broke out of the Indians' seige had an unhappy encounter with some Mormons, and one of the Gentiles was killed. Now a group of the local Mormons began to think the whole affair through. What if those who escaped did tell tales—some of them true and justified—and bring back dreaded retaliation on their heads? The only wise, safe thing to do was unthinkable—and yet, were these not low creatures who had themselves brought nameless suffering upon innocent women and children? So their reasoning turned down pathways of darkness, and at some point—by some—it was decided to strike back.

John D. Lee, local Church agent among the Indians, talked the emigrants into disarming and making an attempt for safe passage to Cedar City. Lee's terse "'Do your duty,' started the massacre—which called for the 50 Iron County militiamen to slaughter the men and the 200 Indians to kill the women and older children. About 120 were killed. Only seventeen small children survived to be eventually returned to the East."[7]

Brigham's response, sent back with all speed, to "not meddle" and "preserve good feeling" was addressed to Isaac Haight, presiding Church authority in Cedar City; but it arrived two days after the fact.

This one isolated tragedy—this one isolated instance of retaliation by any Mormons in face of the overwhelming and varied persecution thousands of them had suffered—was blown out of proportion and worried, as a dog worries a bone, in part because of its tragic timing, in part because it offered one of few legitimate excuses to publish ill tidings of the Mormons. Historian Nels Anderson observed that "'most investigators were not so much interested in the facts as in using the incident to indict Brigham Young.'"[8]

The facts clearly attest to the fact that Brigham was involved neither in the perpetrating nor the condoning of the deed, but the complexities of his feelings and emotional reactions were increased by John D. Lee's involvement. Lee, through the early Nauvoo ceremony of "adoption," was part of Brigham's large family. To see this man he had trusted and nurtured involved in such a heinous activity, hardly within the scope of Brigham's comprehension, was all the more painful because of the ugly light his betrayal cast on the Church. Explaining himself, again in an intimate manner, he said before the gathered Saints:

> I will tell the Latter-day Saints that there are some things which transpire that I cannot think about. There are transactions that are too horrible for me to contemplate. The massacre at Haun's mill, and that of Joseph and Hyrum Smith, and the Mountain Meadow's massacre and the murder of Dr. Robinson are of this character. I cannot think that there are beings upon the earth who have any claim to the sentiments and feelings which dwell in the breasts of civilized men who could be guilty of such atrocities; and it is hard to suppose that even savages would be capable of performing such inhuman acts.[9]

That Brigham had difficulty dealing with the situation and those who had been involved in it—especially in light of the delicate and weighty complexities already claiming his attention and care—reveals mainly "what it may cost an imperfect mortal to be called to the role of prophet."[10]

General Johnston joined his troops the first of November, and they started toward Fort Bridger. The Mormons had actually purchased the fort in 1855; they enlarged and rebuilt it, only to burn it to the ground a scant two months after completion of the new additions.

The Mormon guerrilla bands under Lot Smith and others had been successful in driving off horses and cattle and even burning several supply trains, so the soldiers kept a very scanty subsistence that winter. With temperatures at forty-four degrees below zero, many of the soldiers and teamsters suffered frostbite before reaching the fort. When Brigham learned of their sad straits, he sent a load of salt to Colonel Johnston, who "returned it with every expression of bitterness."[11]

Johnston did not—because he could not—mount a winter campaign, so Brigham set the example. Rather than stewing, or keeping fear and bitterness stirred up, he relaxed, leaving matters for the time being where they belonged: in the hands of the Lord. Wilford Woodruff wrote:

> Through all this President Young has been as calm as a summer's day. The army of Zion is now returning to its home with the same spirit of composure and quietude that it carried with it into the mountains. As the men passed, on their return, by President Young, they gave him a quiet salute and went silently to their homes, while President Young gazed upon them with thanksgiving and praise to the God of Israel.[12]

That winter was one of the brightest in the valley. The harvest had been abundant; the Saints rejoiced, held balls and other social gatherings. As one writer said: "There was the great sagacity and remarkable commonsense leadership of Brigham Young seen in all this jubilee. He was preparing to make his second exodus, if necessary, and did not intend to play his Moses to a dispirited Israel."[13]

Late in February, Colonel Kane arrived as emissary for the government. He was exhausted and in ill health, yet Brigham assured him:

> Brother Thomas, the Lord sent you here, and he will not let you die. No! you cannot die till your work is done; I want to have your name live with the saints to all eternity. You have done a great work, and you will do a greater work still.

He also reminded his visitor, in stirring detail, of the history of the Latter-day Saints, perhaps to remind him of important elements he should not fail to take into consideration when representing this people. "It is not in the power of the United States to destroy this people," Brigham said. "For they [the United States] are in the hands of God, and so are we; and he will do with us as he pleases, and if we do right God will preserve us." These words sum up "the whole policy of Brigham Young in this issue between the Church . . . and the government. It was both Alpha and Omega in his philosophy on the subject; he never deviated from it."[14]

General Johnston's views were adamant: ". . . in view of the treasonable temper and feeling now pervading the leaders and a greater portion of the Mormons, I think that neither the honor nor the dignity of the government will allow of the slightest concession being made to them."[15] One wonders if Johnston recalled these words when he aligned himself with the rebellious and treasonable cause of the Confederacy, for which he eventually gave his life. Nevertheless, through Colonel Kane's ministrations, the newly appointed Governor Cummings agreed to travel unescorted to Utah, where he was graciously and with all due honors received. He immediately formed his own opinion of Governor Young, telling Elder Staines, who asked his opinion of the Mormon prophet, "No tyrant ever had a head on his shoulders like Mr. Young. He is naturally a good man. I doubt whether many of your people sufficiently appreciate him as a leader."[16]

Governor Cummings hoped things would now be resolved, but when it was learned that the troops were to be quartered in the Territory, thirty thousand people began to abandon their homes. In May, he returned to Camp Scott for his wife; when she saw the deserted city it moved her to tears. He reported to the secretary of state:

> The people are moving from every settlement in the northern part of the Territory. The roads are everywhere filled with wagons loaded with provisions and household furniture, the women and children often without shoes or hats, driving their flocks they know not where. Young, Kimball and the influential men have left their mansions without apparent regret, to lengthen the long train of wanderers. The masses announce to me that the torch will be applied to every house indiscriminately throughout the country as soon as the troops attempt to cross the mountains. I shall follow these people and try to rally them.[17]

During these dark days, Brigham wrote to Brother Appleby, president of the Eastern Mission:

> Rather than see my wives and daughters ravished and polluted, and the seeds of corruption sown in the hearts of my sons by a brutal soldiery, I would leave my home in ashes, my gardens and orchards a waste, and subsist upon roots and herbs, a wanderer through these mountains for the remainder of my natural life.[18]

Perhaps Brigham believed it would never come to that; the Lord would not permit it to be so. But his determination was fixed and real: he would do what he had said he would do, if it came to that.

On April 7, with two of his wives already in Provo, Wilford Woodruff loaded his wagons and began his journey to Provo in a severe snowstorm, which caused great suffering to the people and their animals.

Public opinion, as people turned their eyes westward, began to alter. Wrote the *New York Times:*

> When people abandon their homes to plunge with women and children into a wilderness to seek new settlements, they know not where, they give a higher proof of courage than if they fought for them.[19]

And the *London Times:*

> Does it not seem incredible that, at the very moment when the marine of Great Britain and the United States are jointly engaged in the grandest scientific experiments that the world has yet seen, 30,000 or 40,000 natives of these countries, many of them of industrious and temperate habits, should be the victims of such arrant imposition?[20]

With the aid of a peace commission a settlement was reached, which included Johnston's troops marching straight through the city—never pausing, never touching a thing, never breaking ranks. Colonel Cooke bared his head in honor of the men he had led in the Mormon Battalion. The army never stopped till they reached the Jordan River, two miles west of the city, where they camped for three days. Camp Floyd, which would become the largest military post in the country, was established in Cedar Valley, thirty-six miles south of Salt Lake.

President Buchanan, after accusing Brigham and other leaders of treason and additional crimes, extended them a pardon. Tongue in cheek, Brigham thanked the President, saying:

> As far as I am concerned, I thank President Buchanan for forgiving me, but I really cannot tell what I have done. I know one thing, and that is that the people called Mormons are a loyal and a law-abiding people, and have ever been. Neither President Buchanan nor any one else can contradict that statement. It is true Lot Smith burned some wagons containing government supplies for the army. This was an overt act, and if it is for this we are to be pardoned, I accept the pardon.[21]

Brigham went into a period of semi-isolation after Governor Cummings took over, spending much of his time in his homes and offices, running things very much as usual, though more quietly. A soldier stationed at Camp Floyd provided the following delightful insights:

> Some reckless slanderer, destitute of either honor, honesty or truth, says that "Brigham Young remains secluded, never leaving his house, but concealing himself from the rage of the Mormons, who can now

see his duplicity and falsehood." This is untrue, entirely without foundation. Brigham has been here several times, since I came to Camp Floyd, and the Mormons show him the utmost respect wherever he goes. He is still their head-man, and his word is omnipotent wherever Mormonism has a foot-hold. My worthy friend, the Bishop, of whom I spoke to you in my last, introduced me to him, adding that I was a printer; "Ah!" said Brigham, "then I presume you have often put in type 'our own correspondent's' accounts of affairs out here. Now, do you take me for the terrible, treasonable, anathemaizing, many-wived, law-resisting rascal I have been represented?" And, of a truth I should say, no. He has an open, pleasant countenance, that speaks of benevolence, humanity and frankness; there is nothing in his appearance to indicate the bold bad man that the race of Drummonds have represented him to be. . . . He is not very well liked by some of our officers, I admit, but the cause of it is this: He holds the opinion that "the rank is but the guinea's stamp, the man's the gold for a' that," and an honest, upright, sober private soldier is a better man by far than a king without these qualities. . . . I am no friend of Mormonism, or the policy of Brigham Young, but I approve of giving "the devil his due." He is no longer Governor nor is he vested with any civil authority; but Young's moral powers remain quite unaltered and unweakened with the Mormon settlers of Utah.[22]

The Lord turned even the presence of their enemies into good for the Saints. When Johnston's army was called back at the outbreak of the Civil War, the camp was abandoned and the goods sacrificed. Hundreds of wagons valued at $150 to $175 were sold for $10 each. Flour, purchased by the government for $28.40 a sack, sold for fifty-two cents. Many of the officers of the camp called upon Brigham Young before their departure and presented him with the flagstaff as a token of their friendship. Brigham and Colonel Johnston never met face to face. The colonel died when his forces met Grant's at the Battle of Shiloh.

Notes

1. England, *Brother Brigham,* p. 176.
2. Gates and Widtsoe, *Life Story,* p. 174.

3. Spencer and Harmer, *Brigham Young at Home,* p. 91.

4. Secretary's Journal, 20 August 1857, Brigham Young Papers, Church Archives.

5. Proclamation reprinted in frontispiece, *To Utah with the Dragoons and Glimpses of Life in Arizona and California, 1858-1859* (Salt Lake City: University of Utah Press, 1974)

6. Spencer and Harmer, *Brigham Young at Home,* p. 93.

7. England, *Brother Brigham,* p. 180-81.

8. Ibid., p. 181.

9. *JD,* 11:281.

10. England, *Brother Brigham,* p. 183.

11. Spencer and Harmer, *Brigham Young at Home,* p. 98.

12. Cowley, *Wilford Woodruff,* p. 392.

13. Spencer and Harmer, *Brigham Young at Home,* p. 100.

14. *CCH,* 4:345-46.

15. *CCH,* 4:252-53.

16. Spencer and Harmer, *Brigham Young at Home,* p. 103.

17. Ibid., p. 104-109.

18. England, *Brother Brigham,* p. 185.

19. Spencer and Harmer, *Brigham Young at Home,* p. 105.

20. Ibid.

21. Ibid., p. 106.

22. Langley, *To Utah with the Dragoons,* p. 107-108.

Chapter Fifteen

Brother Brigham

*Descriptions, impressions of Brigham – Civil War –
Theatre in Deseret – a new governor and corrupt, non-
Mormon officials – Black Hawk uprising –
the coming of the railroad*

Strive to be righteous, not for any speculation, but because righteousness is lovely, pure, holy, beautiful, and exalting; it is designed to make
the soul happy and full of joy, to the extent of the whole capacity of
man, filling him with light, glory, and intelligence.
Journal of Discourses, 8:172

Of Joseph Smith it was said that if he could once get the ear
of his persecutors and talk with them, even those who hated him
or were prejudiced against him would become his friends. This
was true even in the extreme instance of one of his worst persecutors, Moses Wilson, who said, "He was a very remarkable man. I
carried him into my house, a prisoner in chains, and in less than
two hours my wife loved him better than she did me."[1]

Brigham Young was extraordinary enough that most men
could not fail to recognize and acknowledge his superiority, and

the sincerity of nature which sat behind his more obvious gifts. Captain Richard F. Burton arrived in Salt Lake on August 24, 1860. He was a brilliant scholar, a world traveler, and an enthusiastic, in-depth observer of human nature and social and religious groups. In his book entitled *The City of the Saints* he wrote:

> Such is his Excellency, President Brigham Young, prophet, revelator, translator and seer—the man who is revered as king or kaiser, pope or pontiff never was; who, governing as well as reigning, long stood up to fight with the sword of the Lord, and with his few hundred guerillas, against the then mighty power of the United States, who has outwitted all diplomacy opposed to him; and finally who made a treaty of peace with the President of the great republic as though he wielded the combined power of France, Russia and England.[2]

Burton later added:

> The first impression left on my mind by this short visit, and it was subsequently confirmed, was that the Prophet is no common man and that he has none of the weakness and vanity which characterize the common man.[3]

Mr. Phil Robinson, a *London Times* correspondent in Africa during the first Boer War, praised Burton's treatment of the Mormon people. "I think I can defy anyone to name another book about the Mormons worthy of honest respect," he wrote;

> . . . There is not, to my knowledge, a single Gentile work before the public that is not utterly unreliable from its distortion of facts. Yet it is from these books—for there are no others—that the American public has acquired nearly all its ideas about the people of Utah.[4]

Horace Greeley, founder and editor of the *New York Tribune,* visited Salt Lake in 1859, when he was at the height of his own power, and was able to discern something of what he found there, leaving a detailed description of his encounter with the Mormon prophet:

He spoke readily, not always with grammatical accuracy, but with no appearance of hesitation or reserve, and with no apparent desire to conceal anything; nor did he repel any of my questions as impertinent. He was very plainly dressed in thin, summer clothing, and with no air of sanctimony or fanaticism. In appearance, he is a portly, frank, good-natured, rather thick-set man of fifty-five, seeming to enjoy life, and to be in no particular hurry to get to heaven. His associates are plain men, evidently born and reared to a life of labor, and looking as little like crafty hypocrites or swindlers as any body of men I ever met. The absence of cant or snuffle from their manner was marked and general; yet I think I may fairly say, that their Mormonism has not impoverished them—that they were generally poor men when they embraced it, and are now in very comfortable circumstances.[5]

Greeley's last observation is interesting in view of the many sacrifices made by these leading men of Mormondom, time and time again, when they had turned their backs on even the bare bones of human comfort to answer a call, when they and their wives had laid their all on the altar; and yet, indeed, the Lord had cared for and prospered their way. Even such an enlightened man as Mr. Greeley was pleased to find his suppositions disproved: the Mormons were "industrious, frugal and hard-working," not "ignorant, superstitious and brutalized."[6] He found them honest, sincere, and intelligent—nothing like what he had been led to believe.

So it was with most who came to see for themselves.

Many statesmen and government officials visited the Mormon prophet, among them General Sherman and his daughter; the Emperor of Brazil; members of a Japanese embassy; Prince Frederick of Wittgenstein, accompanied by Baron Rothschild; Ole Bull, a Norwegian violinist; Schuyler Colfax, Speaker of the House—and, in a slightly different vein, the actress Julia Dean Hayne; the Swiss Bell Ringers; and the famous midgets, Mr. and Mrs. Tom Thumb. Some came more out of curiosity than sincere interest; some with political agendas of their own; all were graciously and warmly received—even the American author Mark Twain, who wrote at length, with tongue-in-cheek humor, of his impressions of Salt Lake and Mormonism. In his book *Roughing*

222 Brigham Young: An Inspiring Personal Biography

It, he said, skirting the issue of polygamy, that as he and his brother walked the clean, lovely streets of Salt Lake, boasting gardens and orchards behind each house, they "felt a curiosity to ask every child how many mothers it had and if it could tell them apart." In the account of his meeting with Brigham Young, he goes into charming detail:

> The second day we put on our white shirts and went and paid a state visit to the king. He seemed a quiet, kindly, easy mannered, dignified, self-possessed old gentleman of fifty-five or sixty and had a gentle craft in his eye that probably belonged there. He was very simply dressed and was just taking off a straw hat as we entered. He talked about Utah and the Indians and Nevada and general American matters and questioned our secretary and certain government officials who came with us. But he never paid any attention to me, notwithstanding I made several attempts to "draw him out" . . . But he merely looked around at me at distant intervals, something as I have seen a benignant old cat look around to see which kitten was meddling with her tail . . . . When the audience was ended and we were retiring from the presence, he put his hand on my head, beamed down at me in an admiring way and said to my brother, "Ah—your child, I presume? Boy or girl?"[7]

The historian Bancroft left an excellent word picture of Brigham Young:

> Brigham Young was now in his forty-third year, in the prime of a hale and vigorous manhood, with exuberant vitality, with marvellous energy, and with unswerving faith in his cause and in himself; with deep-set, blue-gray eyes, he was a strong-willed man, one born to be master of himself and many others. In manner and address he was easy and void of affectation, deliberate in speech, conveying his original and suggestive ideas in apt though homely phrase. When in council he was cool and imperturbable, slow to decide, and in no haste to act; but when the time for action came he worked with an energy that was satisfied only with success.[8]

Two Frenchmen, Remy and Brenchly, who traveled throughout the West in those days, wrote extensively of the Mormon prophet in *A Journey to Salt Lake City:*

John Hyde, the apostate, who published a book in New York on Mormonism, in which he does not spare his former co-religionists, nor, at times, even Young himself, represents the latter, on the whole, as a superior man.

Brigham Young is not an ordinary man. With an extensive knowledge of men, and a fine and delicate tact, he combines unusual strength of mind and remarkable energy of character. . . .

One of the severest tests of greatness, says Hyde, is the power to completely centre in oneself a thousand interests and the deep affection of a thousand hearts. All really great men have done this, Philosophy has had its disciples, adventurers their followers, generals their soldiers, kings their subjects, imposters their fanatics. No man ever lived who had more deeply devoted friends than Brigham Young. The magnetism that attracts and infatuates, abounds in him. Even his enemies have to acknowledge a great charm in the influence he throws around him. The clerks in his office, and his very wives, feel the same veneration for the Prophet as the most respectful newcomer. . . . The whole secret of Brigham's influence lies in his *real sincerity*. Brigham may be a great man, greatly deceived, but he is not a hypocrite. . . . For the sake of his religion, he has over and over again left his family, confronted the world, endured hunger, come back poor, made wealth and given it to the Church. He holds himself prepared to lead his people in sacrifice and want, as in plenty and ease. No holiday friend nor summer prophet, he has shared their trials as well as their prosperity. He never pretends to more than the inward monitions of the Spirit, nor, as [Joseph] Smith, to direct revelations and physical manifestations. No man prays more fervently than Brigham Young. No man can more win the hearts nor impress the minds of his hearers than Brigham while in prayer. Few men can persist in believing him a hypocrite, either in his family, or in private meetings, or in public.[9]

What Brigham Young thought of what others—the outside world, in particular—thought of him we can surmise from many of the things he said:

I depend not upon human wisdom or human power. I occupy the position that God our Heavenly Father has placed me in, and . . . I tremble not, I fear not, neither do I care for the insults of the world, for the Lord is my bulwark, my shield and my deliverer.[10]

Let the wicked say what they please, for their breath is in their nostrils, and all their glory is like the grass and the flower of the grass that passeth away. . . . Let not your feelings be afflicted or in anywise troubled by the sayings and doings of the wicked, for they are in the hands of the Almighty, and he will dispose of individuals and nations as seemeth him good.[11]

Assuredly he knew who he was and understood his role in the kingdom.

"My name is held for good and evil upon the whole earth," he told the people. "Thirty years ago Brother Joseph, in a lecture to the Twelve said to me, 'Your name shall be known for good and evil through out the world,' and it is so. The good love me, weak and humble as I am, and the wicked hate me; *but there is no individual on the earth but what I would lead to salvation, if he would let me; I would take him by the hand, like a child, and lead him like a father in the way that would bring him to salvation."[12]*

Here glows the sincerity his observers wrote of, and here resurfaces his image of himself as a father to his people—in a very literal, "working" sense. What is more, he had a perfect understanding and testimony of salvation:

It is sometimes taught among us that we should follow Brother Joseph or Brother Brigham, or some other leader and do as they say, and that is all that is required. Now this is in one sense a false doctrine. No man should trust solely the testimony of another. He should have a direct testimony from God for himself. The obedience is intelligent and not blind. I might have listened to Joseph Smith testify of the truth of the Book of Mormon until I was as old as Methuselah, and in the end I would have gone away in darkness had I not received a testimony from God that he was a prophet and that he knew by revelation whereof he spoke. Men should get the spirit of God and then live by it.[13]

And again he taught his followers:

What earthly power can gather a people as this people have been gathered, and hold them together as this people have been held together?

It was not Joseph, it is not Brigham, nor Heber, nor any of the rest of the Twelve, nor any of the Seventies and High Priests that does this, but it is the Lord God Almighty that holds this people together, and no other power.[14]

"'The Latter-day Saints believe in the Gospel of the Son of God, simply because it is true,' he once declared. 'They believe that Jesus is the Saviour of the World; they believe that all who attain to any glory whatever, in any kingdom, will do so because Jesus has purchased it by His atonement.'"[15]

Certainly Brigham had himself in perspective, and knew that only one opinion of Brigham Young really mattered in the end: "You need have no fear but the fear to offend God."[16]

As the great drama of the Civil War unfolded across American soil, the Mormons were marshalling all their efforts to be admitted into the Union as a state. At the same time much political pressure was brought to bear upon Deseret, in hopes that they might rise in rebellion against the government and in support of the southern cause. Their well-drafted petition was given the runaround on the United States Senate floor; it seem ironic that when so many states were wanting to get out of the Union, one was summarily denied who wanted to get in. Even so, the territory's portion of the war tax was duly levied. Although it was discovered that the type of property being taxed did not exist in this area (the territory was legally exempt), and although the Mormons had requested that the assessment be altered to include payment by means other than coin, which was difficult to come by at that time, no quarter was given. So the taxation without representation was paid, without protest, by people whose obedience to government was based upon a higher allegiance, which lent nobility to their actions, if not to those of the government they supported.[17]

Utah's attitude throughout the Civil War is well expressed by John Taylor's remarks on the 4th of July, 1861:

Shall we join the north to fight against the south? No! Shall we join the south against the north? As emphatically, No! Why? They have both as before shown, brought it upon themselves, and we have had no hand in the matter. Whigs, Democrats, Americans and Republicans have all in turn endeavored to stain their hands in innocent blood, and whatever others may do, we cannot conscientiously help to tear down the fabric we are sworn to uphold. We know no north, no south, no east, no west; we abide strictly and positively by the Constitution, and cannot by the intrigues or sophism of either party, be cajoled into any other attitude.[18]

No volunteers from Deseret Territory were sent into service as fighting soldiers. The only direct line service came when President Lincoln approached Brigham Young directly—not the non-Mormon governor of the state—for the appointment of guards along the mail routes.

Lincoln told a visitor from Utah that the Mormons were like the logs he learned to plow around as a youth clearing timber, "too hard to split, too wet to burn, and too heavy to move," and added, "You go back and tell Brigham Young that if he will let me alone I will let him alone."[19]

Lincoln kept his word, even to the extent of refusing to push prosecution of the Morrill Anti-Bigamy Act of 1862, which would disincorporate the Church and limit its real estate holdings to fifty thousand dollars.

While the majority of the country was torn by internal warfare, comparative peace blessed the secluded mountain valleys, and Brigham used the reprieve well. Over 150 new communities were begun during the 1860s. On July 10, 1861, the first telegraph pole was raised on Main Street in Salt Lake. The Overland company had anticipated trouble with both the Mormons and the Indians, but instead Mr. Street, the general agent, appealed to Brigham for help. The only trees large enough to serve as poles were high in the mountains, and the group of Latter-day Saints who had contracted to supply them realized quickly that they were losing money on the deal, and refused to honor their bargain. When Brigham learned of this, his word to the brethren was: fulfill your agreement if it makes paupers of every one of you. Thus, the line was completed by October 17, 1861, and Brigham was extended the honor of sending the first message, which he addressed to J. H. Wade, president of the Pacific Telegraph Company. After congratulating them for their achievement, he stated: "Utah has not seceded, but is firm for the constitution and laws of our once happy country and is warmly interested in such useful enterprises as the one so far completed."[20]

Brigham once made the statement that "if I were placed on a cannibal island and given the task of civilizing its people, I should straightway build a theatre for the purpose."[21] When the need was brought to his attention, Brigham arranged the elements so that the opportunity became a reality, combining the talents of Hyrum B. Clawson and Phil Margetts to form the Deseret Dramatic Association. The graceful theatre building was dedicated on March 6, 1862, with special musical numbers and hymns composed for the occasion. The first plays performed there were "The Pride of the Market" and "State Secrets." The spiritual overtones expected in the theatre experience were evident, and the prophet himself became president of the Deseret Dramatic Association. In the dedication, Brigham reminded the people that

> every pure enjoyment was from Heaven and was for the saints and when they came together with pure spirit and with faith that they would pray for the actors and actresses that they would be refreshed and benefited in their entertainments and that those on the stage should ever be as humble as if they were preaching the gospel. Truth and virtue must abound and characterize every person engaged on the stage or they should be immediately ejected from the building. No person would be permitted to bring liquor into this edifice.[22]

None of the actors was allowed to smoke, and all rehearsals were opened with prayer. No wonder those involved looked upon their work as assignments from the Lord—as missions. Brigham knew the stage was a place where the study of human nature could take place. He loved Shakespeare, but rejected cheap melodrama and did not prefer tragedies with too much realism in them; he refused the repetition of "Oliver Twist" upon the boards after an overenthusiastic performance by an actress who was being mur-

Said to be the last photo of Brigham Young, taken in the summer of 1877, shortly before his death.

This early view of Nauvoo and the temple rising on the hill above the city shows prominently in the foreground the yard and outhouse of the prophe's mother, Lucy Mack Smith.

Brigham and his daughters

The Salt Lake Temple in process. The scaffolding around the Assembly Hall puts the time of the photo around 1880. The Council House on the corner of Main Street burned down in 1883.

This view of Brigham's residence was taken from the roof of the Salt Lake theatre, looking north.

Brigham Young's house and barns, 1865, looking north on State Street.

The view of Nauvoo taken from Bluff Park Shows the grace and beauty of the Mormon city and its setting.

The Salt Lake Theatre, ca. 1865

dered by Bill Sykes. "If I had my way," he said, "I would never have a tragedy played on these boards. There is enough tragedy in every day life and we ought to have amusement when we come here."[23]

Brigham oversaw many aspects of the theatre himself, making sure that none of the actresses were out alone at night without the protection of a chaperone. He took a personal interest in the productions, even to the point of minor details, as in the case when Sara Alexander was made up as a blonde in a role which originally called for a brunette. When he pointed out this discrepancy to her, she quickly responded that she would be happy to play the part as a brunette if she could have John McDonald's glossy dark curls for a wig. Poor Brother McDonald, proud of his beautiful hair which fell to his shoulders, was approached by the prophet to make the sacrifice, and gallantly responded, "'If the success of the play depends upon my hair, Brother Brigham, you shall have my hair.'"[24] Even the barrels of sand and salt water placed near the lamps were checked nightly by Brigham, and woe to the man who had failed to see to them properly. One night three oil lamps in the footlights caught fire, but before panic could ensue, Brigham stepped across the stage and fanned out the flames with his broad-brimmed hat.

Sara Alexander, a ward in Brigham's house, had received only a reluctant agreement when she requested permission to join the theatrical company, but won Brigham's enthusiastic approval by her excellent performances. His daughter, Clarissa, tells of the time when

> an Eastern actor, who played in the city for a season, fell in love with her, and as she had no other guardian, came and asked for Father's consent to their marriage. Father replied, "Young man, I have seen you attempt Richard III and Julius Caesar with fair success, but I advise you not to aspire to Alexander!"[25]

Julia Dean Hayne, one of the outstanding actresses of the day, spoke the following words at the close of her farewell performance, following a year's residence as leading lady at the Salt Lake theatre:

Ladies and Gentlemen: It is but seldom I lose the artist in the woman, or permit my personal feelings to mingle with my public duties; yet, perhaps, in now taking leave I may be pardoned if I essay to speak of obligations which are lasting . . . To President Young, for very many courtesies to a stranger, lone and unprotected, I return those thanks which are hallowed by their earnestness; and I trust he will permit me, in the name of my art, to speak my high appreciation of the order and beauty that reign throughout this house.

I would the same purity prevailed in every temple for the drama's teachings. Then, indeed, the grand object would be achieved, and it would become a school
>   To wake the soul by tender strokes of art,
>   To raise the genius and to mend the heart.[26]

Things were well with Brigham personally at this time. In the summer of 1862 he remarked:

I am better now than I was 20 years ago. I shall soon be 61 years of age and my spirit is more vigorous and more powerful today than it has been in any day I ever saw. It is more quick to comprehend, more ready to discern, the understanding is more matured, more correct in judgment, the memory more vivid and enduring, and discretion more circumspect.[27]

Near the end of the year, in October, he reported in a letter to George Q. Cannon the progress of the various missions. One of the tasks he took upon himself was to consistently visit the outlying settlements, personally instructing and encouraging them. It was a responsibility he took most seriously:

I made a tour through our southern settlements, visiting nearly all of them, and returning on the 25th, having in that short time traveled some eight hundred miles and held thirty public meetings, in twenty-four of which I addressed the congregations. We found the brethren in Washington County were energetic and zealous in developing the resources of that region, though the unprecedented high water the past season so damaged their dams that they labored somewhat at a disadvantage. They are, however, raising quite an amount of cotton, much of it of excellent quality, a great amount of cane, and starting large vineyards and orchards. The brethren manifested much joy in our visiting them; we are pleased to meet with them in their several localities, and returning with the assurance that our trip had benefited both visitors and visited.[28]

Two and a half months later, George A. Smith wrote the following observation to Brother Cannon:

> President Young enjoys excellent health; cares multiply around him. He personally superintends everything of a public nature as far as possible. To conduct his private affairs would seem work enough for any man. He attends the bishops' meetings, visits the endowment House, on almost every occasion, being as near as a man can be 'everywhere present'; preserving in his communications with the brethren *the same simplicity of intercourse and implicit dependence upon the providence of God, as when he used to travel and preach without purse or scrip.*[29]

"Cares multiplying around him" implied more for Brigham Young than for a comparable leader of a community and a people; overt persecution had become almost a fact of existence to him. The anti-polygamy stirrings must have hovered like a shadow at the borders of his days. Then there was the sending of government troops from California under Colonel Connor, men who should have been serving in the front lines for the Union, but were instead established at a fort (Douglas) less than three miles east of Temple Square, where their artillery had an unobstructed shot at Brigham's private residence. The people were justly indignant at this menace without provocation, but President Young displayed an equanimity which disappointed his enemies: "In regard to their location," he remarked,

> I will say that after all the insult that has been offered, they are in the best place they can be in for doing the least injury. If they were at Camp Floyd or Fort Bridger, they would go unrestrained, but here they cannot do much hurt.[30]

The new governor, Stephen Harding, charged the people of Utah with lack of loyalty to the government and attacked the whole body of territorial laws, urging such revolutionary changes that no copies of his address were printed; the Saints attempted to treat his behavior with "silent contempt throughout." Judges Drake and Waite were even more crude in their attempts to misrepresent and vilify the Mormon people. Judge Drake said to the committee who waited upon him,

> Go back to Brigham Young, your master,—that embodiment of sin and shame and disgust,—and tell him that I neither fear him, nor love him, nor hate him; that I did not come here by his permission, and that I will not go away at his desire, or by his directions.[31]

The Mormons, with evidence in plenty, petitioned for the removal of these officers; a counter petition for their retention was drafted and signed by Colonel Connor and the commissioned officers at Camp Douglas. But change was already taking place. James Duane Doty was appointed to replace Harding; and though the two judges were retained, they were able to obtain no support of their evil designs from the new administration. Doty was described as "a very discreet gentleman," who was willing to fall in line with Lincoln's policy of letting the Mormons alone.

Cautious, even a little on edge, the Latter-day Saints let the opposition know that they could not be caught sleeping. When "a reliable person" overheard Colonel Connor say: "These three men must be surprised," and Judge Waite reply: "Colonel, you know your duty," the Saints moved into action. Within half an hour of reporting the action at the president's office, one thousand armed citizens arrived, followed half an hour later by a thousand more. No attempts at arrest were made at that time. Yet, to prevent all the possible dangers of a military arrest, Brigham allowed himself to be arrested on a "friendly complaint" before Chief Justice Kinney, who bound him over at a bail of two thousand dollars to await the action of the grand jury at the next term. The grand jury found no indictment against him, and he was discharged.[32]

All this to satisfy a law enacted without local representation upon a people perennially abused and misrepresented, with a history of nothing but peaceful compliance and industrious ways. The indignity must have bit cruelly into the hearts of these men and women, who wished nothing more than the freedom of religion guaranteed them by a constitution they believed to be God-inspired. To have strangers, hostile to their own interests, placed in authority over them, while their own qualified and just leaders remained powerless, placed them in an ever trying situation, unique in the annals of American history at this "enlightened" time.

If Brigham had seen his power as political or economical, these circumstances would have jarred him, indeed, and surfaced in his public speech and actions; but the contrary held true. In Ogden near this time, he said to the Saints:

> Brother Kimball and myself have come here . . . to speak the things that are in our hearts. First of all, it is the Kingdom of God in our hearts; it is the Kingdom of God or nothing. The Almighty has commenced his work of sending forth his angels from the heavens, and revealing his will. He gave us Joseph, and others, and bestowed the Holy Priesthood upon his servants. We are sharers in the gifts and graces that God has bestowed upon his people. This is a day of days, and a time of times; this is the fulness of times, in which all things that are in Christ are to be gathered in one. This is a momentous period, and we feel an earnestness to lead the minds of those who profess to believe in Jesus, in Joseph, and in the latter-day work, to comprehend the great duties of life by the spirit of the Lord, that they may be one in heart, one in sentiment, and thereby be made one in action, that we may behold the glory of God; this is my desire and the desire of my brethren.[33]

With such a vision, with such a concern uppermost in his heart, no wonder Brigham was disturbed when a man by the name of Ogilvie in a logging camp in Bingham Canyon set off the mining industry with his discovery of a valuable specimen containing strains of both gold and silver.[34] He spoke eloquently on the subject in October 1863:

> It is a fearful deception which all the world labors under, and many of this people, too, who profess to be not of the world, that gold is wealth. On the bare report that gold was discovered in these west

mountains, men left their threshing machines, and their horses at large, to eat up and trample down and destroy the precious bounties of the earth. . . . Can you not see that gold and silver rank among the things that we are the least in want of? We want an abundance of wheat and fine flour, of wine and oil, and every choice fruit that will grow in our climate; we want silk, wool, cotton, flax and other textile substances of which cloth can be made; we want vegetables . . . the coal and the iron that are concealed in these ancient mountains . . . the lumber from our sawmills and the rock from our quarries; these are some of the great staples to which kingdoms owe their existence, continuance, wealth, magnificence, splendor, glory and power, in which gold and tinsel serve as mere tinsel to give the finishing touch to all this greatness. The colossal wealth of the world is founded upon and sustained by the common staples of life.[35]

The opposing factors were at work, and Brigham knew it. General Connor, writing to a fellow officer, revealed the extent of his malice and intent:

My policy in this territory has been to invite hither a large gentile and loyal population, sufficient by peaceful means, and through the ballot box, to overwhelm the Mormons by mere force of numbers, and thus wrest from the Church—disloyal and traitorous to the core—the absolute and tyrannical control of temporal and civic affairs. . . . I have bent every energy and means of which I was possessed, both personal and official, towards the discovery and development of the mining resources of the Territory, using without stint the soldiers at my command, wherever and whenever it could be done.[36]

"If the Lord permits gold mines to be opened here He will overrule it for the good of His Saints," Brigham assured the people. And, writing to George Q. Cannon, he said:

The troops and others at Camp Douglas remain very quiet, the Lord having thus far thwarted their evil designs. At present the great majority of them are in the mountains getting out wood for camp use. Their past plans having failed, they at present are trying to induce an influx of out-siders by inflated representations of rich gold and silver deposits, in Utah's mountains, awaiting discovery and development. I think they will have to wait a good while.[37]

With the ending of the Civil War and the coming of the railroad, Brigham knew that the influences of the world outside Mormonism could no longer be held at bay. He faced the possibility, now that the slavery issue had been handled, that government attention might be turned to the second "great evil": polygamy. With the untimely death of President Lincoln, the Mormons grieved along with the rest of the country; but Brigham did so in a prophetic dimension, knowing the dangers that did and would beset his people. He was aware of how few men of integrity existed in government, and how few were willing to be friends—as Lincoln had been—to the Latter-day Saints.

Brigham's dealings with men of honor and decency had always been generous and expansive. It would have been understandable for the Mormons to resist the establishment of other religions among them, especially considering the active part ministers of other churches had taken in the persecutions of their people in Missouri and Illinois. But Brigham was not simply a man representing himself and the people he led. As he saw it, he was a literal representative of Jesus Christ, and this sacred trust led his motives and actions to higher planes. To the Saints he said,

> In our intercourse with outsiders do not call them "Gentiles" . . . Let our example be such as is worthy of imitation. . . . Attack no man's religion or his business. Show him better ways, greater light, but do not interfere with his affairs.[38]

In the 1860s he welcomed the Catholic missionaries, and in 1871 presented Father Kelly and Father Walsh with a plot of land and $500 so it would be possible for them to build a church. When they purchased a lot for a second cathedral, a blemish on the title was discovered. Both the seller and Father Kelly agreed to go to Brigham to settle the matter, rather than suffer legal litigation, agreeing to stand by his decision. After examining the deed and listening to the evidence, Brigham ruled that the deed be handed over to the priest. "Father Kelly looked upon Brigham Young as a devoted and sincere friend."[39] He was liberal with all sects, presenting the Episcopal missionaries with money and land as well. When Jewish people began entering the valley following the gold rush, he permitted them to meet and pray in one of the ward houses and donated a burial ground to their people. In an English edition of the works of Benjamin 11, Oscar Handlin, he writes: "A few Jews have joined his [Brigham Young's] church." This was around the year 1861. The Jewish people enjoyed a friendly relationship with the Mormons. In the Sevier River area, the Mormon women helped their Jewish neighbors in their first attempts to bottle fruit. A Mr. Ben Brown helped form the Utah Poultry Association. The Zuckerman brothers developed one of the largest potato farms in the world. Simon Bamberger established, among other things, the recreational park known as Lagoon, and Samuel H. Auerbach, who had been in business in California, was one of the men who furnished goods to Camp Floyd in 1859. His family remained in the area and later established one of the most successful department stores in Salt Lake.

> Carvalho, an important Jewish writer who lived in Utah for a time, wrote of Brigham Young when President Young visited Parowan: "I could never have imagined the deep idolatry with which he is almost worshipped. There is no aristocracy . . . about the governor; he is emphatically one of the people.[40]

By 1865 the government had appointed an Indian agent, Colonel Irish, who determined to form a treaty with the Indians, bringing an end to all difficulties. Terms of the treaty included the Indians giving up title to the lands they were occupying and moving to the Uintah Valley, where farms and mills would be laid out for them. They could hunt, fish, and gather on all unoccupied lands, but they were to cease molesting the whites. As Wilford Woodruff reported in his journal, no one could make any headway until Brigham spoke. The Indians had trusted him for a long time, and they were willing to listen to the counsel he gave. "Colonel Johnston of the United States Army was present," Brother Woodruff recorded, "and Colonel Irish informed him that

he could do nothing with the Indians except through the influence of President Young."[41]

Nevertheless, Chief Black Hawk and some of the subchiefs
had not attended the treaty meetings and did not feel bound to
honor agreements made there. The people they attacked were not
only killed, but horribly mutilated, and the "Black Hawk War,"
the most disastrous of any in Utah, continued for several years.
Twenty-seven settlements in several counties were abandoned,
expenses were estimated at $1,190,000 and loss in stock at
$170,000,000, not to mention the loss in property and crops in
the deserted settlements. But the request for government appro-
priations was denied, as had been Colonel Irish's request, first to
General Connor at Camp Douglas and next to federal military
authorities, for an armed force to protect the settlers and deal with
their foes. The citizens were told they must depend upon the territorial militia; then, when they mustered it into service, the
"Mormons" were criticized and accused of

> finding "new means to organize and drill the militia of the territory,
> and to provide them with arms, under the auspices and authority of
> the Mormon church"; going so far as to say that "an open conflict
> with the representatives of the government is apparently braved, even
> threatened!"[42]

How dispiriting this kind of unjust criticism must have been, in
view of the realities!

When the first transcontinental railroad was completed, the
Union Pacific, starting at Omaha and building westward one
thousand miles, and the Central Pacific, building nearly nine
hundred miles east from San Francisco, met—of all places—in
the heart of Mormondom, at a little spot eighty-five miles north-
west of Ogden called Promontory Summit. In the magnificent
ceremonies, the last tie, made of California laurel wood, French
polished, was driven in with three spikes by the governors of
California, Nevada, and Arizona; the last spike was made of
twenty-three $20 gold pieces, and was therefore worth $460.

Brigham, on his annual visit to southern Utah, missed the festivities. Even the non-Mormon governor, Charles Durkee, had been absent in the east and did not return in time to be represented.

There was much conjecture as to the criticism the railroad would occasion amongst the Mormon people, and it was generally believed that they bitterly opposed it. But Brigham intended to capitalize upon progress and convenience for the good of the kingdom. He wanted to harness the iron horse, that it might work to bring emigrants to Utah, transport the products of the valleys to market, and facilitate growth and prosperity toward noble ends. When he learned that the overland railroad would not pass directly through Salt Lake, he wasted no time in frustrated "mourning." Instead he went to work, securing a contract with the Union to construct a line connecting the city with the main track. He formed the Utah Central in March of 1869, with himself as president and John W. Young, his brother, as direct supervisor of building. No longer subsidized by government monies, this track was built at great sacrifice by men who "left their fields willingly to work on the railroad, with pay a most uncertain factor," and women along the route who "often left their household duties to go out and prepare feasts for the workmen." Because the Union Pacific lacked funds to meet their final payment to President Young, they gave, instead of cash, "six hundred thousand dollars' worth of rails, locomotives, cars, and other equipment, all of which were utilized in the building of the Utah Central."[43]

Right-of-way at times became an issue, as in the case of Brother Wood, who returned from serving a mission to find the railroad running right in front of his house. Furious, he stormed in to see Brigham, who tried to placate him by inquiring about his mission, but Brother Wood was too angry to even reply. "'All right,'" Brigham replied, sizing up the situation, "'we have been hunting for a name for this little place and now we have one. We'll call it Woods Cross.'"[44] Today, well over one hundred years later, it still goes by that name.

The accomplishment was remarkable: a railroad built without government subsidies or contributions from capitalists. When the line was completed, a celebration was held on January 10, 1870. It was the beginning of a new year and a new decade—Brigham's last decade, as events would turn out. It was a cold day, but great crowds of the Saints came to celebrate together. Brigham drove the last spike home with a mallet made of Utah iron, engraved with words which characterized all the Saints' endeavors, be they of a spiritual or material nature; it was Brigham's desire that all be considered one and the same. On the top of the steel mallet was an engraved beehive and an inscription around it: "Holiness to the Lord."[45]

Notes

1. McCloud, *Joseph Smith,* p. 4.
2. Spencer and Harmer, *Brigham Young at Home,* p. 87.
3. Ibid., p. 12.
4. *CCH,* 4:528-29.
5. Ibid., p. 523-24.
6. Arrington, *American Moses,* p. 324.
7. Spencer and Harmer, *Brigham Young at Home,* p. 213-14.
8. Ibid., p. 375.
9. Ibid., p. 375-76.
10. *JD,* 10:305.
11. *JD,* 7:270, 3:93.
12. L. S., p. 377; italics author's.
13. Ibid., p. 378.
14. *JD,* 10:305.
15. Spencer and Harmer, *Brigham Young at Home,* p. 374.
16. *JD,* 4:369.
17. *CCH,* 5:11.
18. Ibid.
19. England, *Brother Brigham,* p. 187.
20. Spencer and Harmer, *Brigham Young at Home,* p. 229.
21. Ibid., p. 147.
22. Ibid., p. 149-50.
23. Ibid., p. 167.
24. Ibid., p. 154.
25. Ibid., p. 164.

26. Gates and Widtsoe, *Life Story*, p. 276.
27. Preston Nibley, *Brigham Young*, p. 379.
28. Ibid., p. 380.
29. Ibid., p. 382.
30. *CCH,* 5:19.
31. Ibid., 5:22.
32. Arrington, *American Moses,* p. 296-97.
33. Journal History of Brigham Young, 11 June 1864, Church Archives.
34. Preston Nibley, *Brigham Young*, p. 383.
35. Journal History of Brigham Young, 25 October 1863. Church Archives.
36. Journal History of Brigham Young, 21 July 1864, Church Archives.
37. Preston Nibley, *Brigham Young*, p. 386.
38. Gates and Widtsoe, *Life Story*, p. 147-48.
39. Beehive House Historical File, "Catholic Church in Salt Lake City," p. 1.
40. Beehive House Historical File, "Jews in Salt Lake City," pp. 1-3.
41. Cowley, *Wilford Woodruff,* p. 442.
42. *CCH,* 5:157-58.
43. Spencer and Harmer, *Brigham Young at Home,* p. 241-42.
44. Ibid., p. 243.
45. Ibid.

Chapter Sixteen

Brigham Young at Home

Descriptions, family habits, customs, relationships –
Brigham's genius for organization and love –
his homes, his wives, his children

This is a world in which we are to prove ourselves. The lifetime of man is a day of trial, wherein we may prove to God, in our darkness, in our weakness, and where the enemy reigns, that we are our Father's friends, and that we receive light from him and are worthy to be leaders of our children—to become lords of lord, and kings of kings—to have perfect dominion over that portion of our families that will be crowned in the celestial kingdom with glory, immortality, and eternal lives.
Journal of Discourses, 8:61

Elder Lorenzo Snow observed: "Brother Brigham has always been willing to sacrifice all he possesses for the good of the people; that is what gives brother Brigham power with God and power with the people. . . ."[1]

How did he do it all with such amazing skill and care? Brigham was extraordinary, but he was still a human being. Picture him as Richard Burton so vividly drew him:

. . . fifty-nine years of age: he looks about forty-five . . . Scarcely a gray thread appears in his hair, which is parted on the side, light coloured, rather thick, and reaches below the ears with a half curl. . . . The forehead is somewhat narrow, the eyebrows are thin, the eyes between grey and blue, with a calm, composed and somewhat reserved expression . . .

His manner is at once affable and impressive, simple and courteous. . . . He shows no signs of dogmatism, bigotry, or fanaticism. . . . He impresses a stranger with a certain sense of power. . . . He is neither morose nor methodistic, and where occasion requires he can use all the weapons of ridicule to direful effect, and "speak a bit of his mind" in a style which no one forgets. . . . His powers of observation are intuitively strong, and his friends declare him to be gifted with an excellent memory and a perfect judgment of character.[2]

Or, as his fifty-first child, Clarissa, described him:

He had the affection and tenderness of a woman for his family and friends. He was good to look at, and I fail to recall an instance when he was not immaculate in person and dress. He had well-shaped hands and feet, a clear white skin, and blue eyes—the kind that radiate love and tenderness—and a mouth that was firm, commanding the respect of all with whom he came in contact. Few could resist the wonderful personality that made him so beloved of his people. He was of medium height, rather large, with beautiful light brown curly hair, a high brow that was broad and intelligent, a long straight nose, and a chin that denoted character and firmness.[3]

Clarissa maintained that her mother "looked upon him as the embodiment of all that was good and noble."[4] Harriet Amelia Folsom, wife number twenty-five, was always purported to be Brigham's favorite, but when reporters anxiously cornered her after his death, her reply to their questions was firm and serene. "I can't say he had any favorites," she said. "He was equally kind and attentive to all in his lifetime, and left each surviving wife an equal legacy." Asked, "do you still believe in polygamy?" she responded, "Certainly I do. If polygamy was once right, it is still right. There is no reason why a polygamous marriage may not be as happy as the ordinary marriage, if it is entered understandingly."[5]

How many wives did Brigham Young have? Fifty-five women were sealed to him: sixteen who had children by him, nine who did not, and, as close as can be judged, thirty who were sealed to him for eternity only. Sealings in the temple at that time could be of several kinds; the most common was for both time and eternity, but a woman could be sealed to a man for eternity only, or sealed to one man for time and another for the eternities to come. Usually this would occur when a woman was sealed to a dead husband for eternity and a living man for this life only. It was also understood that children born to their union, in Biblical fashion, would be thought of as the progeny of the first husband. In this sense, some of Brigham's wives who had been sealed to the Prophet Joseph Smith were made a part of his household for purposes of protection and care, and it has been virtually impossible to ascertain how many he lived with on a conjugal basis.

From June 1842 through May 1844, when the practice of polygamy was first enjoined upon the brethren, Brigham was sealed to four women. Lucy Ann Decker Seeley was his first plural wife and bore him seven children. It was her daughter, Clarissa, who wrote *Brigham Young at Home,* which details so lovingly her father's life. His second plural wife was Augusta Adams Cobb, forty-one years old, who had left her husband and five of her children in Boston, coming to Nauvoo with two of her children, one of whom died on the way. On the same day he married Harriet Elizabeth Cook, who was only nineteen and had no relatives in the Church. She bore Brigham one son. Clara Decker, Lucy's sixteen-year-old sister, became his fourth plural wife. She was one of the three women in the original pioneer company.

From September 1844, following Joseph's death, through May 1845, Brigham was sealed secretly to fifteen women. These sealings were recorded in code in his diary, and have only recently been deciphered and documented. Four of these—Emily Dow Partridge, Louisa Beaman, Olive Gray Frost, and Eliza R. Snow—had been sealed to the Prophet Joseph for eternity; therefore, they were sealed to Brigham for time only, as was Margaret Pierce Whitesides, widowed now, but sealed to her husband for eternity.

Mary Elizabeth Rollins, wife of a non-Mormon, was also sealed to Joseph in 1842, then married to Brigham for time in 1844.

Louisa Beaman, who married Brigham in 1846, bore him five children, none of whom lived through infancy. Emily and Brigham had seven, one of whom died as a child. Margaret bore Brigham one son—his fiftieth child—whose name was Brigham, after his father. Clarissa Chase Ross married Brigham at the age of thirty-two and bore him four children. Mary H. Pierce, Margaret's sister, was sealed to Brigham in January of 1846 and died little more than a year later, in March of 1847. Susan Snively was married to Brigham for thirty-three years before his death, but bore him no children. Emmeline Free married him at the age of nineteen; they had ten children together. Mary Ann Clark and Diana Chase were both childless, as was Eliza Snow, who was married to Brigham "in name only" and never bore a child of her own. Clarissa Blake married him at the age of fifty-nine; Rebecca Holman married him at the age of twenty and died four years later.

After the completion of the Nauvoo Temple, Brigham married nineteen women during a five-week period from January 7 to February 6, 1846. Seven of these were older than himself, among them fifty-nine-year-old Phebe Morton Angell, Mary Ann's mother, and sixty-nine-year-old Abigail Marks Works, mother of his first wife who died of consumption. Fourteen of these women had been married before; three were to divorce him, as did three of the earlier group, although Susa Young claimed that only one woman, Mary Jane Bigelow (her own mother's sister), ever willingly left Brigham, with the noted exception of Ann Eliza. Only two of this group of women bore him children: Zina one daughter, and Margaret Alley, two children.

During the homeless period, while crossing the plains, Brigham was sealed to an additional four women: Jane Terry Young (previously married to a Young not related to Brigham), who died four days after the sealing; sixteen-year-old Lucy Bigelow and her nineteen-year-old sister Mary Jane, who were sealed to him at Winter Quarters; and Sarah Malin, sealed to him when he returned to Iowa after entering the valley. Both she and Mary Jane later left him.

During the Utah years, Brigham married five additional women in the 1850s, four in the 1860s (including Amelia Folsom, the fabled beauty and favorite, and the infamous Ann Eliza Webb), and two in the 1870s. In August of 1852, when Orson Pratt first publicly preached polygamy, ending the uneasy period of secrecy, Brigham was fifty-one years old with thirty-one children and three more to be born that year. Seven of his forty-two plural wives had died; six had left him. At the time of his death fifteen years later, nineteen had died and ten had received divorces. Only sixteen of the fifty-five mothered his fifty-seven children, and six of these had only one child each. Eleven of these women survived him, and none of them, even the very young ones, married again.[6]

Brigham never concealed his reluctance to enter polygamy; as late as 1859, in an interview with Horace Greeley, who asked if the plurality of wives was acceptable to Mormon women, he bluntly replied, "They could not be more averse to it than I was when it was first revealed to us as the Divine will. I think they generally accept it, as I do, as the will of God."[7]

Testimonies from the women themselves matched or exceeded his own. Margaret Pierce, who married Brigham as a young widow, revealed her feelings in her autobiographical sketch. Speaking of the death of her first husband, she wrote:

> But God saw fit to send a great wave of sorrow over my hitherto happy life, and after a few months of blissful married life my dear husband was stricken. . . and died in February 1845, leaving me a widow at the age of twenty years.

Then, concerning plural marriage she wrote:

> The principle of plural marriage as we understood it was revealed for the purpose of exalting the human race. But, through the inability of many to understand the laws that govern it, much uncalled for unhappiness has arisen. We do not think this is caused by any defect in the marriage system, but rather from a want of knowledge in those who were disposed to practice it.

And believing as we did that polygamy was essential to our salvation and being left without a natural protector, I embraced the principle and was married to Brigham Young in 1854. I gave birth to a son whom we named Morris Brigham Young.

. . . It was a grand school of education for those who had embraced it . . . . The children of those polygamous parents loved each other as though of one mother, and that same love continues with them and will through life. They were taught the true and righteous principles of God, and love and truth dwelt in their hearts. I have lived with this wonderful family from 1849 and can truthfully say that I have never had an unpleasant word with any of them.[8]

It was Margaret who would take the children of the family and teach them special songs and dances to perform on Brigham's birthday each year, when a grand celebration would be held. Clarissa remembered one year when her father was presented with a large, elaborate "hair wreath" of flowers woven from the heads of every member of the family.[9]

Emily Dow Partridge, widow of the Prophet Joseph, who bore seven of Brigham's children, wrote:

It was when Brother Pifer had charge of President Young's temporal affairs. He called to see me one day and said Sister Clara D. Young had requested him to look after me and see that I did not lack the comforts of life. He expressed some surprise that one wife should take such an interest in another wife in the same family. Well take them all together, President Young had about as good a family as could be found, and as far as I know the best of feelings exists among them at the present time. We have had our ups and downs. Our trials have been for good, and the longer we live, and the older we grow, we can see that we have no cause to feel sorrowful, but every reason to thank the Lord for his mercies and kind care that has been over us; and that He has deigned to guide us in the right way. Our path may not always have been strewn with thornless roses, but we have been the recipients of many favors. And as for myself, I feel more and more thankful that I took the course that God marked out for me, although to look ahead at the time things looked very dark. And I know that my children will honor and bless my name.[10]

This uncommon amiability was due, in part, to the selfless efforts of the wives themselves. Susa recorded:

> The wives of Brigham Young lived together without outer friction or violent disagreement so far as any of us children knew. That they were all equally congenial could not be expected for they were not weaklings and all "had minds of their own." But their differences, if and when they existed, were their own affairs and were settled amongst themselves without disturbing in the slightest degree the serene tranquility of our family life. They were ladies, and lived their lives as such.[11]

Clarissa pointed out the talents and strengths of the individual wives. Eliza and Zina gave much of their time in building up the Church, though Zina was also the family "doctor" with a store of medicines (camphor, ipecac, hot drops, mustard plasters, and composition tea) and a natural gift for healing. She also was put in charge of the detested cocoonery and mulberry orchard, overcoming her repugnance and tending the cocoons with her own hands. Susan Snively was the best cook of all the women, and for many years had care of the Forest Farm. Eliza Burgess was a wonderful housekeeper and a skilled seamstress and would sew dainty clothing for Clarissa when, as a child, she visited her in her Provo home. When Clarissa was married, Eliza made her wedding cake. Harriet Cook was the schoolteacher, and Clarissa remembered that she would always keep her busy cutting carpet rags. Each woman took care of her own apartment and children, and then had other tasks assigned to her. Aunt Twiss was queen of the Lion House kitchen.

Clarissa's own mother, Lucy Ann Decker, was in charge of the Beehive House, where she boarded the men who worked on the estate, as well as caring for her own seven children. Each day she prepared and served several meals: breakfast for the men at seven, the family at eight, Brigham at ten (he ate but two meals a day, breakfast at ten and dinner at four), a noon meal for the men, a noon meal for the family, and two evening meals—unless there were guests, which happened frequently, and refreshments were required. Once when her daughter asked her how she handled all that was required of her, she replied, "If your father wasn't the most wonderful man in the world, I couldn't do it." Clarissa added,

> She adored Father, but there wasn't a jealous hair in her head. Some of the other wives undoubtedly were jealous at times, but Mother never was. She had previously made a most unhappy marriage, and the contrast between that and her later happiness was so great that she appreciated it to the fullest extent.[12]

Clarissa's aunt, Clara, was best known for her loving, sympathetic nature. She had four children of her own, but also reared the two of Margaret Alley's after her death. "She also had under her protection at the Lion House her own younger sister, a woman and her son by the name of Farnham, and a young Indian girl whom they called Sally."[13]

"Not all these good women were sweet-tempered or unselfish—not by any means," wrote Susa. "They were just mortals. But there were enough of them who radiated love and comradeship in ever-widening circles to humanise the group." Expanding further on the subject, she explained:

> If all wanted to be happy, each must share in unselfish contribution to family harmony; at least they all tried, and all succeeded, as far as my brothers and sisters or I can remember. The joy, the happiness of their lives came through the delightful upspringing growth in spiritual beauty, in the confidence and friendship of each other, and in the reverence and love manifested by their intelligent, God-fearing husband, Brigham Young, who knew the difficult upward path they each were treading because of the strain which justice and mercy put upon him in the adjustments and readjustments necessary for himself.[14]

The constant adjustments, the drain upon inner, as well as outer resources, is not easy to imagine. J. Sterling Morton, who visited Salt Lake in February of 1871, wrote: "Saturday, February 18, 1871: Brigham Young called upon and 'interviewed' for more than one hour. He is a man of wonderful will, forecast, judgment and tact." And, a week later:

> Brigham Young's carriage called for me at 3:30 p.m. Rode with him
> to see Sister Emoline and nine children. Then went to his house and
> was introduced to eleven Mrs. Youngs and thirty young Youngs.
> Dined at 4:30 p.m. About seventy persons, young and old, gathered
> at the family board. The scene was ante-deluvian.[15]

Brigham's genius for organization and detail served him well.
His life and the routine of his family were carefully structured.
But that alone would not account for the spirit of his home life
which is so constantly acknowledged. Susa's words ring with a
depth and sincerity which cannot be belied:

> In all my life in that beloved home I never heard my father speak an
> unkind or irritable word to one of his wives. I never heard a quarrel
> between my father's wives. . . . I never heard one of my father's wives
> chastise or correct another wife's children. I have heard the children
> quarrel, naturally, but very little of that indeed, for we were not a con-
> tentious family. Much less did I ever hear or see anything but the
> utmost courtesy and kindliness between my father and his wives.
> Correct his children he did, but each with that dignity and delibera-
> tion that neither humiliated the child nor lowered his own self-
> respect. . . . No other fact of father's life was so profound a proof of
> his true nobility and greatness as his life at home and the influence
> which he radiated there. He was ever present in spirit, and we were
> not surprised, certainly never alarmed, to see him at any unexpected
> moment or place. [16]

Ellis Shipp, who lived for an extended time in Brigham's
household before her own marriage, observed that

> here there were no discords. This home circle was the pattern of com-
> fort, order, and refinement—he abode of love, sweet peace, and divine
> progression, the blessed offspring of a supreme faith, noble industry,
> and beautiful unselfishness. There was no lavish expenditure and yet
> no need was unprovided for.[17]

Only such consistency, based on high and pure principles,
could have moved Susa to observe and record:

His beautiful courtesy was never more in evidence than when he approached any one of his wives whom he loved and who loved him. Especially was that so when in the company of Mother Young, whose health was rather poor and who had born the heat and burden of the day for him and with him. To her he paid exquisite attention, quiet, composed but sincere. His attitude of consideration towards her was reflected in that of every other wife and child he had. . . . He was so eminently successful in his home life that no one ever related to him, or who benefited from his friendship, ever failed to return in full the measure he gave of love, heaped and running over.[18]

There was an element of magic in being one of Brigham Young's children. The houses he built were filled with features to enrich the spirit and imagination of young people. His "Mansion" or "White House" was the first impressive house he built, situated on East South Temple, overlooking the whole of the city. Mary Ann Angell lived here most of her life, with the exception of a few years spent at the Beehive House; her funeral was held in the White House. The eagle gate was built on South Temple, or Brigham Street, in 1859 and used as a toll gate to City Creek Canyon; it also served as an entrance of sorts to Brigham's estates which spread on either side of it, with the Beehive and Lion houses to the west, as well as the tithing office and storehouse, the bunkhouse, barn and blacksmith shop and, further down the block, Temple Square. On the east side of the gate stood the White House, the schoolhouse, corrals, wood and smokehouses, a lamb barn, and a carpenter's shop.

Other homes which belonged to Brigham and were used by various members of his family included a home on Main Street, which once belonged to Jedediah M. Grant; a home for two wives where the Hansen Planetarium now stands on State Street; a house called the Empey home on South Temple; a home next to the Salt Lake Theatre on State Street; one home in Soda Springs, Idaho, one in Provo, and two in St. George. There was also the Forest Farm, where Brigham conducted his silk worm experiment and planted a variety of trees including ash, locust, walnut, plum, apple, peach, pear, and cherry. He planted alfalfa, sugar beets and a wide variety of vegetables, including experimental crops. "At the 1860 fair sponsored by the Deseret Agricultural and Manufacturing Society, Brigham Young won more prizes than anyone. His apples and strawberries took four awards. Two unusual prizes were Chinese sugar and chufa nut, an edible African root."[19]

The Beehive House was completed in 1854. Mary Ann Angell lived there until 1860, Lucy Ann Decker until after Brigham's death, when the house was willed to her. The Beehive symbol, intertwined with the name *Deseret,* has deeper and more ancient applications than most people realize. Hugh Nibley explains that the

> founders of the Second Civilization of Egypt had the bee as the symbol of their land, their king, and their empire. . . . The bee sign was always regarded by the Egyptians as very sacred . . . the archaic and ritual designation of the bee was *deseret,* a "word of power" too sacred to be entrusted to the vulgar, being one of the keys to "the king's secret." . . . The Jaredites in their wanderings took with them "a honeybee" which they called in their language deseret, as well as "hives of bees." In certain editions of the Book of Mormon . . . the word *deseret* is capitalized, for the editors have recognized that it is really a title. . . . In that case, one might be justified . . . in seeing in Deseret the national symbol or as it were the totem of Jared's people. . . . It is to say the least a very picturesque coincidence that when the Lord's people migrated to a promised land in these latter days, they called the land Deseret and took for the symbol of their society and their government the honeybee.[20]

The Lion House, built in 1856, had a large crouching lion placed on the portico over the front entrance—symbolic of "The Lion of the Lord," as Brigham was called. As early as 1844 this title was applied to him. After one of his powerful sermons in Nauvoo, Wilford Woodruff wrote in his diary, "The lion roared again tonight."[21] It is interesting to note that

> during the early years in the Utah Territory the church members lovingly gave appellations to the General Authorities. Jedediah M. Grant, Salt Lake City's first mayor, called himself "Mormon

Thunder" when he was delivering one of his fiery speeches. In March 1851 the *Deseret News* printed the following appellations for the First Presidency and the Twelve as reviewed by W. W. Phelps:

Presidency

Brigham Young	the Lion of the Lord
Heber C. Kimball	the Herald of Grace
Willard Richards	the Keeper of the Rolls

The Twelve

Orson Hyde	the Olive-branch of Israel
Parley P. Pratt	the Archer of Paradise
Orson Pratt	the Gauge of Philosophy
Wilford Woodruff	the Banner of the Gospel
John Taylor	the Champion of Right
George A. Smith	the Entablature of Truth
Amasa M. Lyman	the Aegis [protector] of Justice
Ezra T. Benson	the Helmet of Righteousness
Charles C. Rich	the Measuring Rule of Patience
Lorenzo Snow	the Mirror of Hope
Erastus Snow	the Evergreen Spring of the Mountain
Franklin D. Richards	the Spy-glass of Faith [22]

The Beehive House was where Brigham did his official entertaining. In the Lion House several of his wives lived at any one time in bedroom/sitting room apartments. Here, in the front parlor, Brigham held family prayers:

> The custom of evening prayer-time in the Lion House was as fixed as the stars. About seven o'clock the rhythmic sound of the prayer-bell was heard as father's hand lifted it in regular lightstroke counts . . . a hymn or two was joyously sung . . . then came the quiet prayer of gratitude and adoration.[23]

After prayers, family councils were sometimes held, or Brigham would linger to talk over current events with wives or older children who had no other commitments. Often he would turn to his daughters and ask for music, and they would gather around the piano and sing his favorites: "Hard Times Come Again No More," or "Auld Lang Syne."

The picture is idyllic, but as Brigham's counsel to his family reveals, there were challenges in making the ideal a consistent reality. In a "Letter for the Perusal of My Family," he wrote:

> I do not wish to complain of you without a cause, but at prayer time lately I have noticed that one has been visiting, another has gone to see Mary, and another to see Emily, etc., etc. My family . . . will acknowledge that my time is precious to me as theirs is to them. When the time appointed for our family devotion and prayer comes, I am expected to be there; and no public business, no matter how important, has been able to influence me to forgo the fulfillment of this sacred duty which I owe to you, to myself, and to God.

> My counsel, which I expect you to receive kindly, is to be home by six-thirty each evening so as to be ready to bow down before the Lord to make . . . acknowledgements to Him for His kindness and mercy and long-suffering towards us. Your strict attendance to my wishes in this respect will give joy to the heart of your Husband and Father.[24]

It is amazing to think that Brigham could organize and control so many diverse and distinct human beings; that he did so with patience, love, and the power of example seems evident.

Daily routines were admirably structured. Lights were usually out by ten o'clock, and everyone up by half past seven in the morning. In good weather the boys slept on the lower porch, the girls on the upper, giggling and telling ghost stories until late into the night. When they were forced to sleep indoors the windows were left open, even in winter, for Brigham believed in the importance of good ventilation at all times. He was always very cautious of fire, and, despite his multitude of cares and responsibilities, would make the rounds each night with his candle, checking the sitting rooms "to see that there were no live coals on the hearth."[25]

Clarissa tells of eating breakfast with her father in the morning where there was corn-meal mush and milk, hot doughnuts and syrup, codfish gravy and squabs from the pigeon house. Brigham drank his own herb brew of composition tea. As he grew older, he began to prefer a more simple diet of buttermilk and Johnny cake, with water to drink. Sometimes Clarissa would go with him to the barber or to meet an immigrant train which had just arrived:

> When he went out he wore a rather high hat, a Prince Albert coat, and either a green cape or a grey shawl over his shoulders. In the summertime he wore light cream prunella cloth suits—sack coats and trousers, with white shirt and neck cloth and a panama hat.[26]

Brigham never left the tithing office grounds, where the early wagon trains unloaded, without being sure each new family had a place to go and someone to care for them that night. Each bishop was assigned a quota of immigrants to be responsible for, and those who had arrived earlier were generous in sharing and helping the newcomers along.

On Saturday afternoons, the family often went to the warm sulphur springs a mile from their home to bathe. Brigham enjoyed entertainment and believed in the pattern of eight hours to work, eight hours to rest, eight hours to relax from the stresses and strains of the day. Picnics were always one of his favorite activities, as well as dances and the theatre. He enjoyed having guests come to dinner, and he was always ready to enjoy music of any uplifting kind. Christmas was a time for modest celebration. The children would receive nuts and raisins, molasses candy, gumdrops, or peppermint sticks. In their stockings each received one toy and items of clothing: scarves, mittens, stockings, garters, and wristers. Pioneer Day was probably the most celebrated day in the valley, with bands, choirs, young girls dressed in white carrying banners, parades and speechmaking, and picnics in the mountains.

Brigham built a large porch on the west side of the Lion House fitted with all sorts of gymnastic equipment: trapezes, vaulting poles, wands, hoops, jumping ropes, and back boards. Many of the girls took dancing lessons or were given opportunities to perform in dramatic productions. Brigham created a "font"—a small pool where the cold canyon water ran constantly. Here the children bathed and played, with separate dressing rooms to protect privacy.

For an extended period of time Karl Maeser, unable to support himself with teaching, acted as private tutor to Brigham's household—which included many who were not members of his immediate family, such as Ellis Reynolds (Shipp), who was to become the second woman doctor in Utah. Brigham considered Maeser the noblest educator in the Church and was grateful for his influence in the lives of his children. Ellis described that rare influence well:

> As a pupil of Professor Maeser how blessed was my life! Every moment in his presence seemed a benediction, so great was his spiritual influence, his intuitive uplift to all that was pure and divine. He was by nature spiritualistic. His implicit faith in *The Living God* was an integral part of his being, indeed the dominant spark of his magnetic influence over mind and morals.[27]

At the north end of the Beehive House was a family store, run by John Haslam and provided with a wide variety of household supplies. Each wife had a running account here, as well as at the ZCMI, where fancier items could be purchased. Children could "shop" at the store, but their lists needed to first be approved. "Whenever I wanted a list of things from the town store I would go to Father rather than to Mother for permission to get them," Clarissa wrote.

> It was a trifle easier to obtain his consent, and he didn't bother to scrutinize my list quite so carefully as Mother did. One day I brought for his approval a long list of things that began with "corn plasters." Father glanced at it and then smiling at me quizzically said, "Well, daughter, if corn plasters is at the top, I guess the rest of it must be all right, so just go ahead." Thereafter I put everything I could think of on my list before I brought it to him.[28]

Brigham had ten daughters who were teenagers at the same

time and called themselves "The Big Ten." Brigham was in the habit of presenting them often with little gifts which might please them. Clarissa tells the story of an occasion when he had given each girl a beautiful grosgrain ribbon sash. Phoebe had set hers out on her bed, along with her dress, gloves and pocketbook, in preparation for a dance. When she entered her room after dinner the sash was missing. Indignant, she went in search of her father. "I know Aunt Eliza has taken it," she claimed.

"All right, daughter, we'll see," Brigham replied, and detained Eliza on her way to the prayer room to ask concerning the sash. "Have you seen anything of it?" he asked.

"Yes, President Young," she replied. 'I felt that you wouldn't approve of anything so frivolous for your girls so I put it away."

"Sister Eliza," said Brigham, "I gave the girls those ribbons, and I am the judge of what is right and wrong for my girls to wear. Phoebe is to have her sash."[29]

Brigham was always accessible to his children; some of them recorded that they would rather go to him with their problems than to their mothers, because of his great tenderness with them. On May 21, 1874, George Cannon Young said of his grandfather: "Brigham Young always had an open door policy with his children. The door was always open to them. He respected them and they respected him."[30] Susa tells of one occasion when Brigham, learning that one of his children was ill, dismissed a council meeting, "declaring to the assembly that the meeting could wait, but his sick child could not."[31]

His understanding of his children and their needs extended even to a mature level. This great leader was so just, so true, so genuine in his domestic relations that those who came into the household to assist, either within the confines of the house itself or without, as helpers in all the many-sided domestic, farm, and field activities which marked his wide circle of home life, felt that each "belonged" to the family. Each man, each woman became a very part of Brigham Young's life and was interwoven into the domestic fabric forever. Two of his daughters married his business manager, another married the telegraph clerk in his office, another his teamster, while still another married a salesman in the shop.[32]

Brigham gave homes to his daughters as well as to his sons. Susa gives us insight into his thinking on the matter:

> I think that father settled his wives into homes of their own in his later years to correct what he esteemed to be a mistake of his early judgment. For when he gave me the deed to my first home in the city, in 1876, he told me that he had made a mistake. If he had his life to live over again, he said, he would give every wife a home of her own and give her the deed to it; for that was every wife's right, and nothing more than justice. He cautioned me not to deed or give away my home, not to anyone; but to remember that a home was a woman's first possession. He brought out and showed to me at that time, the plot of the big tract of land called the Upper Garden, east and north of the Lion House, where he had marked sites for homes for all his children. Especially was he solicitous over his daughters.[33]

Brigham Young had fifty-seven children, eleven of whom died before maturity. Of the forty-six remaining, twenty-nine were daughters, seventeen sons. "The letters of a person," Thomas Jefferson said, "especially one whose business has been chiefly transacted by letters, form the only full and genuine journal of his life."[34] Brigham's letters to his sons give wonderful insight into the thoughts and feelings which motivated him, and into the relationships he shared with his boys.

> Brigham Young's desire for his children was that "they not only walk in the footsteps of their father, but take a course to enjoy life, health, and vigor while they live, and the spirit of intelligence from God, that they may far outstrip their father in long life, and in the good they will perform in their day." And more specifically, "I wish my sons to far exceed me in goodness and virtue."[35]

Joseph, Brigham's eldest, son of Mary Ann Angell, served in the Territorial Legislature for many years and was ordained an apostle in 1864. Brigham Jr. was a mission president, an apostle, and counselor in the First Presidency. John served as a counselor to Brigham, later to the Twelve Apostles, after his father's death.

He also gained great influence in financial circles due to his extensive involvement in railroad construction. Willard became the first
native-born Utahn and the first Mormon to enroll in West Point,
appointed at the age of nineteen by John R. Park, president of the
Deseret University as the "best scholar and strongest boy at the
University."[36] In his military career, he supervised important river
and harbor improvements along the Mississippi and Missouri
rivers, presided over two colleges, and became superintendent of
Church building. He returned to the Academy in 1879 as an assistant professor. Feramorz was appointed to the naval academy at
Annapolis, and Don Carlos served as a member of the State
Legislature and was also Church architect for many years. Eleven
of his sons served missions for the Church.[37]

Brigham explicated a profound principle to his son, Oscar,
who was serving a mission:

> If there be any difference in missions probably the first mission that a
> man takes has more influence on his future than any that he may take in
> after life. On his first mission he lays the foundation and adopts the prin-
> ciples which are to guide him through his future career, and it has sel-
> dom been the case that a young man who has been dilatory and careless
> while upon his first mission has ever recovered the ground he then lost.[38]

Oscar was effusive in response to one of his father's letters:

> [Oh] the joye that it gave me to resived a lettear from my Father . . . If
> God gives me powear I will returne a beatere man than any one in the
> City of Greate Salt Lake thought when I leafte . . . There is a good
> meny of the Elders that will returne some of which are going to make
> grate men in this kingdom they are them which have lived the relinen
> [religion] of Jesus Christ the Survents of the moste High. The Brothen
> teleme that I muste not preach to you. They say that you know all that
> I can teale you and a greadel more but then it is borne in me.[39]

To Don Carlos, newly arrived in New York to study engineer-
ing and architecture, Brigham wrote:

> As you advance in life you will find every position and occupation sur-

rounded by its peculiar temptations, the great strength and bulwark against all of which is prayer to our Heavenly Father. Cultivate this spirit and you will find that it should be a wall of fire around you, and your glory in the midst of you. In its practice you will find a safeguard against the wiles of the adversary, and every good resolution will be fortified by it, and every seductive influence will lose its power to annoy you . . . Our character is not entirely our individual property. It belongs partly to our neighbors and we have no right to shake their confidence in us and in mankind generally by acts inconsistent with the good name we have established.[40]

The scope of his advice touched on every possible subject, such as this counsel to his son Alfales:

I noticed a marked improvement in the plainness of your handwriting. I am very glad to see it, and hope you will continue to take pains to improve. No one will think you any less a good lawyer because you are a plain writer, but rather seeing the clearness of your handwriting will judge therefrom that you are clear in your thoughts and perceptions, two great requisites for a successful lawyer.[41]

To his son Morris, discouraged by his inability to learn the Hawaiian language, he wrote encouragingly:

Your difficulty in learning the language will disappear, I hope, by the study which I know full well you will give it. Never allow your courage to fail you; man's greatest works have been done by men of patience, perseverance, and a determined will which would acknowledge no defeat, rather than by those gifted with a natural ability which made success easy but who lacked the tenaciousness of purpose. Then, my boy, never say fail, but work on in the way you have started and your reward is certain.[42]

To Feramorz in Annapolis, he wrote of a philosophy of life he held dear:

If a man have to drive the plow let him do it well; if only to cut bolts, make good ones; if to blow the bellows, keep the iron hot. It is our attention to our daily duties that makes us men, and if we devote our lives to the service of heaven, our faithfulness therein will eventually fit us with our Heavenly Father in eternity to dwell. Aspire to acquire knowledge that you may be able to do more good and also to progress in your sphere of life; but remember that you will win only by trust in the Lord, by present contentment and by doing faithfully that which you have in hand. This I have confidence you will do. No one advances who imagines himself too good or too big for present duties. Such a one is apt to sink into a smaller and a smaller place. In the long run, and for the most part, men are found in the places they have fitted themselves to fill. It is one of the most cherished hopes of my life to see my sons by faithfulness, diligence, and devotion to God and their duties, fit themselves to be able ministers of salvation to the children of men. This should be the great object of our lives.[43]

With tender insight Brigham observed that "if children knew the feelings of their parents when they did good or evil, 'it would have a salutary influence upon their lives; but no child can possibly know this, until it becomes a parent. *I am compassionate therefore toward children.*'"

I do not believe in making my authority as a husband or a father known by brute force; but by a superior intelligence—by showing them that I am capable of teaching them. . . . If the Lord has placed me to be head of a family, let me be so in all humility and patience, not as a tyrannical ruler, but as a faithful companion, an indulgent and affectionate father, a thoughtful and unassuming superior; let me be honoured in my station through faithful diligence, and be fully capable, by the aid of God's Spirit, of filling my office in a way to effect the salvation of all who are committed to my charge.[44]

He accomplished to an incredible, thrilling degree his noble aim.

"One knew instantly when he was in the room," his daughter, Susa, wrote. "But his penetrating influence had been there all the time, resting peacefully over everything and everybody so that no one was surprised to see him enter. *His presence was like light and sunshine and 'benediction after prayer.'*"[45]

Notes

1. *JD,* 4:246.

2. Richard F. Burton, *The City of the Saints and Across the Rocky Mountains to California* (New York: Alfred A. Knopf, 1861), p. 262-64.

3. Spencer and Harmer, *Brigham Young at Home,* p. 16-17.

4. Ibid., p. 16.

5. Harold Schindler, "In Another Time," Salt Lake Tribune, p. J2, Beehive House Historical Files.

6. Stanley S. Ivins, "Notes on Mormon Polygamy," *Western Humanities Review,* Summer 1956.

7. Jeffrey Ogden Johnson, "Determining and Defining 'Wife': The Brigham Young Households," *Dialogue: A Journal of Mormon Thought,* p. 59.

8. Margaret Pierce Young, Autobiography (1880), Church Archives, p. 7-8, 13-15.

9. Spencer and Harmer, *Brigham Young at Home,* p. 197.

10. Emily Dow Partridge Young, "Written for the Anniversary of President Brigham Young's Birthday, 1897," Church Archives.

11. *Life Story,* p. 340-41.

12. Spencer and Harmer, *Brigham Young at Home,* p. 72.

13. Ibid., p. 75.

14. Gates and Widtsoe, *Life Story,* p. 341.

15. Julius Sterling Morton, Diary Extract, 1832-1902, Church Archives.

16. Gates and Widtsoe, *Life Story,* p. 355.

17. McCloud, *Not in Vain,* p. 57.

18. Gates and Widtsoe, *Life Story,* p. 340.

19. "Forest Farm Tidbits," Utah State Historical Society, February 20, 1979, Beehive House Historical File.

20. Hugh Nibley, *Lehi in the Desert and the World of the Jaredites* (Provo, Utah: Religious Studies Center, Brigham Young University, 1979), p. 187-89.

21. "The Lion House: Its Name," p. 2, Beehive House Historical File.

22. Ibid., p. 1-2.

23. Gates and Widtsoe, *Life Story,* p. 333-34.

24. Arrington, *American Moses,* p. 322.

25. Gates and Widtsoe, *Life Story,* p. 336.

26. Spencer and Harmer, *Brigham Young at Home,* p. 19.

27. McCloud, *Not in Vain,* p. 55.

28. Spencer and Harmer, *Brigham Young at Home,* p. 49.

29. Ibid., p. 83-84.

30. "The Big Ten," *Era,* May 1969; Beehive House Historical File.

31. Gates and Widtsoe, *Life Story,* p. 340.

32. Ibid., p. 339.

33. Ibid., p. 353.

34. Jessee, ed., *Letters of Brigham Young to His Sons,* p. xxi-xxii.

35. Ibid., p. xxx.

36. "West Point," Beehive House Historical File.
37. Jessee, *Letters of Brigham Young,* p. xxxiii.
38. Ibid., p xxxi.
39. Ibid., p. 145.
40. Ibid., p. xxxv.
41. Ibid., p. 235.
42. Ibid., p. 249.
43. Ibid., p. 305-6.
44. Ibid., p. xxiv.
45. Gates and Widtsoe, *Life Story,* p. 337.

Chapter Seventeen

For the Kingdom's Sake

Death of Heber C. Kimball – tabernacle constructed – Brigham's genius in overseeing construction of Salt Lake Temple – Relief Society reorganized – Retrenchment – first Sunday School – University of Deseret – Brigham Young Academy at Provo – Deseret Alphabet – Zion's Cooperative Mercantile – the United Order – prosecution for "lascivious cohabitation" – death of George A. Smith

---

We must watch and pray, and look well to our walk and conversation, and live near to our God, that the love of this world may not choke the precious seed of truth, and feel ready, if necessary, to offer up all things, even life itself, for the Kingdom of Heaven's sake.
Journal of Discourses, 11:111

The *Chicago Times* of February 22, 1871, ran the following description of the famed Mormon colonizer and prophet:

Brigham Young is now seventy years of age. He is of fine physical stature . . . staunchly and compactly built. He stands straight . . . shows no sign of age in his walk. His well-formed mouth gives indication of a great mental energy and indomitable pluck.

Brigham was 5' 10" in height at a time when the average height for men was 5' 7" and 5' 3" for women. B. H. Roberts described him as compactly built and of stately bearing . . . hair light auburn and of soft and fine texture. The forehead was high and broad at the base, the nose slightly aquiline, the eyes full and of a light grey, the mouth well formed and gentle in manner, yet said to be capable of anger that was terrible. In him, indeed, was blended the strong and gentle qualities that go to the making of the highest and truest manhood—your leader of men.[1]

Brigham remained the firm and unquestioned leader of his people until the last day of his life, inspiring and challenging them to the utmost, forming by his own vision and determination a distinct and powerful kingdom, despite the encroachment of worldly influences which increasingly threatened to corrode the purity of his work. Wilford Woodruff, speaking at a Pioneer Day celebration in 1880, said:

On July 24th I drove my carriage with President Young lying on a bed in it into the open valley, the rest of the company following. When we came out of the canyon into full view of the valley I turned the side of my carriage around, open to the west, and President Young arose [leaned up] from his bed and took a survey of the country. While gazing upon the scene before us, he was enwrapped in vision for several minutes. He had seen the valley before in vision and upon this occasion he saw the future glory of Zion and of Israel as they would be planted in the valleys of the mountains. When the vision had passed Brigham Young said, *This is the right place. Drive on.*[2]

The valleys belonged to the Saints by divine decree. When the first territorial governor was appointed in 1857 to replace the true leader of the Latter-day Saints, he was followed by a string of largely disinterested men—fourteen different governors before Brigham Young's death. No wonder the people continued to turn to him for guidance and leadership.

In 1868 Heber C. Kimball died, so Brigham began the last decade of his life without the very real support of this friend, who had been more like a brother to him from his young, awkward, formative days. Heber said before the people in 1857, "I love brother Brigham Young better than I do any woman upon this earth, because my will has run into his, and his into mine."[3]

There were many influences toward change and growth during Brigham's last years, and though sometimes with reluctance or even foreboding, he responded to them.

The amazing elliptical, dome-shaped tabernacle had already become a reality. According to Clarissa's story, Brigham conceived the idea while eating a hard-boiled egg which he cut through endwise and then set it up on toothpicks, intrigued with the design possibilities. He approached Henry Grow, a millwright and bridge builder, to construct it. He figured out the dimensions, with Truman O. Angell, Mary Ann's brother, as architect and William Folsom as his assistant. The building, begun in September, 1865 and first opened for services in 1867, rested on forty-four sandstone piers and was built entirely with wooden pegs and thongs, since nails were so difficult to come by at that time. Today, under its huge unsupported roof it can seat 8,000 people comfortably, often accommodating as many as 10,000. The choir seats have space for three to four hundred people. The magnificent organ which graces the building was constructed by Joseph Ridges, a gifted convert from Australia. Some of the materials for the organ were hauled over four hundred miles, with only native timbers used. Despite alterations for the addition of modern conveniences, the building remains very much as Brigham designed it, though he, if asked who was architect, would have replied:

> "God is the Supreme Architect. We owe all our inspiration, our love of beauty and the knowledge of how to express our views to the Father in Heaven who gives to His children what they ask for and what they need." If the old definition is true, that art is what we feel and science is what we do, Brigham Young was both artist and scientist.[4]

Although the walls of the Salt Lake Temple had reached only a height of twenty-five feet when Brigham died, his influence on the spirit and quality of the building is undeniable. When the walls were only a few feet above the ground, the superintendent of the building came to President Young, disheartened and discouraged:

"Brother Brigham," he said, "I guess we'll have to make a change in our Temple walls. I have been careless, I guess. I find that the men have been occasionally using granite chips in between the blocks to save using so much mortar.

Brigham Young arose, without words, led the way down to the Temple block, found the foundation walls well begun, and the workmen filling in between the great granite blocks with chipped bits of granite only, leaving out the mortar which would cement them and thus solidify the whole.

"This Temple," he rebuked the builders, "is to stand throughout the Millennium. Can you not understand the decay and destruction which would come with the cracking and settling of the massive structure which is to rest upon these walls?"

Two or more tiers of blocks were painfully and slowly dug out, and carefully laid up again. There was no more careless work done on those walls. "Build not for to-day nor tomorrow, but for all eternity," was his constant teaching, both in temporal and spiritual forces.[5]

On another occasion the architect approached the President:

"Brother Brigham," he said, "we have made a serious if not fatal mistake in all our plans. We have planned this whole building without adequate chimneys for heating. What on earth will we do to heat all the halls and rooms in the winter time? We will have to tear part of the walls out, won't we? What shall we do?" Brigham Young sat quietly listening and considering. It was before the day of central heating. After a pause, he said: "Go on, Brother Angell. When the time comes to heat it, there will be a way provided!" So it proved; for when the Temple was completed a central heating plant, two blocks away, furnished the necessary warmth.[6]

As he strove to more perfectly organize the kingdom, Brigham began with the women, reviving the institution established by Joseph Smith in Nauvoo. He gave this "mission" to Eliza R. Snow, who, in 1866, began to establish branches of the Relief Society in every ward, until it was made uniform and universal throughout the stakes of the Church. This work naturally expanded. Suffrage societies were organized; women's co-operative stores and a Woman's Exchange were established. Nursing classes were instituted in every ward, and an organized attempt was made to encourage and assist women to go east and study medicine, that they might return as physicians prepared to minister to their sisters. Eliza R. Snow stressed how vital this training was: "so that we can have our own practitioners, instead of having gentlemen practitioners. In ancient times we know that women officiated in this department, and why should it not be so now?"[7]

Ellis Shipp, despite Eliza's urgings that she study medicine and the seeming confirmation of her patriarchal blessing, still desired the benediction of the man she thought of as her "beloved, her honored foster father."[8] He received her personally and listened while she recounted her hopes and fears. Then he stood, walked over and took her hand in his own. "I say go, Ellis," he told her, his keen gaze holding her own. "Go, and God bless you."[9]

In keeping with his awareness of the intrinsic strength in the female sex, Brigham turned next to organizing the young women— and what better place to start than with his own daughters? He was concerned to see his girls following the fashions of the times: bustles, ruffles, shingled hair, and the mincing gait of the sixties. He knew the "retrenchment" he was asking would be a sacrifice for young minds and spirits; it was proper that his own family should lead out.

Eliza again became his counselor and assistant as the project materialized. He requested the assistance of the mothers as well as their daughters, and, on November 28, 1869, they met in the parlor of the Lion House to organize the Retrenchment Association. He warned against the "silly rivalry" that induced women to compete with one another in the acquiring of showy and costly possessions, which at times forced families into debt and made women slaves to petty fashions and desires. He had seen where this kind of wordliness would lead, and deeply desired something higher for them. "There is need for the young daughters of Israel to get a living testimony of the truth. I wish our girls to obtain a knowledge of the gospel for themselves," he explained.

I want you to vote to retrench in your dress, in your tables, in your speech, wherein you have been guilty of silly, extravagant speeches and light-mindedness of thought. Retrench in everything that is not good and beautiful. *Not to make yourselves unhappy, but to live so that you may be truly happy in this life and the life to come.*[10]

In 1888, the name of the society was changed to the Young Ladies Mutual Improvement Association, and it became a charter member of the National Council of Women and the International Council of Women. In 1974, the designation became simply that of Young Women.

Six years later, in the summer of 1875, Brigham organized the young men of the Church, calling Junius, the son of Daniel H. Wells, to head the work, with the following instructions:

We want to have our young men enrolled and organized throughout the Church, so that we shall know who and where they are, so that we can put our hands upon them at any time for any service that may be required. We want them to hold meetings where they will stand up and speak—get into the habit of speaking—and of bearing testimony. These meetings are to be for our young men . . . for their mutual improvement. There is your name: The Young Men's Mutual Improvement Soci—Association.[11]

In 1849, Richard Ballantyne had organized the first Sunday school in the valley, which was attended by children of many of the leading families in the Church. Others were started up, but with no central organization or authority. In 1866, George Q. Cannon, a secretary of Brigham's, published a magazine called the *Juvenile Instructor,* aimed at assisting young people of Sunday school age. This perhaps prompted Brigham to organize what was called the Parent Sunday School Union, changed in 1872 to the Deseret Sunday School Union, with Elder Cannon as president. A year following Brigham's death, in August of 1878, John Taylor organized the Primary Association.

In 1850, only three years after the Saints entered the Valley, the "University of Deseret" was established. In 1855 Congress issued a land grant, but there were no funds and no public buildings, so the first classes were held in the home of Julia Ives Pack, with a fee of eight dollars per quarter. The school later moved to the upper room of the Council House, and accepted students of both sexes; indeed, it was called a "Parent School," and was intended for the training of heads of families, as well. Brigham himself was among the pupils. "I want to have schools," he said,

> to entertain the minds of the people and to draw them out to learn the arts and sciences. Send the old children to school and the young ones also; there is nothing I would like better than to learn chemistry, botany, geology, and mineralogy, so that I could tell what I walk on, the properties of the air I breathe, what I drink, etc.[12]

The scope of Brigham's educational insight is suggested in the many statements he made to the Saints on the subject: "Every true principle, every true science, every art, and the knowledge that men possess, or that they ever did or ever will possess, is from God. We should take pains and pride to . . . rear our children so that the learning and education of the world may be theirs."[13] And to what end? "We try to so live as to gain more information, more light, more command over ourselves . . . until we can comprehend the great principles of existence and eternal progression."[14]

There were many literary and debating societies founded during the early years, but Brigham was frustrated at the delay in establishing serious institutions of learning, due in part to the death or preoccupation of some of the most qualified men, and in part to drought, grasshopper plagues, Indian troubles, and the Utah War, which consumed what time remained from the plain, overwhelming task of colonization—building homes, planting fields and gardens, establishing businesses and industry, and feeding and clothing families.

All the schools of Utah were established as coeducational; the attendance record of 1869 shows 307 males, 239 females. The new university prospered with Daniel H. Wells as chancellor and John R. Park, a graduate of Wesleyan University and a well-known scholar, as president. Brigham made it his business to know every schoolteacher in the valley personally, and explored all new angles and concepts which came to his attention.

Distressed by the influx of non-Mormon miners and business-men who were creating a noticeable division of educational interests, Brigham attempted to fashion a visionary ideal of education into reality. Religious studies, book-learning, and manual work would be offered "in about equal proportions, and all teaching was to be per-meated with a formal attempt to have the pupils understand their relation to their God as well as their duty to their fellow men."[15]

The first such school was established in Provo, called the Brigham Young Academy, and opened August 27, 1876. When he selected the man to be the moving spirit behind the work, Brigham chose well. Karl G. Maeser was a German convert from Saxony, "reared and educated under superior masters in the land of traditional intellectual love." As a teacher he possessed incredi-ble gifts, further empowered by the purity of spirit and dedication to high principles upon which they rested. "Under his superior tutelage," Ellis Reynolds (Shipp) wrote, "I realized a truly great blessing in sharing the immensity of his knowledge, his power to impart the wealth of his intelligence and superior wisdom to the world about him. He helped me to higher ideals in so many ways."[16] He would do likewise for thousands of students after her.

When Dr. Maeser asked Brigham for instructions, the prophet replied simply, "Brother Maeser, whatever you teach, even the multiplication tables, do it with the spirit of the Lord."[17] In his own "masterly definition of education (which was inscribed on the portals of the Utah Building in the California Exposition): 'Education is the power to think clearly, the power to act well in the world's work, and the power to appreciate life.'"[18]

This power, as all others, Brigham desired the Saints to possess.

As Colonel Kane noted, the Mormons had a peculiar fondness for music. From the beginning of the Church's history, exquisite hymns of the most sacred nature were composed, among these W. W. Phelp's "The Spirit of God," William Clayton's "Come, Come,

Ye Saints," and Eliza R. Snow's "O My Father." Bands and orchestras were introduced early into the lives of the Saints. Brigham urged each of his children to learn to play a musical instrument, and there were several pianos and harpsichords in his households; one of his daughters played the harp.

John Tullidge and Professor George Careless both emigrated from Great Britain and blessed the kingdom with their musical gifts, presenting classical performances of excellent quality. Lavinia Careless was Brigham's favorite singer. When she and her husband presented Handel's oratorio, "The Messiah," Brigham took the time to seek him out for instruction on the principle of counterpoint, that he might all the better appreciate the triumphant "Hallelujah Chorus." Brigham had always enjoyed singing himself; music ran deep in his soul.

> But that he should give it the breadth, and freedom of expansion, while yet keeping proper balance between the harmony that lifts the soul and the cheap, vulgar and mechanical music that debases and demoralizes art—this is indeed a tribute to the innate refinement and grace of spirit not often found in rugged men who are both pathfinders and state builders.[19]

Many of Brigham's enterprises could be termed experimental in nature. In an attempt to help the many immigrants from non-English speaking countries, Brigham organized a committee, under direction of the Board of Regents of the University of Deseret, to create a phonetic alphabet. The committee included Parley P. Pratt, Heber C. Kimball, and George D. Watt, who was skilled in shorthand and had transcribed many of the major addresses of Church leaders for the Journal of Discourses. This attempt to make English spelling sensible consisted of thirty-eight characters with sounds broken down into six long vowels, six short vowels, one aspirate ("h" sound) and twenty-one articulate sounds (consonants). "Bancroft described the characters as 'borrowed from the Greek and Book of Mormon characters,'" but actually they were a "Mormon invention."[20]

The result was so successful and complete that articles appeared in the *Deseret News* written in the new alphabet, two elementary readers were produced in 1868, and the entire Book of Mormon was written in Deseret text. Many young people entering the valley who learned this language (or rather this alphabet for English) preferred it and found it much simpler to use. But it was not practical in a growing, expanding society where common English would always be the means of communication, and by the 1870s it faded from use. Brigham's attitude toward the endeavor, as summarized by a clerk, was typical:

> He was very anxious that we should lay aside the old and mysterious way of spelling the English language, as we have laid aside the mystery in the religious dogmas of the day. We will continue to improve in the whole science of Truth; for that is our business; our religion circumscribes all things, and we should be prepared to take hold of whatever will be a benefit and blessing to us.[21]

Brigham, it will be remembered, had in his young life experienced speaking in tongues—in what Joseph identified as the pure Adamic tongue. Perhaps he recalled Joseph Smith's expanded view on the weaknesses of the English language as expressed so beautifully in a letter to W. W. Phelps: "O Lord, deliver us in due time from the little, narrow prison, almost as it were, total darkness, of paper, pen and ink;—and a crooked, broken, scattered and imperfect language."[22]

Another visionary concept was the cooperative plan of merchandising, whose purpose was to avoid the concentration of wealth in the hands of the few and enable people to, in effect, "become their own merchants, and share in the profits of the business by a wide distribution of the shares of stock among the people."[23] It was attempted in Brigham City in 1864 and enjoyed its greatest success there. The Provo movement also forged forward, enough to get the attention of Salt Lake merchants and stir them to action. The Zion's Cooperative Mercantile Institution was incorporated March 1, 1869. Part of the intent of the "co-ops" was to "draw the reins so tight as not to let a Latter-day Saint trade with an outsider,"[24]—a declared boycott against the non-Mormons who were, very literally, seeking the destruction of the Latter-day Saints. In June of 1866, nearly three years earlier, the Wade bill had been introduced in the senate, "aimed at nothing short of complete destruction of local self-government in Utah."[25] It did not become a law, but it made glaringly clear the imminent dangers. As Leonard Arrington explained,

> The cooperative movement fulfilled its purposes, both financially and in broader economic terms. ZCMI made immediate profits, with dividends by 1873 amounting to more than $500,000, on an original investment of $280,000. Many smaller non-Mormon merchants were squeezed out of the competition, and the larger non-Mormon firms such as Walker Brothers and Auerbach Brothers experienced temporary declines and less expansion than otherwise expected upon the completion of the railroad.[26]

The Prophet Joseph Smith had introduced, both in Kirtland and Missouri, an ideal form of communal life known as the Order of Enoch, or the United Order—not after the pattern of men, but after the pattern of God. Brigham himself had participated in this, giving all his property in Kirtland to aid the Prophet and the necessary development of the Church. This system revolved around righteous use of agency, focusing upon the wise steward who increased his means without being at the mercy of the idle and the uncaring. Commenting on this subject, Brigham said:

> If we were to divide up our substance now equally amongst this people we would have to do it all over again in a year from now, for the thrifty and careful would have a surplus while the extravagant and shiftless would be without hope and in debt.

Bringing to bear his delightful humor, he added:

> For you remember what Bishop Hunter used to say, "there are the Lord's poor and the devil's poor and the poor devils, and we have all three kinds in this Church."[27]

In 1874, a severe depression in the national economy was causing high unemployment and food shortages in Utah. This intensified Brigham's distress at the lack of unity and dedication he had perceived in the Saints. As he wrote to his son, Morris, on May 5: "During the winter the spirit strongly impressed us that the time had arrived when gathered Israel should take more unified and effectual steps for more rapidly performing the great work before us, and we began by organizing St. George."[28]

Brigham understood perfectly the principle of agency, of consecration freely given, and longed to assist his people to reach a level where all would prosper and have the luxury of working and progressing without restraint. He spoke to the Saints on the vision, the motivation behind the principle, and often in eloquent, impassioned terms:

> This co-operative movement is only a stepping-stone to what is called the Order of Enoch, but which in reality is the Order of Heaven. . . . If we would work together in our farming, in our mechanism, be obedient and work as a family for the good of all, it would be almost impossible for anyone to guess the success we would have. But we have got to do it in the Lord, always ready and willing that He should have it all, to do with it as He pleases. I have asked a favour of the Lord in this thing, and that is not to place me in such circumstances that what he has given me shall go into the hands of our enemies. But let it go for the preaching of the Gospel, to sustain and to gather the poor, to build factories, make farms, and set the poor to work, as I have hundreds and thousands that had not anything to do. I have fed and clothed them and taken care of them until they have become comparatively independent. I have made no man poor, but thousands and thousands rich; that is, the Lord has through me.

> We see servants that labour early and late and have hardly enough clothing to go to meetings in on the Sabbath. I have seen many cases of this kind in Europe, when the young lady would have to take her clothing on a Saturday night and wash it, in order that when the young lady would have to take her clothing on a Saturday night and wash it, in order that she might go to the meeting on the Sunday with a clean dress on. Who is she labouring for? For those who, many of them, are living in luxury. And to serve the classes that are living on them, the

poor labouring men and women are toiling, working their lives out to earn that which will keep a little life within them. Is this equality? No. What is going to be done? The Latter Day Saints will never accomplish their mission until this inequality shall cease on the earth.[29]

Transition proved to be the prime difficulty when setting up these cooperative ventures. Orderville, one of the longest, most successful of these communities, was comprised largely from a colony on the Muddy River which had failed and suffered privation and hardship to such a degree that they could view the cooperation of holding things in common, and the security this brought, in a positive light. Although they enjoyed different degrees of success, Brigham's vision had its impress upon each. Economic difficulties, social "human" difficulties, the government polygamy raid of the 1880s, and the death of Brigham himself contributed to the ongoing demise of the system. As Brigham's son, John R., wrote much later:

> President Young was the pilot, the guiding star. When he died the master mind was gone.
>
> The visible leader, who said, "Unless you are one in temporal things, how can you be one in spiritual things?" and "The way the world does business is sin, the strong build themselves up by putting the weak ones down." That was the voice of the Good Shepherd to that people, and when that voice was hushed in death, the light was gone—and the community dissolved.[30]

With the beginning of Brigham's last decade, in 1871, Vice President Colfax appointed James B. McKean as chief justice of Utah's territorial supreme court with implied, if not stated, instructions to root out polygamy, the second "relic of barbarism." McKean violated the established judicial procedures, "denied criminal jurisdiction to the Mormon probate courts, and refused to grant citizenship to aliens who were involved in plural marriages or who believed them to be acceptable."[31]

Brigham was arrested October 2, 1871, on charges of "lascivious cohabitation." When he was taken to court October 9, his sometimes caustic tongue was under careful control, and his quiet, respectful demeanor disconcerted his expectant opponents. Interestingly, local non-Mormons came to his defense. Major Charles Hemstead, who had formerly edited an anti-Mormon publication, *Union Vedette*, offered to serve as his attorney, galled more by the advantage taken of political office than he had been by the power and position of local Mormon authority.

Brigham was experiencing ill health at the time and requested to spend the winter in his St. George home as usual; he was at this time seventy years old. Trial was set for the following March. But, as Brigham made his slow way south, stopping at Mormon communities along the way, McKean rescheduled the trial date for December 4—a date Brigham could not possibly make. The judge set yet another date, January 2, 1872, anticipating again that Brigham would find it impossible to comply. But when the court convened the Mormon prophet was in attendance, having traveled through deep snow and bitter weather to keep the appointment. Brigham was put in custody, though allowed to remain in his own home under guard of a U. S. Marshall, for whose "services" he was required to pay $10 a day, and who remained at his post for a full 120 days. He was, however, never brought to trial, for McKean's decisions and the errors found in them were taken before the U. S. Supreme Court, where "it was ruled that McKean had permitted the marshall to draw juries illegally. The court quashed all other pending indictments, including the charges against Brigham."[32]

But a more contrived, more distressing and humiliating encounter was yet to come. Brigham's estranged wife, Ann Eliza Webb, encouraged by the "Gentile Ring," took measures to sue Brigham for divorce. She demanded $1,000 a month pending the case's hearing, $6,000 in lawyer's fees, a payment of $14,000 when divorce was granted—all hefty sums for that time—and a "final award" of $200,000, based on her personal estimate of Brigham's income at $40,000 a month.[33]

In February of 1875, Judge McKean happily ordered Brigham Young to pay costs of $3,000 and, in addition, $500 a month to

Ann Eliza. Brigham's lawyers contrived a clever defense based on a technicality which was suited to enrage his enemies:

> They alleged that when the so-called "marriage" had taken place, Ann Eliza, unbeknownst to Brigham, was the undivorced wife of another man and that she knew Brigham had a legal wife living. Brigham refused to pay the bill as the judge ordered, for which McKean held him in contempt of court. He was fined $25 and sentenced to a day in prison. March 1, 1875, the day of the sentence, was cold and stormy, but the seventy-three-year-old Brigham was taken to the penitentiary for twenty-four hours.[34]

Already in the custody of a U.S. Deputy, Brigham went home briefly to collect clothing and other necessities. Then, accompanied by Seymour B. Young, his physician, Daniel H. Wells, mayor of Salt Lake, and a Mr. Rossiter, one of his clerks, he drove through a heavy snowstorm to the prison. At first he was placed with a group of convicted criminals, but was later taken to a private room attached to the warden's quarters, where he spent the night. It was the closest he would come to personally experiencing what the Prophet Joseph had suffered to such a humiliating degree. His dignity did not fail him and, as he had learned at a young age, he kept his tears to himself.

Five days after sentencing Brigham, McKean was removed from office in relative disgrace, but he continued his residence in Utah, practicing law for about three and a half years until he died of typhoid fever in January, 1879.[35]

Ann Eliza's case against Brigham dragged on, suspended like a shadow above him, until Chief Justice Michael Shaeffer proposed a compromise which was settled upon, and Brigham paid $3,600—a fifth of the alimony that was due. The case was not dismissed until April of 1877, scarcely a few months before Brigham's death.[36]

During 1875, when this sensational case raged, President Ulysses S. Grant visited Salt Lake City. He and his wife spent pleasant time conversing with Brigham Young, who reminded him openly that this was the first time he had ever seen a president of his country. As Grant's party rode from the depot up South Temple toward Temple Square, the streets were lined with literally thousands of Sunday School children. The president asked Governor Emery, his escort, whose children they were.

> Emery replied, "Mormon children." "For several moments the president was silent," wrote Edward Tullidge, "then he murmured, in a tone of self-reproach, 'I have been deceived." Tullidge also wrote that Mrs. Grant attended an organ recital in the tabernacle and was much moved by what she saw and heard. She is reported to have told ex-delegate Hooper, "Oh, I wish I could do something for these good Mormon people."[37]

To add to the weight of these last years, Emmeline Free Young, Brigham's wife and mother of ten of his children, died in July of 1875, and Joseph Angell, Brigham's and Mary Ann Angell's oldest son, died at the young age of forty-one. Interestingly, Emmeline was only eight years older than Joseph Angell when she died. Joseph was one who had gone to assist the handcart pioneers. He had served a mission in England, and a special mission in New York where he was in charge of Church emigration. He owned a lumber business in Salt Lake and superintended many major building projects in the valley, including the Salt Lake Theatre.

At the time of his death, Joseph was presiding over the Sevier district, where his brilliant leadership was recognized and appreciated. He had three wives and nineteen children, and possessed one of the finest private libraries in Utah. He had worked as a partner with his father in building the transcontinental railroad. Upon his death, his brother, Brigham Jr., wrote:

> Oh, my brother, my brother. In many things he was superior to any man I ever saw. The Lord giveth and the Lord taketh away. . . . He was a great man tho' possessing many weaknesses, but he was humble and full of faith. It seemes like one half of me had been torn away and I deprived of a mighty counsellor. . . . All the people mourned his loss, and I felt to say in the language of David, "Know ye not that a prince has fallen this day in Israel?"[38]

Less than a month later, on September 1, George A. Smith, Brigham's first counselor, died at the age of fifty-eight. Corpulent, jolly, loyal, and sensitive, this cousin of the Prophet Joseph's had been with Brigham in England when they were young men; their friendship had spanned nearly the whole of their lives. "His sense of loss . . . caused him to weep openly during the funeral. For many Saints, it was the first time they had seen Brigham cry."[39]

Concerning the things he had passed through, Brigham's perspective never faltered. "Instead of crying over our sufferings," he told the people,

> I would rather tell a good story and leave the crying to others. I do not know that I have ever suffered; I do not realise it. . . . As I said to the brethren the other night, the only suffering I ever realized in this Church was to preserve my temper toward my enemies. But I have even got pretty much over this. Do what they please, we will not be angry; it is not becoming in saints to be so. Let us do right, ourselves, and we will find honour.[40]

The scope of Brigham's prophetic insight and understanding stood behind every act of his life. With masterful feeling and language he endeavored to share the depth of this understanding and commitment with those whom he loved and led:

> All intelligent beings who are crowned with crowns of glory, immortality, and eternal lives must pass through every ordeal appointed for intelligent beings to pass through, to gain their glory and exaltation. Every calamity that can come upon mortal beings will be suffered to come upon the few, to prepare them to enjoy the presence of the Lord. If we obtain the glory that Abraham obtained, we must do so by the same means that he did. If we are ever prepared to enjoy the society of Enoch, Noah, Melchizedek, Abraham, Isaac, and Jacob, or of their faithful children, and of the faithful Prophets and Apostles, we must pass through the same experience, and gain the knowledge, intelligence, and endowments that will prepare us to enter into the celestial kingdom of our Father and God. How many of the Latter-day Saints will endure all these things, and be prepared to enjoy the presence of the Father and the Son? You can answer that question at

your leisure. Every trial and experience you have passed through is necessary for your salvation.[41]

Succinctly, with the buoyant assurance of his nature, he taught:

> As to trials, why bless your hearts, the man or woman who enjoys the spirit of our religion has no trials: but the man or woman who tries to live according to the Gospel of the Son of God, and at the same time clings to the spirit of the world, has trials and sorrows acute and keen, and that, too, continually. Cast off the yoke of the enemy, and put on the yoke of Christ, and you will say that his yoke is easy and his burden is light. This I know by experience.[42]

Notes

1. "Brigham Young—Height-Description—Pen Pictures," Beehive House Historical File.
2. "This Is the Place," Beehive House Historical File,
3. Stanley B. Kimball, "Brigham and Heber," *BYU Studies*, vol. 18:3 (1978), p. 396, 409.
4. Gates and Widtsoe, *Life Story*, p. 226, 229.
5. Ibid., p. 232.
6. Ibid., p. 233.
7. McCloud, *Not in Vain*, p. 100.
8. Ibid., p. 52.
9. Ibid., p. 103.
10. Gates and Widtsoe, *Life Story*, p. 303-6; italics author's.
11. Arrington, *American Moses*, p. 370.
12. Gates and Widtsoe, *Life Story*, p. 287-88.
13. *JD*, 12:326.
14. *JD*, 9:167.
15. Gates and Widtsoe, *Life Story*, p. 291.
16. McCloud, *Not in Vain*, p. 52-55.
17. Gates and Widtsoe, *Life Story*, p. 292.
18. Ibid., p. 291.
19. Ibid., p. 249.
20. "The Deseret Alphabet of the English Language," p. 1, Beehive House Historical File.
21. Arrington, *American Moses*, p. 397.
22. *HC*, 1:299.

23. *CCH,* 5:223.
24. Ibid., p. 228.
25. Ibid.
26. Arrington, *American Moses,* p. 351.
27. Gates and Widtsoe, *Life Story,* p. 201.
28. Dean L. May, "United Order Founded," *Deseret News,* Church Section, February 1975, Beehive House Historical File.
29. Gates and Widtsoe, *Life Story,* p. 204.
30. England, *Brother Brigham,* p. 222.
31. Arrington, *American Moses,* p. 371.
32. Ibid., p. 373.
33. Ibid.
34. Ibid., p. 374.
35. Jessee, *Letters of Brigham Young to His Sons,* p. 343.
36. Ibid., p. 330.
37. Ibid., p. 5-6.
38. Gates and Widtsoe, *Life Story,* p. 123.
39. Arrington, *American Moses,* p. 371.
40. *JD,* 8:151.
41. *JD,* 8:150.
42. *JD,* 16:123.

Chapter Eighteen

The Prophet and His People

Journeys and teachings – support of education and women's rights –
The Woman's Exponent – *befriending B. F. Grant –*
cornerstone of Salt Lake Temple laid – Dedication of St. George Temple,
Manti and Logan Temple sites – reorganization of priesthood –
death of Brigham Young – aftermath – testimony

It was asked me by a gentleman how I guided the people by revelation. I teach them to so live that the Spirit of revelation may make plain to them their duty day by day that they are able to guide themselves. To get this revelation it is necessary that the people live so that their spirits are as pure and clean as a piece of blank paper that lies on the desk before the inditer, ready to receive any mark the writer may make upon it.

Journal of Discourses, 11:240

"I know that Joseph Smith was a Prophet of God," Brigham testified before the Saints in Ogden, "and that he had many revelations. . . .

I have had many revelations; I have seen and heard for myself, and know these things are true, and nobody on earth can disprove them. . . . What I know concerning God, concerning the earth, concerning government, I have received from the heavens, not alone through my natural ability, and I give God the glory and the praise.[1]

The powerful combination of God working through the man, Brigham, utilizing his rare and magnificent spirit, rendered his contribution unique. And the fascination of his personality, his inner force and magnetism, has not diminished. The light of this monumental figure yet has power to penetrate to the depths of our being. We are imprudent, indeed, if we judge the man too quickly or shallowly. Hugh Nibley, one of the few scholars in the Church with a mind magnificent enough to fathom Brigham Young's, explains:

> No man ever spoke his mind more frankly on all subjects. All his days he strove to communicate his inmost feelings, unburdening himself without the aid of notes or preparation in a vigorous and forthright prose that was the purest anti-rhetoric. It has been common practice to dismiss any saying of his of which one disapproves (and he makes no effort to please) by observing that he said so much on so many things that he was bound to contradict himself, and therefore need not be taken too seriously all the time. No view could be more ill-advised, for there never was a man more undeviatingly consistent and rational in thought and utterance.[2]

Observations regarding Brigham's mental and spiritual acuity are numerous and impressive, and would fill an entire volume of themselves. John Taylor, known for his own scholarly abilities, said of Brigham,

> President Young's memory is remarkable in regard to names and persons. I have traveled with him throughout the length and breadth of this Territory, and I do not know that I have ever seen him come in contact with a man whose name he did not remember and the circumstances connected with him. There is something remarkable in this.[3]

Substantiating Elder Taylor's observation is the delightful account left by Colonel Kane's wife, relating in detail her family's travels with Brigham Young on one of his journeys through the southern Utah communities of the Church. This experience took place in 1872. Her intimate glimpse into Mormondom was first published by her father in a limited edition in 1874.

When we reached the end of a day's journey, after taking off our outer garments and washing off the dust, it was the custom of our party to assemble before the fire in the sitting-room, and the leading "brothers and sisters" of the settlement would come in to pay their respects . . . and the circle round the fire varied constantly as the neighbors dropped in or went away. At these informal audiences, reports, complaints, and petitions were made; and I think I gathered more of the actual working of Mormonism by listening to them than from any other source. They talked away to Brigham Young about every conceivable matter, from the fluxing of an ore to the advantages of a Navajo bit, and expected him to remember every child in every cotter's family. And he really seemed to do so, and to be at home, and be rightfully deemed infallible on every subject. I think he must make fewer mistakes than most popes, from his being in such constant intercourse with his people. I noticed that he never seemed uninterested, but gave an unforced attention to the person addressing him, which suggested a mind free from care. I used to fancy that he wasted a great deal of power in this way; but I soon saw that he was accumulating it. Power, I mean, at least as the driving-wheel of his people's industry.[4]

Her powers of observation provide us with a unique and valuable description of the Mormon prophet, as well:

I strolled out on the platform afterwards, to find President Young preparing for our journey—as he did every morning afterwards—by a personal inspection of the condition of every wheel, axle, horse and mule, and suit of harness belonging to the party. He was peering like a well-intentioned wizard into every nook and cranny, pointing out a defect here and there with his odd, six-sided staff engraved with the hieroglyphs of many measures; more useful, though less romantic, than a Runic wand. He wore a great surtout, reaching almost to his feet, of dark-green cloth [Mahomet color?] lined with fur, a fur collar, cap, and pair of sealskin boots with the undyed fur outward. I was amused at his odd appearance; but as he turned to address me, he removed a hideous pair of green goggles, and his keen, blue-gray eyes met mine with their characteristic look of shrewd and cunning insight. I felt no further inclination to laugh. *His photographs, accurate enough in other respects, altogether fail to give the expression of his eyes.*[5]

Hugh Nibley reports his grandfather's firsthand account of Brigham's method of dealing with visitors by placing them in a big black leather chair, situated so that it faced the window—and "the calm blue eyes of Brother Brigham" who sat, usually for a space of three minutes or so, "quietly waiting for his guest to say something." At the end of that time he was able to discern the exact nature of the man or woman who sat opposite him, which "always put him on top of the situation. Brigham Young used to say that no man, if allowed to speak, could possibly avoid revealing his true character, 'For out of the abundance of the heart the tongue speaketh.'"[6]

On women's rights, as with many other issues, Brigham was ahead of his times. During the early days of the Church in Utah, the women were given the civil franchise. "Now, sisters, I want you to vote," Brigham told them, "because you are the characters that rule the ballot box." This privilege was withdrawn when Utah entered the Union as a territory, and not restored until 1870, due to the untiring efforts of leading women and men.[7]

Brigham appreciated the breadth of a woman's influence, and did not doubt that her intellectual gifts could match man's. While acknowledging the sacred nature of women's duties in the home, he supported their entering a variety of fields of endeavor—from the arts to trading, merchandising, and bookkeeping. He counseled them to study

> law, medicine, civic government, to accept public office when compatible with their home duties. Someone asked him if he thought there should be women sheriffs. With a twinkling eye he replied: "Well I think if Sister Harriet [one of his wives] went out after a man she would get him."[8]

Appreciating the power of the press, Brigham supported the establishment in 1872 of *The Woman's Exponent,* a semi-monthly paper founded by Eliza R. Snow, whose first editor was his own young niece, Lula Green (Richards).[9]

And yet, where the marriage relationship was concerned— that most sacred and binding, and potentially confining of states—he demonstrated consistent concern for the rights and protection of women. "'It is not my general practice to counsel the sisters to disobey their husbands,'" he said. "'My counsel is obey your husbands. . . . But I never counselled a woman to follow her husband to the Devil.'"[10] He was often requested to counsel his people, by letter and in person, and he loved to give the ladies practical advice on the entire scope of their duties, remembering the days of his own young wife's illness when he had had practical experience in doing a woman's work, and understanding chemical laws well enough to take it upon himself to teach

> inexperienced women emigrants crossing the plains how to set "risings" overnight and to mould the upspringing dough into suitable loaves. "It is the calling of the wife and mother," he firmly believed, "to know what to do with everything that is brought into the house, labouring to make her home desirable to her husband and children, making herself an Eve in the midst of a little paradise of her own creating, securing her husband's love and confidence, and tying her offspring to herself, with a love that is stronger than death, for an everlasting inheritance."[11]

It distressed him when people allowed petty problems to get in the way of eternal values and insights which would free the energies of an individual to move upward. At times he would gently advise toward resignation and acceptance of conditions which were less than desirable, reminding both parties that in the eternities petty differences would be swept aside, and they would view each other in a more expanded, comprehensive way. Nevertheless, he understood the nature of women's needs and the order of the priesthood, which placed the responsibility squarely on the man's shoulders:

> Woman's nature craves affection, she must have man's love and society, or she cannot be thoroughly happy, and nothing will disappoint her more than to be denied this. Treat her lovingly, take her to your bosom, give her every privilege a wife ought to have.[12]

> It is for the husband to learn how to gather around his family the comforts of life, how to control his passions and temper, and how to

command the respect, not only of his family but of all his brethren, sisters, and friends.[13]

Let the husband and father learn to bend his will to the will of his God, and then instruct his wives and children in this lesson of self-government by his example as well as by precept.[14]

Now let me say to the First Presidency, to the Apostles, to all the Bishops in Israel, and to every quorum, and especially to those who are presiding officers, Set that example before your wives and your children . . . that you can say, "Follow me, as I follow Christ."[15]

Surely Brigham possessed a vivid and comprehensive understanding of the principle Joseph had taught, that "if a man cannot learn in this life to appreciate a wife and do his duty by her, in properly taking care of her, he need not expect to be given one in the hereafter"[16]—a concept he expressed often and eloquently. "The Prophet Joseph Smith often referred to the feelings that should exist between husbands and wives," wrote Lucy Walker Kimball,

that they, his wives, should be his bosom companions, the nearest and dearest objects on earth in every sense of the word. He said men should beware how they treat their wives, that they were given them for a holy purpose. . . . He also said many [men] would awake on the morning of the resurrection sadly disappointed; for they, by transgression, would have neither wives nor children, for they surely would be taken from them and given to those who should prove themselves worthy.[17]

Speaking before the assembled Saints, Brigham taught:

But the whole subject of the marriage relation is not in my reach, nor in any other man's reach on this earth. It is without beginning of days or end of years; it is a hard matter to reach. We can tell some things with regard to it; it lays the foundation for worlds, for angels, and for the Gods; for intelligent beings to be crowned with glory, immortality, and eternal lives. In fact, it is the thread which runs from the beginning to the end of the holy Gospel of salvation—of the gospel of the Son of God; it is from eternity to eternity.[18]

The extent of Brigham's ability to succor his people was astounding; in some ways beyond our grasp. After living intimately in his household, Ellis Shipp was able to write of him:

> How kind and fatherly Brigham Young was to me. My heart warms and my eyes moisten to the big heart, the generous consideration of that great man who lived to bless all the world as far as mortal power could reach. Directed by what seemed a divine instinct he could read and understand the human heart. His vision could encompass all of mortal need in the great and vital things, and even unto the smallest detail of everyday life.[19]

This high-sounding praise was borne out time after time in his everyday dealings with the Saints. Ellis tells of a Sunday in 1872 when she was particularly disheartened and discouraged. Walking home with her two little sons, she passed the Beehive House and was moved to go in, in hopes of kindness and comfort from "Sister Lucy" and the rest of the family. She was no sooner settled in the familiar front parlor when

> Brigham himself walked in. He greeted her with warmth and kindness. It was the Sabbath—surely his precious hours were marked for something. But for a wonderful half hour he sat with her, doing little things to amuse the children, making her feel remarkably relaxed and accepted. As she rose to leave he caught her gaze and his blue eyes held hers, deep and guileless, sincere as a child's. He said, and his voice was tender with feeling, "Peace be unto you." The words entered Ellis's heart like a shaft of warm light. She later recorded: "Methinks if ever there was a heavenly look in man it can be seen in his countenance."[20]

B. F. Grant, son of Brigham's beloved friend and counselor, Jedediah M. Grant, returned to Utah when he was between fourteen and fifteen years old, a waif and a wayfarer, doing odd jobs for his keep. When Brigham learned of his presence, he sent for the boy and took him under his wing, offering him work and tutelage, an opportunity to go to school, for he did not yet know how to read and write, and patience and parental direction time after time. He was one of six orphaned boys and girls living with various of Brigham's families at that time. "I was treated most royally by all the members; in fact, I felt I was indeed a real member of the family so far as treatment was concerned," he wrote. Once when the lad was driving teams and found himself summarily dismissed by a foreman for being late (despite his explanation of milking cows, feeding chickens, and doing chores, and sometimes having to wait a little when breakfast was served late), he found the prophet himself intervening. When he told the great man that the boss had dismissed him, Brigham replied,

> "Oh, the boss? Who is he?" I gave the foreman's name. He laughed and said, "No, my boy, I am the boss. Didn't I make arrangements for you to come and live with me? . . . Remember, when you are discharged I will attend to it myself; now, go back, get your team and go to work."

When B. F. decided to go to California to seek his fortune, Brigham did his best to talk him out of it:

> "My boy, haven't you had enough ups and downs in life to know that the most important thing for you to do is to remain in school? You should know from your past experience that in this cold world no one will have any personal interest in you. Remember, that I am your friend, and you had better remain with me."

When Brigham realized that he could not persuade the youth, in his great wisdom he then did all he could to love and support him, sending him to the ZCMI with one of his wives to be outfitted royally, with a new trunk as well as new clothes, and a gift of $100 to get started.

> When he shook hands with me . . . . I broke down and wept. He put his arm around me as he would one of his own sons, and said, "Goodbye, God bless you, my boy. . . . Remember, if you want to come home and haven't the money, write to me and I'll send it to you." That was the last time I ever saw President Young. He died while I was in California.

> My recollection of President Young was that he had two great outstanding personalities; one a very stern and positive way of saying and

doing things, and at other times he had a kind and loving way that would be worthy of a loving mother for her child. However, he was possessed of that wonderful spirit of discernment that it seemed to me, at all times he was able to decide which of these attitudes to use in order that justice and right should prevail. . . . I would to God I had the ability and words to express my great appreciation and love for this great Pioneer who led his people, under the inspiration and direction of Almighty God. . . . God bless his memory and posterity to the last generation of time.[21]

Brigham loved to personally supervise the work on the St. George temple; even when in poor health he would ride daily to the site, encouraging and aiding the workers, "moving George A. Smith to write in a letter, 'President Young is our only architect.'"[22] On January 1, 1877, the first day of the last year of his life, he participated in the dedication of the lower story of the temple. He spoke only a few words, among them: "All of the angels of heaven are looking at this little handful of people, and stimulating them to the salvation of the human family. . . . When I think upon this subject I want the tongues of Seven Thunders to wake up the people."[23] By April the entire structure was ready for dedication, and Brigham decreed that a special April conference be held from the site. Part of his remarks at the last conference he was to attend reconfirmed the basic elements of his vision and testimony:

We have no business here other than to build up and establish the Zion of our God. . . . We will continue to grow, to increase and spread abroad . . . the Lord Almighty has said [to our enemies] Thus far thou shalt go and no farther, and hence we are spared to carry on his work. . . . The hearts of all living are in his hands and he turns them as the rivers of water are turned.[24]

On April 25, Brigham laid the cornerstone and dedicated the site of the Manti Temple; on May 18 he did the same in the lovely Cache Valley, where the Logan Temple would rise.

Temples and priesthood organization were the final thrusts of the work Brigham did. In the final months of his life he reorganized stakes, formed new ones, set up quarterly stake conferences and monthly priesthood meetings, and organized the quorums as they had never been organized before, defining the duties of the apostles, seventies, high priests, elders, and "those of the lesser priesthood, with plainness and distinctness and power—the power of God—in a way that it is left on record in such unmistakable language that no one need err who has the Spirit of God resting upon him."[25]

Box Elder Stake was organized on August 19. On August 23, Brigham spent the day in business as usual, though he was not well. In the evening he attended a priesthood conference and gave instructions "regarding the duties of bishops, priests, and teachers, urging all to attend faithfully to the sacred responsibilities resting upon them," and "appointed a committee to superintend the building of a new hall in the Temple enclosure which resulted in the erection of a smaller Assembly Hall. After prayers that evening he sat in council with Aunt Eliza R. Snow in the prayer-room." They reviewed material Edward Tullidge had prepared on women of the Church, as well as Eliza's concept of sending women out to lecture on Mormonism. "'It is an experiment,' he responded, 'but one that I should like to see tried.'"[26]

He retired to bed shortly afterward. Around eleven o'clock he was seized with a violent attack of what was believed to be "cholera morbus," but which was later identified as appendicitis; death itself was caused from infection resulting from a ruptured appendix. He suffered greatly the last few days with vomiting, cramps, and purgings. But he endured the pain cheerfully, occasionally making humorous remarks, and seemed to recognize his family members, responding to the prayers said in his behalf with a distinct "amen."

On Wednesday, August 29, 1877, Brigham Young passed from this life. His daughter, Zina, described the intimate particulars of the scene:

> He seemed so restless that Dr. Seymour B. Young, his nephew, thought it best for him to be removed from the canopy bed he occupied which stood in an alcove of the room and placed him before the

open window where he would get the air and where his beloved ones could be around him.

> ... When he was placed on the bed in front of the window he seemed to partially revive, and opening his eyes, he gazed upward, exclaiming: "Joseph! Joseph! Joseph!" and the divine look in his face seemed to indicate that he was communicating with his beloved friend, Joseph Smith, the Prophet. This name was the last word he uttered.[27]

As death approached, the family had knelt round his bed and his brother, Joseph, offered a prayer for the assembled group. "I knelt where I had full view of his countenance," Zina confided,

> and in the middle of the prayer I was impelled to open my eyes, and father's face was radiant with an inward glory. It seemed a cloud of light surrounded him. . . . Gazing upon that noble face, I thought he looked like a God. Peace and serenity and grandeur were enthroned upon his countenance. . . .

> As father's breath grew shorter and the prayer was finished, the Doctor said, "He is gone." The multitude who stood respectfully beneath the window heard the words and a murmuring sigh of grief went up like incense to heaven from the loving heart.[28]

On September 1, Brigham's body was removed from the Lion House to the tabernacle, and until noon the following day over 25,000 of the Saints came to pay their last tributes to the man who had been prophet, leader, counselor, friend—and father to his people. He had fulfilled well the trust his beloved Joseph had set upon him. In the October conference of 1864, in the old bowery, he had said:

> I have never particularly desired any man to testify publicly that I am a Prophet; nevertheless, if any man feels joy in doing this, he shall be blest in it. I have never said that I am not a Prophet; but, if I am not, one thing is certain, I have been very profitable to this people.[29]

On Sunday, September 2, the Tabernacle was filled to capacity, with over twelve thousand people somehow finding room.

Services began at noon with the organist, Joseph J. Daynes, play-ing "The Dead March in Saul," "Mendelssohn's Funeral March," and a special piece he had composed himself entitled "Brigham Young's Funeral March." George Careless led the 225-voice choir in singing "Hark, from Afar a Funeral Knell," "Thou Dost not Weep to Weep Alone," and an original piece of his own composi-tion, "Rest." Daniel H. Wells, Wilford Woodruff, Erastus Snow, John Taylor, and George Q. Cannon all addressed the assembled people. Brother Cannon lovingly reminded them:

> Naturally he was a man of indomitable courage, of an unyielding will; and he could not submit even to the conquerer Death without strug-gling against him . . . but his natural feelings . . . were that he would hail the day of his release from his mortal existence as the happiest day of his life. . . .

> He has been the brain, the eye, the ear, the mouth and hand for the entire people of the Church of Jesus Christ of Latter-day Saints. . . . Nothing was too small for his mind; nothing was too large. His mind was of that character that it could grasp the greatest subjects, and yet it had the capacity to descend to the minutest details. This was evi-dent in all his counsels and associations with the Saints; he had the power, that wonderful faculty which God gave him and with which he was inspired.[30]

The service was simple and dignified, the mourning dignified and respectful as well: ". . . some four thousand persons, none of whom, at his request, was dressed in black, marched eight abreast to the grave"[31]—"up to the small private cemetery on the hill, where, in accordance with his instructions, he was laid away with-out pomp and ceremony in the silent hillside to await the voice of the Master on the Resurrection Day."[32]

On one occasion, Brigham observed:

> I never have professed to be Brother Joseph, but Brother Brigham try-ing to do good to this people. I am no better, nor any more impor-tant than any other man who is trying to do good. . . . If I improve upon what the Lord has given me, and continue to improve, I shall

become like those who have gone before me; I shall be exalted in the celestial kingdom, and be filled to overflowing with all the power I can wield; and all the keys of knowledge I can manage will be committed unto me. What do we want more?[33]

In 1862, Congress passed an act disincorporating the Mormon Church and limiting the amount of real estate which any church in a territory could hold to a mere $50,000. This rendered it necessary for the Church to make some provisions, for they dared not play into the hands of their enemies and be seen in open violation of the act. Thus Church properties were placed

in the hands of the Church President and other trustworthy individuals, to be administered by them on behalf of the Church, but in a private capacity. After Brigham Young's death, an auditing committee was set up to separate the accounts of Brigham Young and the Church. The committee found it necessary "to go back to the commencement of accounts" in Salt Lake Valley. These were found to be "strictly correct," with "very slight exception" and vouchers were produced which authenticated the settlements of President Young and demonstrated "the accuracy of his accounts," as "supervised and adjusted" by his clerical staff. One clause of President Young's will gave ample powers to the executors to fully settle everything of a trust character, so that the interests of the Church would be fully protected.[34]

On April 10, 1878, a settlement agreement was readied among all parties. A year later, seven out of Brigham's literally hundreds of heirs contested the settlement. But this suit was eventually settled by the Church out of court. Susa, in her account of Brigham's life, noted:

The will was a model of equity and justice. Each wife was provided with a home of her own or a life-suite in the Lion House, with ample provision for maintenance in comfort to the end of her days. Each daughter, married or single, of first or last wife, inherited equally with the boys and each other; each also had a building lot given them in the Upper Garden. Mothers were given ample powers to disinherit any child who proved unworthy of inheritance and all were enjoined to use their substance in righteous living. A fair monthly income was to be paid to the mothers until the property was settled up, when they were to receive an increased amount, according to the increased possible values of the property.

No mother dispossessed a child. The will was just, it was more: it was full of the kind protecting thought and over-arching sympathy which had suffused the life-association of a loving father with his family.[35]

With only eleven days of formal education, Brigham possessed an incredible mastery of language. He also possessed incredible leadership skills. Hugh Nibley calls him "the greatest leader of modern times,"[36] and expounds on some of the outstanding qualities of his leadership:

For him, getting things done was incidental. The important thing was that the people should know what they were doing and why. His orders and recommendations are never without full and persuasive explanations. . . . the first principle of leadership, as he declares it, is to lead. You do not drive.[37]

As Brigham himself explained:

You can gain and lead the affections of the people, but you cannot scare them, nor whip them, nor burn them to do right against their wills. The human family will die to gratify their wills. Then learn to rightly direct those wills, and you can direct the influence and power of the people.[38]

And again: "Gather the Saints, but do not flatter; invite, but do not urge, and by no means compel any one."[39] He understood that he, or any other man, had very little power to "control"; the only power one could really achieve in this world was power over self. The great secret lay in the overriding power of God in the acts of all men. "If you Elders of Israel can get the art of preaching the Holy Ghost into the hearts of the people, you will have an obedient people."[40]

What earthly power can gather a people as this people have been gathered, and hold them together as this people have been held together?

It was not Joseph, it is not Brigham, nor Heber, nor any of the rest of the Twelve . . . but it is the Lord God Almighty that holds this people together, and no other power.[41]

Absolutely key to this leadership from heaven was the necessity of personal revelation:

How do we know that prophets wrote the word of the Lord? By revelation. . . . Without revelation direct from heaven, it is impossible for any person to understand fully the plan of salvation. . . . I say that the living oracles of God, or the Spirit of revelation must be in each and every individual, to know the plan of salvation and keep in the path that leads them to the presence of God.[42]

It was simple, straightforward counsel:

Take a course to open and keep a communication with your Elder Brother or file-leader—our Savior. Were I to draw a distinction in all the duties that are required of the children of men, from first to last, I would place first and foremost the duty of seeking unto the Lord our God until we open the path of communication from heaven to earth—from God to our own souls.[43]

And, in doing so, Brigham knew we would come to a necessary knowledge of the nature of God, and our relationship to him. In practical, deftly drawn terms, he brought this knowledge down to the personal, intimate level:

No human being has had power to organize his own existence. Then there is a greater than we. Are we our own in our bodies? Are we our own in our spirits? We are not our own. We belong to our progenitors—to our Father and our God.[44]

I want to tell you, each and every one of you, that you are well acquainted with God our Heavenly Father, or the great Elohim. You are all well acquainted with him, for there is not a soul of you but what has lived in his house and dwelt with him year after year; and yet you are seeking to become acquainted with him, when the fact is, you have merely forgotten what you did know. There is not a person here to-day but what is a son or a daughter of that Being. In the spirit world their spirits were first begotten and brought forth, and they lived there with their parents for ages before they came here. This, perhaps, is hard for many to believe, but it is the greatest nonsense in the world not to believe it. If you do not believe it, cease to call him Father, and when you pray, pray to some other character.[45]

In order to achieve any of the things Brigham taught, in order to incorporate eternal principles into our beings, we must be filled with love for that God we are attempting to serve—love for ourselves as his children, and love for those who are literally our sisters and brothers.

Away with all little meannesses, and deal out kindness to all. From the high and from the lower circles of life find if you can on the face of the earth a gentleman or lady, in the strict sense of the word, and you will find a man or woman that would border very closely on an angel. . . . To be gentle and kind, modest and truthful, to be full of faith and integrity, doing no wrong is of God; goodness sheds a halo of loveliness around every person who possesses it, making their countenances beam with light, and their society desirable because of its excellency. They are loved of God, of holy angels, and of all the good on earth.[46]

This power of love, weaving souls together, would create the unity, the oneness, necessary to growth and salvation: "It is folly in the extreme for persons to say that they love God; when they do not love their brethren,"[47] Brigham counseled. "Ye mighty men of God, make sure the path for your own feet to walk to eternal life, and take as many with you as you can. Take them as they are, understand them as they are, and deal with them as they are; look at them as God looks at them, and then you can judge them as he would judge them."[48] . . . "If we are united, we are independent of the powers of hell and of the world."[49] . . . "I wish the people to understand that they have no interest apart from the lord our God. The moment you have a divided interest, that moment you sever yourselves from eternal principles."[50]

We have come here to build up Zion. How shall we do it? I have told you a great many times. There is one thing I will say in regard to it. We have got to be united in our efforts. We should go to work with a united faith like the heart of one man; and whatsoever we do should be performed in the name of the Lord, and we will then be blessed and prospered in all we do. We have a work on hand whose magnitude can hardly be told.[51]

Brigham, the "Lion of the Lord" gave his life to that work. His words, his actions, his legacy stand forever, immovable and unassailable.

Hugh Nibley, in preparing a volume on the teachings of Brigham, told his editors: "I feel like a mental midget to the side of Brigham Young."[52] He does not qualify or apologize for his respect and admiration of the two great prophets of our era: "I am thinking of the two greatest men of our dispensation, the one the devoted disciple and boundless admirer of the other—Joseph Smith and Brigham Young. They are practically out of reach as exemplary figures."[53]

Let Brother Brigham himself have the closing words—eloquent in their expression, thrilling in their conviction, and powerful in their representation of the essence of the man:

"God bless the humble and the righteous, and may He have compassion upon us because of the weakness that is in our nature. And considering the great weakness and ignorance of mortals, let us have mercy upon each other."[54]

"This is a world in which we are to prove ourselves. The lifetime of man is a day of trial, wherein we may prove to God—in our darkness, in our weakness, and where the enemy reigns—that we are our Father's friends."[55]

Notes

1. *JD*, 16:46.
2. Hugh Nibley, *Brother Brigham Challenges the Saints* (Salt Lake City: Deseret

Book,1994), p. 307-308.

3. John Taylor, *The Gospel Kingdom: Writings and Discourses of John Taylor,* collector's edition (Salt Lake City: Bookcraft,1987), p. 55.

4. Mrs. Thomas L. Kane, *Twelve Mormon Homes* (Philadelphia: William Wood, 1874), p. 113-14.

5. Ibid., p. 5; italics author's.

6. Hugh Nibley, *Brother Brigham Challenges the Saints,* p. 307.

7. Gates and Widtsoe, *Life Story,* p. 297.

8. Ibid., p. 303.

9. Ibid., p. 301.

10. Ibid., p. 297.

11. Ibid., p. 306-7.

12. Arrington, *American Moses,* p. 313.

13. *JD,* 10:28.

14. *JD,* 9:256.

15. *JD,* 15:229.

16. *They Knew the Prophet,* p. 145.

17. Ibid., p. 139-40.

18. *JD,* 2:90.

19. McCloud, *Not in Vain,* p. 52.

20. Ibid., p. 85.

21. B. F. Grant, "Brigham Young's Kindness to a Boy," in *Faith-Promoting Stories,* p. 149-54.

22. England, *Brother Brigham,* p. 227.

23. Ibid., p. 228.

24. *JD,* 18:356-7.

25. *CCH,* 5:508.

26. Gates and Widtsoe, *Life Story,* p. 360-61.

27. Ibid., p. 362.

28. Ibid., p. 362.

29. *JD,* 10:339.

30. Gates and Widtsoe, *Life Story,* p. 363-4.

31. Arrington, *American Moses,* p. 401.

32. Gates and Widtsoe, *Life Story,* p. 364.

33. Ibid., p. 367-8.

34. "Brigham Young Estate," p. 1, Beehive House Historical File.

35. Gates and Widtsoe, *Life Story,* p. 364-5.

36. Hugh Nibley, *Brother Brigham Challenges the Saints,* p. 449.

37. Ibid., p. 450-53.

38. *JD,* 8:363.

39. *JD,* 8:72.

40. *JD,* 12:257.

41. *JD,* 10:305.
42. *JD,* 14:209, 9:279.
43. *JD,* 8:339.
44. *JD,* 8:67.
45. *JD,* 4:216.
46. *JD,* 11:240, 12:259.
47. *JD,* 4:297.
48 *JD,* 8:10.
49. *JD,* 5:257.
50. *JD,* 4:31.
51. *JD,* 13:155.
52. Hugh Nibley, *Brother Brigham Challenges the Saints,* p. x.
53. Ibid., p. xiv-xv; italics author's.
54. *JD,* 9:158.
55. *JD,* 8:61.

Selected Bibliography

Anderson, Karl Ricks. *Joseph Smith's Kirtland: Eyewitness Accounts.* Salt Lake City: Deseret Book, 1989.

Arrington, Leonard J. *Brigham Young: American Moses.* Urbana and Chicago: University of Illinois Press 1986.

Arrington, Leonard J., and Jolley, JoAnn. "The Faithful Young Family: The Parents, Brothers, and Sisters of Brigham," *Ensign,* August 1980.

Barron, Howard H. *Orson Hyde: Missionary, Apostle, Colonizer.* Bountiful, Utah: Horizon Publishers, 1977.

Bloxham, V. Ben, Moss, James R., and Porter, Larry C., eds. *Truth Will Prevail: The Rise of the Church of Jesus Christ of Latter-day Saints in the British Isles 1837-1987.* University Press, Cambridge, England: University Press. Published by The Corporation of the President, The Church of Jesus Christ of Latter-day Saints. U.S. distribution by Deseret Book, Salt Lake City.

Campbell, Eugene E. *The Essential Brigham Young.* Salt Lake City: Signature Books, 1992.

Cannon, Donald Q., and Cook, Lyndon W., eds. *Far West Record.* Salt Lake City: Deseret Book, 1983.

Cannon, Janath R. *Nauvoo Panorama.* Nauvoo: Nauvoo Restoration, Inc., 1991.

Cowley, Matthias F. *Wilford Woodruff: History of His Life and Labors.* Salt Lake City, Utah: Bookcraft, 1964.

Curtis, Eunice E. The Ancestors of Enos Curtis and Ruth Franklin: Utah Pioneers, 1783-84, and Related Families, Church Archives.

England, Eugene. *Brother Brigham*. Salt Lake City: Bookcraft, 1980.

—. *Why the Church Is as True as the Gospel: Personal Essays on Mormon Experience*. Salt Lake City: Bookcraft, 1986.

Faith-Promoting Stories. Comp. by Preston Nibley. Salt Lake City: Bookcraft, 1977.

Firmage, Edwin Brown and Mangrum, Richard Collin. *Zion in the Courts: A Legal History of The Church of Jesus Christ of Latter-day Saints*. Urbana and Chicago: University of Illinois Press, 1988.

Gates, Susa Young, ed. *The Young Woman's Journal*. Vol. 4, no. 1, October 1892.

Gates, Susa Young and Widtsoe, Leah D. *The Life Story of Brigham Young*. New York: The MacMillan Co., 1931.

Godfrey, Kenneth W., Godfrey, Audrey M., and Derr, Jill Mulvay. *Women's Voices: An Untold History of the Latter-day Saints, 1830-1900*. Salt Lake City: Deseret Book, 1982.

Holzapfel, Richard Neitzel, and Holzapfel, Jeni Broberg. *Women of Nauvoo*. Salt Lake City: Bookcraft, 1992.

Gowans, Fred R., and Campbell, Eugene E. *Fort Bridger: Island in the Wilderness*. Provo, Utah: Brigham Young University Press, 1975.

Holzapfel, Richard Neitzel and Cottle, L. Jeffrey. *Old Mormon Nauvoo and Southeastern Iowa: Historic Photographs and Guide*. Santa Ana, CA: Fieldbrook Productions, Inc., 1990.

Jessee, Dean C. "Brigham Young's Family, Part 1, 1824-45," *BYU Studies* 18:3.

—, ed. *Letters of Brigham Young to His Sons*. Salt Lake City: Deseret Book, 1974.

The Journal of Brigham: Brigham Young's Own Story in His Own Words. Comp. by Leland R. Nelson. Provo, Utah: Council Press, 1980.

Journal of Discourses, 26 vols. London: Latter-day Saints' Book Depot, 1854-86.

Kane, Mrs. Thomas L. *Twelve Mormon Homes*. Philadelphia: William Wood, 1874.

Kimball, Stanley B. "Brigham and Heber," *BYU Studies.* Vol. 18:3, 1978.

Langley, Harold D., ed. *To Utah with the Dragoons and Glimpses of Life in Arizona and California 1858-1859.* Salt Lake City: University of Utah Press, 1974.

Larson, Gustive O. *Prelude to the Kingdom.* Francestown, New Hampshire: Marshall Jones Co., 1947.

Little, James A. "Biography of Lorenzo Dow Young," *Utah Historical Quarterly.* Vol. 14, 1946.

Madsen, Truman G. *Defender of the Faith.* Salt Lake City: Bookcraft, 1980.

Maxfield, Miriam. "A Compiled History of Phinehas Howe Young," typescript, Church Archives.

McCloud, Susan Evans. *Joseph Smith: A Photobiography.* Salt Lake City: Aspen, 1992.

—. *Not in Vain.* Salt Lake City: Bookcraft, 1984.

McConkie, Mark L. *The Father of the Prophet.* Salt Lake City: Bookcraft, 1993.

My Kingdom Shall Roll Forth: Readings in Church History. Salt Lake City: published by the Corporation of the President, The Church of Jesus Christ of Latter-day Saints, 1979.

Nibley, Hugh. *Brother Brigham Challenges the Saints.* Salt Lake City: Deseret Book, 1994.

Nibley, Preston. *Brigham Young: The Man and His Work.* Salt Lake City, Deseret Book, 1970.

Nibley, Preston. *The Presidents of the Church.* Salt Lake City, Deseret Book, 1974.

Palmer, Richard F., and Butler, Karl D. *The New York Years: Brigham Young.* Charles Redd Center for Western Studies, Brigham Young University, 1982. (Dist. by Signature Books, Midvale, Utah).

Pratt, Parley P. *Autobiography of Parley P. Pratt.* Ed. Parley P. Pratt, Jr. Salt Lake City, Deseret Book, 1938.

Roberts, B. H. *A Comprehensive History of the Church of Jesus Christ of Latter-day Saints,* 6 vols. Provo, Utah: Brigham Young University Press, 1965.

—. *The Missouri Persecutions*. Salt Lake City, Bookcraft, 1965.

—. *The Rise and Fall of Nauvoo*. Salt Lake City: Bookcraft, 1965.

Robinson, E., ed. *Times and Seasons* 5 vols. November 1839 - January 1844.

Smith, Joseph, Jun. *History of the Church of Jesus Christ of Latter-day Saints,* 7 vols. Ed. B. H. Roberts. Salt Lake City: Deseret Book, 1951.

Smith, Lucy Mack. *History of Joseph Smith by His Mother.* Salt Lake City: Bookcraft, 1958.

Smith, Joseph Fielding. *Essentials in Church History.* Salt Lake City, Deseret Book, 1950.

Spencer, Clarissa Young and Harmer, Mabel. *Brigham Young at Home.* Salt Lake City: Deseret Book, 1940.

Stegner, Wallace. *The Gathering of Zion: The Story of the Mormon Trail.* Lincoln and London: University of Nebraska Press, 1964, 1981.

Stewart, John J. *Brigham Young and His Wives and the True Story of Plural Marriage.* Salt Lake City, Utah: Mercury Publishing Co., 1961.

Talmage, James E. *The House of the Lord.* Salt Lake City: Deseret Book, 1969.

Taylor, John. *The Gospel Kingdom: Selections from the Writings and Discourses of John Taylor.* Ed. G. Homer Durham. Salt Lake City: Bookcraft, 1987.

They Knew the Prophet, compiled by Hyrum Andrus and Helen Mae Andrus. Salt Lake City: Bookcraft, 1974.

Whitney, Orson F. *Life of Heber C. Kimball.* Salt Lake City: Bookcraft, 1945.

Widtsoe, John A., ed. *Discourses of Brigham Young.* Salt Lake City: Deseret Book, 1954.

Young, Brigham, Manuscript History of, 1801-1844. Comp. Elden J. Watson. Salt Lake City, 1967.

Young, S. Dilworth. *Here Is Brigham: Brigham Young, the Years to 1844.* Bookcraft: Salt Lake City, 1964.

Index